Library and Resource Centre
Ravenswood House
Fareham Hants
PO17 5NA
Tel:02382 310889
library.ravenswood@southernhealth.nhs.uk
www.hantshealthcarelibrary.nhs.uk

PLEASE ENTER DETAILS BELOW ON LOAN SLIP

Author ~~SEX AND VIOLENCE~~ FARRINGTON. D

Title SEX AND VIOLENCE

Accession No.   030152

Sex and Violence

Sex and Violence

THE PSYCHOLOGY OF CRIME AND RISK ASSESSMENT

Edited by

David P. Farrington
Cambridge University, UK

Clive R. Hollin
Leicester University, UK

and

Mary McMurran
Cardiff University, UK

London and New York

First published 2001 by Routledge
11 New Fetter Lane
London EC4P 4EE

Simultaneously published in the USA and Canada
by Routledge
29 West 35th Street, New York, NY 10001

© 2001 Routledge

Routledge is an imprint of the Taylor & Francis Group

Typeset in Sabon and Optima
by Keystroke, Jacaranda Lodge, Wolverhampton
Printed and bound in Great Britain
by MPG Books Ltd, Bodmin

British Library Cataloguing in Publication Data
A catalogue record for this book is available from the British Library

ISBN 0–415–26890–7

Contents

C. Violent Offenders and Offences   195

List of Figures

List of Tables

List of Contributors

Klaus-Peter Dahle, Institute for Forensic Psychiatry, Free University of Berlin, Germany

Mats Dernevik, Department of Psychiatry, University Hospital, Linköping, Sweden

Michael Donnelly, Institute of Clinical Science, Queen's University, Belfast, Northern Ireland

Eric B. Elbogen, Law/Psychology Program, University of Nebraska, Lincoln, United States

Mikael Falkheim, Regional Forensic Psychiatric Clinic, Birgittas Hospital, Vadstena, Sweden

David P. Farrington, Institute of Criminology, University of Cambridge, England

Clive R. Hollin, Centre for Applied Psychology, University of Leicester, England

Rolf Holmqvist, Department of Education and Psychology, University of Linköping, Sweden

Stephen M. Hudson, University of Canterbury, New Zealand

Margaret A. Jackson, School of Criminology, Simon Fraser University, Burnaby, Canada

John Q. La Fond, School of Law, University of Missouri, Kansas City, United States

Stephen J. Lally, American School of Professional Psychology, Arlington, United States

Rosaleen McElvaney, The Children's Hospital, Dublin, Ireland

Nicholas McGeorge, Department of Psychology, University of Portsmouth, England

Sinéad McGilloway, Department of Psychology, National University of Ireland, Maynooth, Ireland

Mary McMurran, School of Psychology, Cardiff University, Wales

Cynthia Mercado, Law/Psychology Program, University of Nebraska, Lincoln, United States

John Murray, Queensland Corrective Services Commission, Brisbane, Australia

Emma J. Palmer, Centre for Applied Psychology, University of Leicester, England

Devon L. L. Polaschek, School of Psychology, University of Victoria, Wellington, New Zealand

Susan J. Sachsenmaier, Mendota Mental Health Institute, Madison, United States

Rolf Sandell, Department of Education and Psychology, University of Linköping, Sweden

Mario J. Scalora, Law/Psychology Program, University of Nebraska, Lincoln, United States

Richard J. Siegert, School of Psychology, University of Victoria, Wellington, New Zealand

Andrew Silke, Scarman Centre, University of Leicester, England

Anna L. Stewart, School of Criminology and Criminal Justice, Griffith University, Queensland, Australia

Masayuki Tamura, National Research Institute of Police Science, Chiba, Japan

Alan J. Tomkins, Law/Psychology Program, University of Nebraska, Lincoln, United States

Bryan Tully, Psychologists at Law Group, London, England

Tony Ward, University of Melbourne, Australia

Kazumi Watanabe, National Research Institute of Police Science, Chiba, Japan

Hartmut-Michael Weber, Department of Criminology, University of Applied Science, Fulda, Germany

Introduction

David P. Farrington, Clive R. Hollin and Mary McMurran

Forensic psychology is a booming topic in the United Kingdom and in many other countries. In recent years, there has been an enormous increase in demand and employment opportunities for psychologists working with offenders, and parallel increases in undergraduate and graduate courses and in the volume of research, journals and books on this topic. Forensic psychology is also a very international topic. The European Association of Psychology and Law (EAPL) was founded in 1993 to bring together researchers from different European countries, and it currently has over 350 members. The EAPL has signed an agreement with Harwood Academic Publishers to publish books of selected papers from its conferences and also to designate *Psychology, Crime and Law* as the house journal of the EAPL.

As an innovation, it was decided that the Ninth European Conference on Psychology and Law would be a joint conference between the EAPL and the American Psychology-Law Society (Division 41 of the American Psychological Association). This joint conference was held in Trinity College, Dublin, Ireland, in July 1999, and was mainly organized by David Carson and his colleagues from Southampton University. The conference was a huge success, being attended by over 600 delegates from 27 countries. It was opened with a welcoming address by Irish President Mary McAleese.

So many good papers were given at the conference that it was decided that two books would be published based on selected papers. This volume focuses on sex and violence, while the other volume covers *Psychology in the Courts: International Advances in Knowledge* (edited by Ronald Roesch, Raymond Corrado and Rebecca Dempster). There were over 30 papers submitted for this volume, and unfortunately we had space to accept only about half of them. The chapters in this book are revised versions of papers originally presented at the conference. The selected chapters are grouped into three sections, on risk assessment, sex offenders and violent offenders respectively. They represent contributions from ten different countries: Australia, Canada, England, Germany, Ireland, Japan, New Zealand, Northern Ireland, Sweden and the United States. We hope that this book will contribute to the international advancement of forensic psychology.

Section A is devoted to the important topic of risk assessment. It will not have escaped the attention of anyone working with offenders that risk assessment has become a hot issue over the past few years. As the research develops, so there is the opportunity to influence practice and help practitioners, clients, and the public by increasing the likelihood of making accurate decisions regarding the risk an individual poses to the community.

Chapter 1, by Emma J. Palmer, reviews the use of psychometric measures in informing the process of risk assessment. This chapter highlights the applicability of scales that, based on records and interviews, offer an assessment of factors shown empirically to be related to criminal behaviour. Chapter 2, by Susan J. Sachsenmaier and Stephen J. Lally, takes on the theme of a scientific approach to risk assessment, specifically in the area of sex offenders. This chapter discusses the value of guidelines, based on research, to inform practice in this area.

After sex comes violence – Chapter 3, by Eric B. Elbogen, Cynthia Mercado, Alan J. Tomkins and Mario J. Scalora, considers clinical practice and risk assessment with sex offenders. Based on data generated by the MacArthur Risk Assessment Study, this chapter considers the critical practical issue of whether the risk cues for violence identified in the MacArthur study are readily available in everyday clinical practice. The study concludes that they are and discusses the clinical implications.

Chapter 4, by Margaret A. Jackson, moves to the assessment of the risk of child abuse. This chapter considers the unfolding of practice and how that has informed current policies and assessment procedures. Chapter 5, by Sinéad McGilloway and Michael Donnelly, and Chapter 6, by Mats Dernevik, Mikael Falkheim, Rolf Holmqvist and Rolf Sandell, are both concerned with risk assessment with mentally disordered offenders. Both examine current procedures and consider their effectiveness in practice.

The overwhelming theme that emerges from the chapters in Section A is the need for a scientist-practitioner approach to the difficult task of risk assessment. Rather than fighting battles claiming the superiority of research-based predictors or of clinical judgement, it is clear that an informed approach will seek to draw on both research and clinical experience in order to make the best assessments.

Section B covers issues relating to the investigation and understanding of sexual offences. In Chapter 7, John Q. La Fond describes American commitment laws for sexually violent predators, which allow for the detention, after the end of their prison sentence, of those sexual offenders deemed to be high risk and who suffer from a personality disorder or mental abnormality. Concerns regarding the validity of diagnoses, the accuracy of risk assessment, and the effectiveness of treatment exercise the minds of clinicians, lawyers, and politicians. Bryan Tully in Chapter 8 examines issues related to 'recovered memories', with particular reference to 'memories' of sexual abuse. Sexual abuse, particularly of children, is of enormous concern, and society naturally seeks justice through the conviction of abusers. It is imperative, however, that convictions are based upon reliable evidence, and the development of psychological science along with sensitive assessment techniques are required to inform the courts appropriately about the status of 'recovered memories'.

Rosaleen McElvaney in Chapter 9 reviews research on why victims of sexual crimes are reluctant to report their victimization at the time, and the problems that ensue from reporting sexual abuse after a long delay. Not least are the problems caused to traumatized individuals by protracted legal proceedings after disclosure. The justice system could alter distressing practices that deter disclosure by victims. In Chapter 10, Devon L. L. Polaschek, Tony Ward, Stephen M. Hudson and Richard J. Siegert investigate rapists' accounts of their offences, tracing the chain of events that lead to the offence and beyond. A model of rape is presented, graphically representing the process of offending from background triggers, through goal-setting, approach, preparation, and offending, to post-offence behaviour and self-appraisal. This new, dynamic model allows for fertile theoretical development of the understanding of the variety of behaviours that are evident in the rape process.

In Chapter 11, John Murray focuses on the situational aspects of sexual offending, bringing this neglected area into line alongside psychological and cultural factors. Acknowledging the role of situational factors in sexual offending leads logically to the development of situational crime prevention approaches. A survey of over 6,000 women revealed that victimization is often repeated; victims of sexual violence are vulnerable to further sexual violence. Women at risk of sexual violence could be advised about risk minimization through alteration of situational factors.

Section C reviews violent offenders and offences. Klaus-Peter Dahle in Chapter 12 studies criminal careers of different types of offenders in a sample of about 400 male prisoners. In general, the serious violent crimes were committed by persistent offenders who had long criminal careers. In Chapter 13, Anna L. Stewart considers the effectiveness of police and criminal justice methods in preventing domestic violence. She concludes that traditional approaches involving deterrence, incapacitation and re-habilitation are ineffective, and recommends community crime prevention methods that strengthen informal social control processes.

Chapter 14, by Kazumi Watanabe and Masayuki Tamura, and Chapter 15, by Andrew Silke, are both concerned with offender profiling, which has attracted a great deal of attention in recent years. Chapter 14 reports the first detailed analysis of mutilation—murder cases in Japan; such cases have increased considerably in the 1990s. Interestingly, the authors show how characteristics of the offence and of the victim are related to characteristics of the offender. Chapter 15 reviews recent developments in offender profiling and investigates how far it might be applicable to terrorist violence. Andrew Silke describes a number of famous cases of terrorism where offender profiling was used, but concludes that its impact on the investigation was either negligible or detrimental.

In the final chapter 16 Nicholas McGeorge and Hartmut-Michael Weber investigate policies in different European countries regarding imprisonment and release procedures for homicide cases. In general, countries with indeterminate sentences use risk assessment in deciding when to release offenders. The authors consider various justifications for life sentences and also how far these sentences might involve infringement of human rights.

Taken together, the following 16 chapters include a great deal of interesting information about understanding and controlling sexual and violent offences and about related topics such as risk assessment and offender profiling. We believe that they should be of interest not only to scholars in criminology and psychology but also to policy-makers and practitioners who have to deal with sexual and violent offences on a day-to-day basis.

A
RISK ASSESSMENT

Chapter 1

RISK ASSESSMENT: REVIEW OF PSYCHOMETRIC MEASURES

Emma J. Palmer

RISK ASSESSMENT

Much research in criminology has concentrated on the prediction of criminal behaviour, seeking to establish those factors that are reliably associated with the criterion behaviour (Hollin & Palmer, 1995). Of this work, a substantial proportion has been concerned with the prediction of re-offending, or recidivism. It is important that the risk factors for predicting re-offending are known, as this knowledge allows measures that assess these to be generated and gives a direction for treatment programmes within both prisons and the community.

Before reviewing the literature on risk assessment and predicting recidivism, it is necessary to consider the issue of 'hits and misses' when making predictions of this type (Hollin & Palmer, 1995). This refers to the importance of making sure that the predictors identified produce high levels of *true positive* decisions (correct identification of re-offending when the predictors are present) and *true negative* decisions (correct prediction of no re-offending in the absence of the predictors). These are known as 'hits', while incorrect decisions are known as 'misses', with *false positives* occurring when presence of the predictors is associated with no re-offending and *false negatives* occurring when re-offending happens despite the absence of the predictors.

The literature reveals a number of factors to be associated with an increased likelihood of re-offending (for a review, see Bonta, Law & Hanson, 1996; Gendreau, Little & Goggin, 1996; Hanson & Bussiere, 1996). These include criminal history (offence type and severity, previous convictions), demographic variables, family background, social factors, situational factors, and psychological variables such as attitudes to offending. These factors can be split into two types of predictors: *static* variables that do not change (for example, criminal history and family background), and *dynamic* variables that may change over time (for example, social, situational and psychological factors), and lead to a change in risk (Simon, 1971). The advantage of including dynamic variables in risk assessment measures is their ability to account for changes that may have been brought about by rehabilitation programmes or other criminal justice interventions.

Early methods of predicting risk of re-offending were pioneered in the 1920s, tending to use information from official files containing demographic and criminal history variables (e.g. Burgess, 1928; Hart, 1923). These types of prediction measures are generally referred to as *statistical or actuarial* prediction, and the information used is mostly of a static nature, e.g. criminal history and family background. Later measures of risk to predict re-offending have incorporated dynamic factors. Another method of prediction is *clinical* prediction, which is based on the clinical judgement of individual clinicians or clinical teams. One continuing debate in this area concerns the effectiveness of these two types of prediction, and although it is generally accepted that statistical prediction is the more accurate (Gottfredson, 1987; Meehl, 1954), it can also be argued that the inclusion of clinical variables does add something to a purely statistical method. Furthermore, there are very few measures that are purely statistical in nature (Hollin & Palmer, 1995).

Actuarial prediction

Actuarial instruments to assess risk of re-offending are typically developed by examining a range of possible variables that may predict recidivism – these may include demographic, criminal history, and psychological variables. Multivariate statistics are then used to identify those that best predict risk of re-offending (for an example of this, see Harris, Rice & Quinsey, 1993). Once these variables have been identified, offenders can be assigned a risk score by either summing their scores on the individual variables, or using a system whereby some variables are weighted.

Over the years many actuarial measures attempting to predict risk of re-offending have been developed in this way. Examples of these for general offender populations include the California Base Expectancy Scale (Gottfredson & Ballard, 1965), the Salient Factor Scale (Gottfredson, Wilkins & Hoffman, 1978), the Wisconsin Juvenile Probation and Aftercare Instrument (Ashford & LeCroy, 1988), and the Recidivism Prediction Score (Nuffield, 1982). Other instruments have been developed for more specific populations, for example, the Contra Costa Risk Assessment Instrument, the Arizona Juvenile Risk Assessment Form, and the Orange County Risk Assessment Instrument are all aimed at young offenders (Ashford & LeCroy, 1990), while Harris et al. (1993) have developed an instrument for predicting violent offending among mentally disordered offenders.

One instrument mentioned above that has been the subject of a degree of research is the Salient Factor Scale, which was developed by the U.S. Parole Commission (Gottfredson et al., 1978; Hoffman, 1983; Hoffman & Stone-Meierhoefer, 1979) using only statistical information. It is a checklist consisting of 6 items, which are combined to give a score ranging from 0 to 10, with high scores indicating a higher risk of reconviction. Within this range, there are categories of risk as follows: 0–3 is low risk, 4–5 is fair risk, 6–7 good risk, and 8–10 very good risk. The checklist items and scoring are shown in Table 1.

An initial 5 year follow-up evaluation study among released prisoners by Hoffman and Beck (1985) demonstrated that scores on the Salient Factor Score predicted re-offending. This is supported by more recent research reporting a long-term follow-up of prisoners that suggests its predictive ability was retained over the seventeen years covered by the study (Hoffman, 1994).

Moving the focus to measures developed in England, Nuttall (1977) produced the Reconviction Prediction Score (RPS), which aimed to give a percentage probability of reconviction of male offenders within 2 years of release from prison. This identifies 16 predictors, covering a number

Table 1: Salient Factor Score (from Hoffman & Beck, 1985).

Item A	Prior convictions/adjudications None = 3; One = 2; Two or three = 1; Four or more = 0
Item B	Prior commitment(s) of more than 30 days None = 2; One or two = 1; Three or more = 0
Item C	Age at current offense/prior commitments Age at current offense: 26 years or more = 2; 20–25 years = 1 19 years or less = 0
Item D	Recent commitment-free period (three years) No prior commitment of more than 30 days (adult or juvenile), or released to the community from last such commitment at least 3 years prior to the commencement of the current offense = 1; Otherwise = 0
Item E	Probation/parole/confinement/escape status violator this time Neither on probation, parole, confinement or escape status at the time of current offense; nor committed as a probation, parole, confinement or escape status violator this time = 1; Otherwise = 0
Item F	History of heroin/opiate dependence No history of heroin or opiate dependence = 1; Otherwise = 0

of demographic and criminal history variables (see Table 2). Unlike the Salient Factor Score, it assigns a weighting to the different variables measured, which are then summed to give the raw total score (range –31 to +31). These are then converted to the final score which has a range from 0 to 100, which corresponds to the probability of reconviction with higher scores indicating a higher risk. A large validation study of the RPS by Ward (1987) concluded that it is generally robust, with the exception of a few minor statistical points.

Table 2: Predictors in the Reconviction Prediction Score (from Ward, 1987)

Main offence	Interval at risk since last release
Age at offence	Juvenile custodial treatment
Value of property stolen	Probation history
Number of associates	Prison offences
Offences during current sentence	Occupation (Registrar-General's class)
Number of previous convictions	Employment at time of offence
Age at first conviction	Time in last job
Number of previous imprisonments	Living arrangements at time of offence

A more recent scale developed in England and Wales used to identify those offenders who are suitable for parole is the Risk of Reconviction Scale (ROR) (Copas, Marshall & Tarling, 1996). They used the statistical technique of survival analysis to model the length of time it took offenders to be reconvicted. This analysis identified six items which are weighted to produce two final scores; one to indicate risk for any re-offending; the other for serious re-offending (see Table 3).

The authors of the ROR have also developed a similar tool for use in the English and Welsh Probation Service, known as the Offender Group Reconviction Scale (OGRS: Copas & Marshall, 1998). This provides

Table 3: Items on the ROR and their Weights (from Copas et al., 1996)

		WEIGHTS	
	Variable	Any re-offending	Serious re-offending
1.	Age at conviction	–1	–1
2.	No. of juvenile custodial sentences	+3	+4
3.	No. of adult custodial sentences	+2	+3
4.	No. of previous convictions (max. 25)		
5.	Current offence type:		
	Violence	–1	+1
	Sexual	+1	+8
	Drugs	–8	–11
	Burglary	+4	+3
	Theft	+8	+9
	Other	–4	–10
6.	If female	–13	–1

probabilities of reconviction at least once within 2 years, using information from six demographic and criminal background items (see Table 4). Launched nationally in 1997 it is anticipated OGRS will become the standard risk assessment tool used in writing Pre-Sentence Reports for the courts.

Table 4: Items on the OGRS (from Copas & Marshall, 1998)

1.	Age	
2.	Sex (coded 1 if female and 0 if male)	
3.	No. of juvenile custodial sentences	
4.	Total number of appearances in court	
5.	Years since first conviction	
5.	Current offence type:	
	Sexual	−12
	Drugs	−6
	Violence (includes arson & robbery)	−5
	Fraud/forgery	−2
	Criminal damage	+3
	Theft	+6
	Vehicle theft	+6
	Burglary	+7
	Other offences	+3

Similar research in the Scottish prison service has been carried out by Cooke and Michie (1998) which identified similar predictor variables. An evaluation of this measure showed it to correctly predict level of reconviction within two years of release in 83% of cases and predict re-imprisonment in 74% of cases (Cooke & Michie, 1998).

Measures incorporating dynamic, clinical predictors
Clinical prediction of recidivism varies from research examining the predictive validity of a measure of a single psychological construct through to that which attempts to develop classification schemes based on knowledge of a number of psychological variables (Hollin & Palmer, 1995). These are known as simple predictors (one psychological construct) and complex predictors (a number of psychological variables). These can arguably be said to use actuarial methods, in that they look for the variables that best predict recidivism, but they are notable for the inclusion of clinical variables.

Simple predictors
The prediction of recidivism literature reveals a huge number of studies relating various psychological factors to recidivism. These have included personality variables, psychometric scales and intelligence tests (Hollin &

Palmer, 1995). McGurk, McEwan and Graham (1981) used a number of psychometric tests to explore whether personality types were differentially related to recidivism among young offenders. Cluster analysis of scores from the Hostility and Direction of Hostility Questionnaire (Caine, Foulds & Hope, 1967), the Psychological Screening Inventory (Lanyon, 1973), and the 16 Personality Factor Questionnaire Form E (Cattell, Eber & Tatsuoka, 1970) revealed four personality clusters: an 'anxious' type, a 'normal' type, a 'disturbed' type and a 'truculent' type. Comparison of the recidivism rates of the four clusters showed that the young offenders in the 'anxious' group re-offended the least, while those in the 'truculent' group had the highest rate of re-offending.

There is also a long tradition of personality research investigating the utility of the Minnesota Multiphasic Personality Inventory (MMPI) to predict recidivism (e.g. Ingram, Marchioni, Hill, Caraveo-Ramos & McNeil, 1985). However, despite the wealth of studies that have used it, the results produced are mixed and inconsistent concerning its predictive validity with respect to recidivism.

In conclusion, the research on 'simple' clinical predictors of recidivism does not show any such measures to be strongly associated with re-offending (for a review, see Andrews & Bonta, 1998). Such evidence that does exist tends to be marred by a lack of replication, small sample sizes, and, especially in the case of the MMPI, highly inconsistent findings. Therefore, more complex clinical predictors will be reviewed next.

Complex predictors
Complex predictors of recidivism typically consist of instruments that classify offenders into categories which may be related to a level of risk (for reviews, see Andrews & Bonta, 1998; Andrews, Bonta & Hoge, 1990). Examples of these include Quay's Behavioral Typology (Quay, 1984); the Interpersonal Maturity (I-Level) system (Sullivan, Grant & Grant, 1957), the Jesness Inventory (Jesness, 1971, 1988), the Conceptual Level (CL) classification (Brill, 1978; Leschied, Jaffe & Stone, 1985) and the Client Management Classification (CMC) system (Dhaliwal, Porporino & Ross, 1994; Lerner, Arling & Baird, 1986).

The majority of these are based on 'personality' classifications (Quay's Behavioral Typology, the I-Level and the CL), and the evidence regarding their predictive utility is limited. In a review Andrews and Bonta (1998) pointed out that so far their effectiveness has generally only been demonstrated with respect to institutional behaviour rather than recidivism after release. As behaviour in prisons does not always correspond to that outside of the institution (Bonta & Gendreau, 1992), this issue needs to be addressed by empirical research before any final judgements on the use of these measures can be made.

The other 'complex' predictor mentioned above, the CMC, is different from the other systems in that it gathers information on background factors and criminogenic variables in order to inform correctional treatment plans. This approach allows for a range of variables covering background, social, criminogenic and psychological factors to be taken into consideration. Originally developed by the Wisconsin Bureau of Community Corrections, it involves a semi-structured interview after which four of the criminogenic factors are highlighted as being important in that offender's criminal behaviour. These are then targeted in rehabilitation programmes. Table 5 shows the criminogenic variables in the CMC.

Table 5: Criminogenic Variables in the CMC

Academic/Vocational skills	Alcohol usage
Employment pattern	Mental ability
Financial management	Health (physical)
Marital/family relations	Sexual behaviour
Companions	Values/attitudes
Emotional stability	

Evaluations of the CMC's ability to reduce recidivism have shown positive results (e.g. Eisenberg & Markley, 1987; McManus, Stagg & McDuffie, 1988). However, an evaluation of the Canadian version (known as Case Management Strategies, CMS) by Dhaliwal et al. (1994) over an 18 month follow-up period found no significant impact upon recidivism rates. It was noted, though, that there were a number of methodological problems that may have contributed to these findings, including low completion rate and inconsistent application of the CMS principles.

Static versus dynamic predictors
A number of studies have examined the question of which type of information – static or dynamic variables – is most efficient at predicting recidivism. This has generally found that actuarial scales using social information history are more accurate than clinical or psychometric scales (e.g. Cowden & Pacht, 1967; Gendreau, Madden and Leipciger, 1980; Smith & Lanyon, 1968). In a comparison of social history information and the MMPI, Gendreau et al. (1980) also found the data on social

history variables to be more stable and reliable than the psychometric data. Other research has investigated whether the combination of static and dynamic data increases the accuracy of risk prediction. Again, results show that dynamic data only adds a minimal amount to the accuracy that could be obtained from using social history data alone (Gendreau et al., 1980; Gough, Wenk & Rozynko, 1965; Hassin, 1986; Wormith & Goldstone, 1984).

However, one such study that revealed a potentially important finding was reported by Holland, Holt, Levi and Beckett (1983). They found that the efficiency of static and dynamic factors in prediction differed according to the criterion used. Thus, when they considered general recidivism (numbers of arrests and reconvictions), the static variables (in this case the Salient Factor Scale) were the most accurate. However, the clinical judgements of mental health practitioners proved to be more accurate in predicting violent recidivism.

The general conclusion from the comparison of statistical and dynamic predictors of risk would appear to be that actuarial scales using demographic and criminal history variables offer the best option, with dynamic information having little to add. However, in their review Hollin and Palmer (1995) suggest that this can be interpreted in one of two ways. Firstly, if the evidence is taken at face value, it can be accepted that actuarial variables are far superior to dynamic information in the prediction of risk of re-offending. Alternatively, it may be argued that the existing measures of dynamic variables are not sophisticated enough for the job in hand.

The need to solve this issue is highlighted by Hoffman and Stone-Meierhoefer (1979), who point out that if dynamic predictors have no role to play in prediction then individual differences between offenders will not influence level of recidivism. Taking this further, it could be argued all offenders are likely to respond to their sentence in a similar way. Conversely, it may be that there are dynamic variables which can not only predict risk of re-offending, but can also offer insights into which conditions this is most likely to occur under and what sort of interventions are best suited to help reduce this risk (Hollin & Palmer, 1995).

The promising results found with the CMC (as discussed above), which combines both actuarial and dynamic clinical variables, suggest that combining the two types of predictors may yet be valuable. This is further supported by research on two more measures that incorporate both static and dynamic variables, and have been found to have good predictive power of recidivism. These are the Level of Service Inventory-Revised

(Andrews & Bonta, 1995) and the Psychopathy Checklist-Revised (Hare, 1991).

The Level of Service Inventory (LSI)

The LSI was developed in Canada by Andrews and his colleagues (Andrews, 1982; Andrews & Bonta, 1995) to assess risk and needs of offenders in order to help planning of treatment and level of supervision. It is based on social learning theory, rather than the personality approach favoured by many clinical instruments of risk, and takes into account the research literature on what factors predict criminal behaviour. The most recent version, the LSI-R, consists of 54 items, which are split into 10 components (see Table 6). These are answered either by a 'Yes – No' or a rating of 0–3, and cover a range of both static and dynamic variables meaning that scores on the LSI-R are sensitive to change over time.

Table 6: Components in the LSI-R

Criminal History (10)*	Leisure and Recreation (2)
Education and Employment (10)	Companions (5)
Financial (2)	Alcohol and Drug Problems (9)
Family and Marital (4)	Emotional and Personal (5)
Accommodation (3)	Attitudes and Orientation (4)

* Number of items in each component

This latest version is seen by Andrews and Bonta (1995) as providing criteria for the following:

- the identification of treatment targets and monitoring of offender risk while they are under supervision or being treated;
- making decisions regarding probation supervision;
- making decisions about placing offenders into halfway houses;
- decisions about security level classifications within prisons;
- assessment of the probability of recidivism.

There is a substantial research literature on the LSI-R (for a review, see Andrews & Bonta, 1998) which shows it is psychometrically sound in terms of reliability and validity, and provides empirical support for its use as an instrument in predicting and monitoring offender risk.

A number of studies have investigated whether the LSI-R can be collapsed into factors (Andrews & Bonta, 1995). Although the findings have been inconsistent, Loza and Simourd (1994) found two factors that appeared to correspond to the factors of the PCL-R (Hare, 1991), namely criminal lifestyle and emotional/personal problems. Furthermore, in the same study, LSI-R scores were shown to be significantly correlated with PCL-R scores. Other studies have examined the relationship between the LSI-R's subcomponents and related measures, and concluded that the subcomponents show good validity (Andrews, Kiessling, Mickus & Robinson, 1986; Andrews & Robinson, 1984; Bonta & Motiuk, 1985).

As noted above, the LSI-R has a number of uses, something which is supported by empirical research. Studies have shown that scores can successfully predict whether parole is granted, the violation of parole, and the placement of offenders in halfway houses (Bonta & Motiuk, 1985, 1987, 1990, 1992). Other studies have demonstrated its ability to predict behaviour both in and out of prison, including prison misconduct and reconviction within a year of release (Andrews & Bonta, 1995; Bonta, 1989; Bonta & Motiuk, 1987, 1992).

A version of the LSI-R has been adapted for young offenders (YLSI; Andrews, Robinson & Hoge, 1984) and been demonstrated to be psychometrically sound (Ilacqua, Coulson, Lombardo & Nutbrown, 1999; Shields, 1993; Simourd, Hoge, Andrews & Leschied, 1994). In another study by Shields and Simourd (1993) it was also shown to be capable of distinguishing between individuals exhibiting predatory and non-predatory behaviour in custody. Finally, adapted versions of the LSI-R have also been successful with female offenders, successfully predicting recidivism, parole violation, and placements in halfway houses and rehabilitation programmes (Coulson, 1993; Coulson, Ilacqua, Nutbrown, Giulekas & Cudjoe, 1996; Coulson, Nutbrown & Giulekas, 1993). However, as yet the YLSI and female version of the LSI-R have not been properly validated as clinical tools.

Psychopathy Checklist-Revised (PCL-R)
The Psychopathy Checklist (PCL) was originally developed by Hare (1980) as a 22 item checklist, and was subsequently revised to form the 20 item PCL-R (Hare, 1991). These items on the PCL-R are summarised in Table 7. Factor analysis has revealed there to be two factors within the PCL-R (Harpur, Hakstian & Hare, 1988):

> "Factor 1: Selfish, callous and remorseless use of others. . . . described a constellation of personality traits that many clinicians consider to be at the heart of psychopathy, including habitual lying, lovelessness and guiltlessness; Factor 2: Chronically unstable and antisocial lifestyle. . . . defines a lifestyle that is aimless, unpredictable and parasitic" (Harpur et al., 1988, p. 745).

Therefore, it would seem that the PCL-R measures 2 associated factors, one to do with personality traits, and the other more general persistent antisocial and criminal lifestyle. Further, while the two factors are correlated (about r = 0.50), they have different external correlates (Hare, 1991; Hare et al., 1990; Hart, Hare & Harpur, 1992).

Table 7: Items on the Psychopathy Checklist-Revised (from Hare, 1991)

	Item	Factor
1.	Superficial charm/glibness	1
2.	Grandiose sense of self-worth	1
3.	Need for stimulation/easily bored	2
4.	Pathological lying	1
5.	Manipulative	1
6.	Lack of remorse or guilt	1
7.	No emotional depth	1
8.	Callous/lack of empathy	1
9.	Parasitic lifestyle	2
10.	Poor behavioural controls	2
11.	Promiscuous sexual behaviour	—
12.	Early behaviour problems	2
13.	Lack of long-term planning	2
14.	Impulsive	2
15.	Irresponsible	2
16.	Failure to accept responsibility for own actions	1
17.	Frequent marital failures	—
18.	Delinquent as a juvenile	2
19.	Poor record on probation or other conditional release	2
20.	Versatile as a criminal	—

Since the PCL-R was developed there has been a great deal of research on its use, which demonstrates that psychopaths are among the most serious and persistent offenders, typically having a number of convictions for a wide variety of offences (Hare, McPherson & Forth, 1988). Furthermore, they are also more likely to violate release conditions and be reconvicted within a year of release from prison, especially of a violent offence (Hart, Kropp & Hare, 1988; Hart et al., 1990; Serin, 1991; Serin, Peters & Barbaree, 1990). This has also been found to hold true among male young offenders (Forth, Hart & Hare, 1990; Gretton, 1997; Gretton, McBride, O'Shaughnessy & Hare, 1995; Toupin, Mercier, Dery, Cote & Hodgins, 1996), female offenders (Loucks, 1995; Zaparniuk & Paris, 1995) and sex offenders (Rice and Harris, 1997). Even though it was not designed as a risk prediction instrument, it has been found to be highly associated with scores on other actuarial measures of risk and be as good as or better at predicting recidivism (Harris, Rice & Cormier, 1991; Hemphill, Hare & Wong, 1998; Serin, 1996; Serin et al., 1990).

Unlike many instruments in this area, assessing an individual on the PCL-R requires a fair amount of work and training, including a semi-structured interview that usually lasts 90 to 120 minutes, and a detailed trawl through case history records (Hart, Hare & Forth, 1994). Therefore, more recently a shorter version of the PCL-R has been developed with 12 items, that takes less training, time and effort to administer. This is known as the Psychopathy Checklist: Screening Version (PCL:SV) and appears to be psychometrically robust (Hart et al., 1994). Its factor structure has also been analysed and been found to be isomorphic to that of the full PCL-R (Hart, Cox & Hare, 1995).

CONCLUSION

In a meta-analysis of predictors of recidivism among adult offenders, Gendreau, Little and Goggin (1995) concluded that dynamic predictors can be as efficient as static ones. Furthermore, they suggest that the LSI-R is the best 'off-the-shelf' risk assessment instrument currently available, with the PCL-R offering the best measure of antisocial behaviour. However, they point out that two things the LSI-R does lack are a direct measure of antisocial behaviour, and a measure of institutional behaviour.

Despite this though, in terms of predicting recidivism, the strength of the LSI-R and PCL-R would seem to lie in the wide array of criminogenic factors they assess, including factors related to lifestyle, behaviour, and attitudes. Unlike many other instruments designed to assess risk, their development was evidence driven rather than theory driven. Therefore they are based on known criminogenic factors rather than assessing psychological constructs hypothesised to be related to offending.

REFERENCES

Andrews, D. A. (1982). *The Level of Supervision Inventory (LSI): The first follow-up*. Toronto: Ontario Ministry of Correctional Services.

Andrews, D. A. & Bonta, J. (1998). *The psychology of criminal conduct*. 2nd edition. Cincinnati, OH: Anderson Publishing.

Andrews, D. A. & Bonta, J. (1995). *LSI-R: The Level of Service Inventory-Revised*. Toronto: Multi-Health Systems.

Andrews, D. A., Bonta, J., & Hoge, R. D. (1990). Classification for effective rehabilitation: Rediscovering psychology. *Criminal Justice and Behavior, 17*, 19–52.

Andrews, D. A., Kiessling, J. J., Mickus, S., & Robinson, D. (1986). The construct validity of interview-based risk assessment in corrections. *Canadian Journal of Behavioral Science, 18*, 460–470.

Andrews, D. A. & Robinson, D. (1984). *The Level of Supervision Inventory: Second Report*. A report to Research Services (Toronto) of the Ontario Ministry of Correctional Services.

Andrews, D. A., Robinson, D., & Hoge, R. D. (1984). *The Youth Level of Service Inventory (YLSI): Scoring manual*. Unpublished manuscript. Ottawa, Ontario: Department of Psychology, Carleton University.

Ashford, J. B. & LeCroy, C. W. (1988). Predicting recidivism: An evaluation of the Wisconsin Juvenile Probation and Aftercare Risk Instrument. *Criminal Justice and Behavior, 15*, 141–151.

Ashford, J. B. & LeCroy, C. W. (1990). Juvenile recidivism: A comparison of three prediction instruments. *Adolescence, 25*, 441–450.

Bonta, J. (1989). Native inmates: Institutional response, risk and needs. *Canadian Journal of Criminology, 31*, 49–62.

Bonta, J. & Gendreau, P. (1992). Coping with prison. In P. Suedfeld & P. E. Tetlock (Eds.) *Psychology and social policy*. New York: Hemisphere Publishing.

Bonta, J., Law, M., & Hanson, K. (1996). *The prediction of criminal and violent recidivism among mentally disordered offenders: A meta-analysis*. Ottawa, Canada: Solicitor General of Canada.

Bonta, J. & Motiuk, L. L. (1985). Utilization of an interview-based classification instrument: A study of correctional halfway houses. *Criminal Justice and Behavior, 12*, 333–352.

Bonta, J. & Motiuk, L. L. (1987). The diversion of incarcerated offenders to halfway houses. *Journal of Research in Crime and Delinquency, 24*, 302–323.

Bonta, J. & Motiuk, L. L. (1990). Classification to halfway houses: A quasi-experimental evaluation. *Criminology, 28*, 497–506.

Bonta, J. & Motiuk, L. L. (1992). Inmate classification. *Journal of Criminal Justice, 20*, 343–353.

Brill, R. (1978). Implications of the conceptual level matching model for treatment of delinquents. *Journal of Research in Crime and Delinquency, 15*, 229–246.

Burgess, E. W. (1928). Factors determining success or failure on parole. In A. A. Bruce, A. J. Harno, E. W. Burgess & J. Landesco (Eds.) *The workings of the indeterminate sentence law and the parole system in Illinois*. Springfield, IL: Illinois State Board of Parole.

Caine, T. M., Foulds, G. A., & Hope, K. (1967). *Manual of the Hostility and Direction of Hostility Questionnaire*. London: University of London Press.

Cattell, R. B., Eber, H. W., & Tatsuoka, M. M. (1970). *Handbook for the Sixteen Personality Factor Questionnaire*. Windsor: NFER.

Cooke, D. J. & Michie, C. (1998). Predicting recidivism in a Scottish prison sample. *Psychology, Crime and Law, 4*, 169–211.

Copas, J. & Marshall, P. (1998). The Offender Group Reconviction Scale: A statistical reconviction score for use by probation officers. *Applied Statistics, 47*, 159–171.

Copas, J., Marshall, P., & Tarling, R. (1996). *Predicting reoffending for discretionary conditional release*. London: HMSO.

Coulson, G. (1993). Using the Level of Supervision Inventory in placing female offenders in rehabilitation programs or halfway houses. *IARCA Journal, 5*, 12–13.

Coulson, G., Ilacqua, G. Nutbrown, V., Giulekas, D., & Cudjoe, F. (1996). Predictive utility of the LSI for incarcerated female offenders. *Criminal Justice and Behavior, 23*, 427–439.

Coulson, G., Nutbrown, V., & Giulekas, D. (1993). Using the Level of Supervision Inventory in placing female offenders in rehabilitation programs or halfway houses. *IARCA Journal, 5*, 12–13.

Cowden, J. E. & Pacht, A. R. (1967). Predicting institutional and post release adjustment of delinquent boys. *Journal of Consulting Psychology, 31*, 377–381.

Dhaliwal, G. K., Porporino, F., & Ross, R. R. (1994). Assessment of criminogenic factors, program assignment and recidivism. *Criminal Justice and Behavior, 21*, 454–467.

Eisenberg, M. & Markley, G. (1987). Something works in community supervision. *Federal Probation, 51*, 28–32.

Forth, A. E., Hart, R. D, & Hare, S. D. (1990). Assessment of psychopathy in male young offenders. *Psychological Assessment: A Journal of Consulting and Clinical Psychology*, 2, 342–344.

Gendreau, P., Little, T., & Goggin, C. (1995). A meta-analysis of the predictors of adult offender recidivism: Assessment guidelines for classification and treatment. *User Report submitted to the Corrections Branch, Minister Secretariat, Solicitor General of Canada.*

Gendreau, P., Little, T., & Goggin, C. (1996). A meta-analysis of the predictors of adult offender recidivism: What works! *Criminology, 34*, 575–607.

Gendreau, P., Madden, P. G., & Leipciger, M. (1980). Predicting recidivism with social history information and a comparison of their predictive power with psychometric variables. *Canadian Journal of Criminology, 22*, 328–336.

Gottfredson, S. D. (1987). Statistical and actuarial considerations. In F. Dutile & C. Foust (Eds.) *The Prediction of Violence*. Springfield, IL: C. C. Thomas.

Gottfredson, S. D. & Ballard, K. B. (1965). *The validity of two parole prediction scales: An eight year follow-up study*. Vacaville, CA: Institute for the Study of Crime and Delinquency.

Gottfredson, S. D., Wilkins, L. T., & Hoffman, P. B. (1978). *Guidelines for parole and sentencing: A policy control method*. Toronto: Lexington Books.

Gough, H. G., Wenk, E. A., & Rozynko, V. V. (1965). Parole outcome as predicted from the CPI, MMPI and a base expectancy table. *Journal of Abnormal Psychology, 70*, 432–441.

Gretton, H. M. (1997). Psychopathy and recidivism from adolescence to adulthood: A ten year retrospective follow-up. Unpublished dissertation. University of British Columbia, Vancouver, Canada.

Gretton, H. M., McBride, M., O'Shaughnessy, R., & Hare, R. D. (1995). Psychopathy in adolescent sex offenders: A follow-up study. Paper presented at the Fourteenth Annual Research and Treatment Conference for the Association for the Treatment of Sexual Abusers, New Orleans, LA, October.

Hanson, K. & Bussiere, M. T. (1996). *Predictors of sexual offender recidivism: A meta-analysis*. Ottawa, Canada: Solicitor General of Canada.

Hare, R. D. (1980). A research scale for the assessment of psychopathy in criminal populations. *Personality and Individual Differences, 1*, 111–119.

Hare, R. D. (1991). *The Hare Psychopathy Checklist-Revised*. Toronto: Multi-Health Systems.

Hare, R. D., Harpur, T. J., Hakstian, A. R., Forth, A. E., Hart, S. D., & Newman, J. P. (1990). The Revised Psychopathy Checklist: Reliability and factor structure. *Psychological Assessment: A Journal of Consulting and Clinical Psychology, 2*, 338–341.

Hare, R. D., McPherson, L. E., & Forth, A. E. (1988). Male psychopaths and their criminal careers. *Journal of Consulting and Criminal Psychology, 56*, 710–714.

Harpur, T. J., Hakstian, R., & Hare, R. D. (1988). Factor structure of the Psychopathy Checklist. *Journal of Consulting and Clinical Psychology, 56*, 741–747.

Harris, G. T., Rice, M. E., & Cormier, C. A. (1991). Psychopathy and violent recidivism. *Law and Human Behavior, 15*, 625–637.

Harris, G. T., Rice, M. E., & Quinsey, V. L. (1993). Violent recidivism of mentally disordered offenders: The development of a statistical prediction instrument. *Criminal Justice and Behavior, 20*, 315–335.

Hart, H. (1923). Predicting parole success. *Journal of Criminal Law and Criminology, 14*, 405–413.

Hart, S. D., Cox, D. N., & Hare, R. D. (1995). *Manual for the Psychopathy Checklist: Screening Version (PCL:SV)*. Toronto: Multi-Health Systems.

Hart, S. D., Hare, R. D., & Forth, A. E. (1994). Psychopathy as a risk marker for violence: Development and validation of a screening version of the Revised Psychopathy Checklist. In J. Monahan & H. Steadman (Eds.) *Violence and mental disorder: Developments in risk assessment*. (pp. 81–98). Chicago: University of Chicago Press.

Hart, S. D., Hare, R. D, & Harpur, T. J. (1992). The Psychopathy Checklist: Overview for researchers and clinicians. In J. Rosen & P. McReynolds (Eds.) *Advances in psychological assessment*. Volume 7 (pp. 103–130). New York: Plenum.

Hart, S. D., Kropp, P. R., & Hare, R. D. (1988). Performance of psychopaths following conditional release from prison. *Journal of Consulting and Clinical Psychology*, 56, 227–232.

Hassin, Y. (1986). Two models for predicting recidivism. *British Journal of Criminology*, 26, 270–286.

Hemphill, J. F., Hare, R. D., & Wong, S. (1998). Psychopathy and recidivism: A review. *Legal and Criminological Psychology*, 3, 139–170.

Hoffman, P. B. (1983). Screening for risk: A revised salient factor score (SFS 81). *Journal of Criminal Justice*, 11, 539–547.

Hoffman, P. B. (1994). Twenty years of operational use of a risk prediction instrument: The United States Parole Commission's salient factor score. *Journal of Criminal Justice*, 22, 477–494.

Hoffman, P. B. & Beck, J. L. (1985). Recidivism among released federal prisoners: Salient factor score and five-year follow-up. *Criminal Justice and Behavior*, 12, 501–507.

Hoffman, P. B. & Stone-Meierhoefer, B. (1979). Post release arrest experiences of federal prisoners: A six-year follow-up. *Journal of Criminal Justice*, 7, 193–216.

Holland, T. R., Holt, N., Levi, M., & Beckett, G. E. (1983). Comparison and combination of clinical and statistical predictions of recidivism among adult offenders. *Journal of Applied Psychology*, 68, 203–211.

Hollin, C. R. & Palmer, E. J. (1995). *Assessing prison regimes: A review to inform the development of outcome measures*. Commissioned report for The Planning Group, HM Prison Service.

Ilacqua, G. E., Coulson, G. E., Lombardo, D., & Nutbrown, V. (1999). Predictive validity of the Young Offender Level of Service Inventory for criminal recidivism of male and female young offenders. *Psychological Bulletin*, 84, 1214–1218.

Ingram, J. C., Marchioni, P., Hill, G., Caraveo-Ramos, E., & McNeil, B. (1985). Recidivism, perceived problem-solving abilities, MMPI characteristics and violence: A study of black and white incarcerated male adult offenders. *Journal of Clinical Psychology*, 41, 423–432.

Jesness, C. F. (1971). The Preston Typology Study: An experiment with differential treatment in an institution. *Journal of Research in Crime and Delinquency*, 8, 38–52.

Jesness, C. F. (1988). The Jesness Inventory classification system. *Criminal Justice and Behavior*, 15, 78–91.

Lanyon, R. I. (1973). *Manual of the Psychological Screening Inventory*. New York: Research Psychologists Press.

Lerner, K., Arling, G., & Baird, S. C. (1986). Client management strategies for case supervision. *Crime and Delinquency*, 32, 254–271.

Leschied, A. W., Jaffe, P. G., & Stone, G. L. (1985). Differential response of juvenile offenders to two different environments as a function of conceptual level. *Canadian Journal of Criminology*, 27, 467–476.

Loucks, A. D. (1995). Criminal behavior, violent behavior and prison maladjustment in federal female offenders. Unpublished doctoral dissertation. Queen's University, Kingston, Ontario, Canada.

Loza, W. & Simourd, D. J. (1994). Psychometric evaluation of the Level of Supervision Inventory (LSI) among male Canadian federal offenders. *Criminal Justice and Behavior*, 21, 468–480.

McGurk, B. J., McEwan, A. W., & Graham, F. (1981). Personality types and recidivism among young delinquents. *British Journal of Criminology*, 21, 159–165.

McManus, R. F., Stagg, D. I., & McDuffie, C. R. (1988). CMC as an effective supervision tool: The South Carolina perspective. *Perspectives*, 4, 30–34.

Meehl, P. E. (1954). *Clinical versus statistical predictions: A theoretical analysis and a review of the evidence.* Minneapolis, MN: University of Minnesota Press.

Nuffield, J. (1982). *Parole decision-making in Canada: Research towards decision guidelines.* Ottawa: Minister of Supply and Services, Canada.

Nuttall, C. P. (1977). *Parole in England and Wales.* London: HMSO.

Quay, H. C. (1984). *Managing adult inmates: Classification for housing and program assignments.* College Park, MD: American Correctional Association.

Rice, M. E. & Harris, G. T. (1997). Cross-validation and extension of the Violence Risk Appraisal Guide for child molesters and rapists. *Law and Human Behavior, 21,* 231–241.

Serin, R. C. (1991). Psychopathy and violence in criminals. *Journal of Interpersonal Violence, 6,* 423–431.

Serin, R. C. (1996). Violent recidivism in criminal psychopaths. *Law and Human Behavior, 20,* 207–217.

Serin, R. C., Peters, R. D., & Barbaree, H. E. (1990). Predictors of psychopathy and release outcome in a criminal population. *Psychological Assessment: A Journal of Consulting and Clinical Psychology, 2,* 419–422.

Shields, I. W. (1993). The use of the Young Offender-Level of Service Inventory (YO-LSI) with adolescents. *IARCA Journal, 5,* 10–26.

Shields, I. W. & Simourd, D. J. (1991). Predicting predatory behavior in a population of incarcerated young offenders. *Criminal Justice and Behavior, 18,* 180–194.

Simourd, D. J., Hoge, R. D., Andrews, D. A., & Leschied, A. W. (1994). An empirically-based typology of male young offenders. *Canadian Journal of Criminology, 36,* 447–461.

Simon, F. H. (1971). *Prediction measures in criminology.* London: HMSO.

Smith, J. & Lanyon, R. I. (1968). Prediction of juvenile probation violators. *Journal of Consulting and Clinical Psychology, 32,* 54–58.

Sullivan, C., Grant, M. Q., & Grant, J. D. (1957). The development of interpersonal maturity: Application to delinquency. *Psychiatry, 20,* 373–385.

Toupin, J., Mercier, H., Dery, M., Cote, G., & Hodgins, S. (1996). Validity of the PCL-R for adolescents. In D. J. Cooke, A. E. Forth, J. Newman & R. D. Hare (Eds.) *Issues in Criminological and Legal Psychology: No. 24. International perspectives on psychopathy.* (pp. 143–145). Leicester: British Psychological Society.

Ward, D. (1987). *The validity of the Reconviction Prediction Score.* London: HMSO.

Wormith, J. S. & Goldstone, C. S. (1984). The clinical and statistical prediction of recidivism. *Criminal Justice and Behavior, 11,* 3–34.

Zaparniuk, J. & Paris, F. (1995). Female psychopaths: Violence and recidivism. Paper presented at a conference entitled 'Mental Disorder and Criminal Justice: Changes, Challenges and Solutions', Vancouver, British Columbia, Canada, April.

Chapter 2

TOWARD A SCIENTIFIC FOUNDATION OF SEX OFFENDER RISK ASSESSMENT

Susan J. Sachsenmaier and Stephen J. Lally

In the United States there has been an increased focus on sexual offenders both by legislators and the general public. This attention has led to the passage of Megan's Law and Violent Sexual Predator Laws (La Fond & Winick, 1998). Megan's Law requires the registration of sexual offenders and notification of the community when high-risk individuals move into the area. While Megan's Law is applied nationwide, states vary on how they rate risk and how a community is notified. There have been many constitutional challenges to sexual offender registration legislation. In general, these challenges have not been upheld (Walsh & Cohen, 1998). It is likely that once sexual offenders have exhausted appellate issues based on constitutional grounds, they will look to challenge the scientific validity of the expert's assessment of an offender as high-risk.

Sexual Predator Laws in the United States arose because states were reluctant to release high-risk sexual offenders into the community after they completed their prison sentence. This civil commitment procedure can result in a de facto life sentence. Though criticized both in terms of double jeopardy and for their unscientific definition of mental abnormality, the United States Supreme Court recently upheld these laws (*Kansas v. Hendricks*, 1997). California's law survived the initial constitutional challenges (*Hubbart v. Superior Court*, 1999), and now at the trial level there have been challenges towards the admissibility of risk assessment instruments (A. Phenix, personal communication, July 19, 1999). At this point, the courts have not upheld these challenges; however, it is predicted that these rulings will in the near future be appealed.

Both Megan's Law and the Sexual Predator Laws require offenders to be evaluated to determine their risk to reoffend. Frequently in this context, psychologists are called by the courts to provide expert testimony about a sexual offender's risk to reoffend. As an expert witness in the United States, a psychologist's opinions must be based on a solid scientific foundation. In a recent case, *Daubert v. Merrell Dow Pharmaceuticals, Inc.* (1993), the United States Supreme Court described the standards for admissibility. Basing their decision on the Federal Rules of Evidence 702, they established a two-pronged test to determine whether an expert's testimony can be admitted. Testimony must be both scientifically valid and relevant. They also articulated criteria which trial judges should use to decide whether the reasoning and methodology underlying the testimony is scientifically valid. The four criteria are: 1) whether the theory or technique can be, and has been tested – falsifiability; 2) whether the theory or technique has been subjected to peer review and published in professional journals; 3) whether there is general acceptance of the theory and technique in the scientific community; and 4) which really has two sub-criteria within it, asks whether the theory or technique has a known error rate and whether there exist standards to control the technique's operation. These four criteria were not meant to be exhaustive, and the Court did not state that testimony had to meet all four elements. Meeting one of the criteria can be enough to show that the expert relied on evidence that had sufficient scientific underpinning to allow testimony. This standard for admission is relatively low, and even imperfect or relatively weak scientific evidence can meet the threshold. The Court felt that once testimony gained admission, its relative strengths or weaknesses would come out in cross examination and determine the weight given to that testimony.

This paper examines whether eight of the most well known instruments used by experts to measure sexual offenders' risk of reoffending have the necessary scientific foundation, in terms of the *Daubert* criteria, to meet the standard for admission into court (See Tables 1 and 2). Their relative

Table 1: Rating of Risk Assessment Instruments According to the *Daubert* (1993) Criteria.

Daubert Criteria _____1.	Abel: VRT	Abel: Questionnaire	Abel: RPS	VRAG	SORAG	FedRAG
1. Falsifiability	+	–	–	+ +	+	– –
2. Peer review and published in professional journal	–	– –	– –	+ +	–	– –
3. General acceptance by scientific community	–	–	+	+ +	+	–
4. a. Known error rate	– –	–	–	+	+	– –
b. Standards for administration	+ +	+	–	+	+	+

Note. + + = fully meets the criteria, + = partially meets the criteria, – = largely does not meet the criteria, – – = does not meet the criteria.

Table 2: Rating of Risk Assessment Instruments According to the *Daubert* (1993) Criteria.

Daubert Criteria	SVR-20	Penile Plethysmograph	PCL-R	RRASOR
1. Falsifiability	+	+	+ +	+
2. Peer review and published in professional journal	– –	+ +	+ +	–
3. General acceptance by scientific community	+ +	+ +	+ +	+ +
4. a. Known error rate	– –	–	+ +	–
b. Standards for administration	–	– –	+ +	+

Note. + + = fully meets the criteria, + = partially meets the criteria, – = largely does not meet the criteria,
   – – = does not meet the criteria.

strengths and weaknesses, and the factors that may affect how much weight the trier of fact gives an opinion will also be reviewed. Finally, guidelines will be presented on how psychologists can enhance the scientific foundation of their risk assessments.

The Abel Screen for Sexual Interests

The Abel Screen for Sexual Interests (Abel Screen) (Abel et al., 1994) is composed of three processes, including: 1) visual reaction time (VRT) to slides representing 22 sexual categories, 2) a self-report questionnaire of sexual history and 3) a risk prediction score (RPS). Studies have shown VRT increases with a client's interest in the subject matter and correlates highly with arousal as measured by plethysmography (Abel et al., 1998). The RPS is partially based on variables reported by Hanson and Bussière (1996) to have relatively high correlations with recidivism. The method of calculating the RPS has not been published in any peer-reviewed journal. Abel offers an explanation in his newsletter (Abel, 1997) and in a handout entitled "Calculations of Twenty Components" (G. Abel, personal communication, June 23, 1999). Hanson (personal communication by e-mail, July 14, 1999) stated, "the main problem with Abel's method of calculating risk is that he fails to consider the intercorrelations of the items." In summary, many, if not most, of Abel's claims regarding the utility of the Abel Screen have not been empirically validated.

In one study (Abel et al., 1998), using a different set of slides than is currently employed, VRT correctly classified 76.7% of subjects with interest in female adolescents, with 20.8% false positives; 91.2% of subjects with interest in male adolescents, with 6.5% false positives; 65.6% of subjects with interest in female children, with 35.2% false positives; and 90.7% of subjects with interest in male children, with 4.4% false positives. In a recent American Psychiatric Association task force report (1999), Abel and others report that currently VRT is not standardized.

Officials at the Abel center reported in personal communication (D. Jones, June 8, 1999; G. Abel, June 23, 1999) that they are aware of no cases in which courts have conducted a hearing on the admissibility of the Abel Screen. This paper will examine the Abel Screen with regards to the *Daubert* criteria; each of the three parts of the Screen will be evaluated separately.

Abel's Visual Reaction Time, or VRT, minimally meets the first *Daubert* criterion, which asks whether the method has been tested. However, these studies (Abel et al., 1994; Abel et al., 1998) did not use the current set of slides. As regards the second criterion, the VRT has only been peer reviewed and published in two articles (Abel et al., 1994; Abel et al., 1998), all other data is provided in narrative format on Abel's website. In spite of its flaws, the VRT is used widely by practitioners in the field (e.g. according to www.abelscreen.com it is used at 102 testing sites) but it is not readily accepted by scientists due to lack of published data. Regarding the fourth criterion, the VRT has a known error rate only when used with admitted sex offenders, and that error rate was determined using a different slide set. It has not been cross validated or used with normal controls or deniers. The VRT's administration is standardized, but only when using Abel's prepared slides.

Abel's self-report questionnaire fares even less well with the *Daubert* criteria. Other than showing positive correlations with a client's VRT measure, it has not been tested, and so fails to meet the first criterion. It does not meet the second criterion, of being subjected to peer review. In fact, the only way to know the content of the questionnaire is to buy the Abel Screen and read one of the questionnaires that is sent with it. The questionnaire, like the Abel Screen itself, is used widely but lacks general acceptance and because of that meets the third criterion. It does not meet the fourth criterion, as it does not have a known error rate; and while there are standards for administration, these standards are problematic if the instrument has to be verbally administered by a clinician to a client with reading and comprehension problems.

The Risk Prediction Score (RPS), while it could be tested, has not been, and so does not fully meet the first *Daubert* criterion. Nor does it meet the second criterion of being subjected to peer review and publication. It partially meets the third criterion, in that it appears to have gained some acceptance in the field; however, some have felt this is premature (M. Rice, personal communication by e-mail, June 8, 1999). As Hanson (personal communication by e-mail, July 14, 1999) stated, "I assume that the individual's score is based on a ratio of some sort, but since Abel is never explicit about how the scores are created, it is impossible to adequately evaluate the credibility of the measure." In terms of the fourth criterion, the RPS does not have a known error rate; and, while there seem to be standards to control its use, these standards are not published (personal communication, G. Abel, June 23, 1999).

Violence Risk Appraisal Guide

The Violence Risk Appraisal Guide (VRAG) is an actuarial instrument developed to predict violence among serious offenders (Harris et al., 1993). A complete review of the literature on appraising and managing risk is provided by the authors in their recent text (Quinsey et al., 1998). Development of the VRAG was based on the fact that actuarial predictions outperform unaided human judgement (Meehl, 1954; Mossman, 1994). The initial subject pool for the VRAG consisted of 618 men, all of whom had undergone pretrial assessment. The final analysis identified 12 variables (Rice, 1997) that yielded a classification accuracy of 74%, and performed equally well for treatment and prison groups. A later study (Rice & Harris, 1995) expanded the sample size, broadened the sample population, extended the follow-up time, included other measures of violence, and yielded an accuracy rate virtually identical to that of the original sample. The VRAG was then cross validated on a sample of sexual offenders (Rice & Harris, 1997), and again yielded an accuracy rate very close to that of the original sample.

A revision was made to replace some of the variables of the VRAG with others that were found to be especially useful for sex offenders (Quinsey et al., 1995). In the original sample, the definition of violent recidivism included all sex offenses. The VRAG was tested on an expanded sample of sex offenders, and performed well in both the cross validation and extended follow-up samples. The instrument performed moderately well in the prediction of sexual recidivism. Rice and Harris (1997) report, "present data support the use of the VRAG for both sex offenders and other violent offenders, and the prediction of violent, rather than specifically sexual, recidivism (page 239)."

The admissibility of the VRAG appears not to have been challenged by the courts (personal communication by e-mail, M. Rice, May 25, 1999). In terms of the *Daubert* criteria, the VRAG meets all four criteria. It has been tested, subjected to peer review and publication, has gained general acceptance, has a known error rate, and has standards to control administration. However, as regards the standards to control administration, there may be some minor variability in individual clinicians' scoring of the VRAG.

Sex Offender Risk Appraisal Guide

The authors of the VRAG later developed the Sex Offender Risk Appraisal Guide (SORAG). Their goal was to develop an actuarial instrument that would be more effective than the VRAG in predicting recidivism in sexual offenders (Quinsey et al., 1998). Quinsey et al. (1998) report that in developing the SORAG, they encountered problems in defining the outcome variables. Frequently, sexual offenders are charged with crimes that are non-sex-related, such as homicide, kidnaping, assault, or burglary. Fourteen variables were identified as having predictive utility with sex offenders. Studies indicate that the SORAG is only marginally better than the VRAG in predicting violent recidivism in sexual offenders (Quinsey et al., 1998).

The admissibility of the SORAG appears not to have been challenged by the courts (personal communication by e-mail, M. Rice, May 25, 1999). In terms of the *Daubert* criteria, the SORAG certainly lends itself to testing, but in terms of the published research, it has only been tested in a limited fashion (Quinsey et al., 1998; Harris et al., 1998). Similarly for the second criterion, peer review and publication, the SORAG only meets this to a limited degree. Though there has been criticism of its method (Boer, Hart, et al., 1997), the SORAG does meet the third criterion of general acceptance. As regards the fourth criterion, the SORAG has a known error rate for the sample from which it was developed, but this may vary when applied to other samples. Also, the SORAG has standards to control administration, but there may be some minor variation between clinicians' scoring.

Federal Sex Offender Registration Act Risk Assessment Guidelines

All states and the federal government have enacted their own version of Megan's Law (Walsh & Cohen, 1998). Among state legislatures, statutes providing for sex offender registration and community notification do not simultaneously provide for an objective standardized method of sex offender risk assessment. The Federal Sex Offender Registration Act Risk Assessment Guidelines (FedRAG) is an objective guide designed to help states rate a sexual offender's risk to reoffend. The guide includes 15 factors with a range of scores, four automatic overrides, and an opportunity to depart downward from the presumptive risk level. Offenders are rated as having a low, moderate, or high risk for reoffense. The FedRAG were developed by consulting with several experts on sex offenders. It is not clear how the weight of the factors was determined and whether there was any testing of the FedRAG's accuracy. In spite of no apparent empirical support, the FedRAG has been used by a number of states to rate a sexual offender's risk to reoffend.

The FedRAG do not fare well with regards to the *Daubert* criteria. The FedRAG have not been tested, but could be; they have not been subjected to peer review or publication; they have gained some acceptance, but more within the federal system than the scientific community; they have no known error rate. They do have standards to control administration but there may be significant variation among different clinicians' scoring.

The Sexual Violence Risk-20

The Sexual Violence Risk-20, or SVR-20, is described, by its authors (Boer, Hart, et al., 1997), as a professional guideline rather than a test. It is a list of twenty factors that research has correlated with increased risk of sexual offending. These factors include both static as well as dynamic factors. Factors are coded on a three point scale, for whether the factor is absent, possibly present, or definitely present. The authors recommend that the user summarize across the factors to rate overall risk as low, moderate, or high. It is left up to the evaluator to decide how many factors or how much of any factor determines the overall risk rating. The authors recommend against just adding up the factors, and instead recommend that the SVR-20 be used to guide the evaluation. For research purposes, they acknowledge that it might be useful to simply summarize the factors.

In terms of the *Daubert* criteria, the SVR-20's ability to predict sexual reoffending could be tested, if, as the authors suggest for research purposes, the factors are merely summarized. In fact, there are studies examining it in this manner (P. R. Kropp, personal communication, June 28, 1999; Dempster, 1999); however, none at this point have been published. If the SVR-20 were used just as a guide for an overall evaluation in which factors are given either greater or lesser weight, then it would be much more difficult to evaluate the guide's falsifiability. At this time, the ability of the SVR-20 to predict recidivism has not been subjected to peer review, and other than a description of the development of the scale (Boer, Wilson, et al., 1997), there is no published literature. The SVR-20 does, to a degree, meet the third *Daubert* criterion – whether the theory or technique is generally accepted. The guidelines for the SVR-20 are based on a comprehensive review of the current sexual offender literature. The SVR-20 does not fare so well with the fourth criterion. Specifically, there is no known error rate. While the SVR-20 manual is very detailed, and it does provide information on how to rate the factors, there is considerable room for subjectivity among evaluators when determining the rating on many of the factors.

The Penile Plethysmograph

The penile plethysmograph provides a measure of penile tumescence, or arousal. Plethysmographic, or phallometric, assessment was developed in the 1950s (Freund, 1991) to evaluate the sexual preferences of individuals; in recent years, the research with the instrument has focused on its potential ability to identify sexual offenders. There have been a large number of studies (i.e., Annon, 1988; Haywood et al., 1990; Malcolm et al., 1993; Ruedrich & Wilkinson, 1992) conducted with the plethysmograph, and it has been found to differentiate sex offenders from non-offenders, and to separate out different types of offenders (i.e., child molesters versus rapists). Deviant sexual interest, as measured by the plethysmograph, has been found to correlate highly with sexual reoffending (i.e., Rice et al., 1990; Rice et al., 1991). In fact, in a recent meta-analysis (Hanson & Bussière, 1998), deviant sexual interest in children was the variable with the highest correlation with sexual recidivism. This test has been criticized on a number of fronts. These criticisms are relevant to this examination of admissibility.

The plethysmograph has been criticized (Simon & Schouten, 1991) for its lack of standardized stimulus materials. There is no one standard set of slides, audio, or videotapes. Studies have demonstrated that more explicit material generates greater response, and auditory material is more effective than visual slides. However, explicit, sexual photographs of children are illegal to possess, or transport, within the United States. In a large number of studies (i.e., Looman et al., 1998), there is a significant percentage (20 to 75%) of individuals who are non-responders – individuals who demonstrate little to no arousal to any of the material. It is not clear whether these non-responders are just faking their response or if they are just not interested in the material. But it is clear that the plethysmograph is vulnerable to conscious efforts to control arousal (McAnulty & Adams, 1991; Sewell & Salekin, 1997). There are relatively few studies of non-offenders, so there is little data about how normal, non-sex offenders respond (Harris & Rice, 1996). What information is available suggests that non-offenders do demonstrate arousal to deviant materials. To separate out offenders from non-offenders, researchers have had to look at the degree of arousal to deviant material relative to non-deviant material (Harris et al., 1998). Using this technique, there has been some success in identifying child molesters. The results with rapists, however, are equivocal, and many non-offenders are not distinguishable from rapists (Howes, 1998).

The admissibility of the plethysmograph has been challenged in several court cases (*United States v. Powers*, 1995; *Berthiaume v. Caron*, 1998; *Parker v. Dodgion*, 1998), and the courts have been divided about whether the method meets the *Daubert* standard. It is also important to note that these cases did not assess the instrument's scientific reliability in terms of predicting recidivism, but rather its ability to diagnose a sexual offender. For example, in *United States v. Powers* (1995), an attorney argued that his client's lack of deviant arousal, as measured by the plethysmograph, was proof that his client did not commit the crime. The appellate court did not support this argument and stated that the plethysmograph's ability to identify an individual as a sexual offender did not satisfy the scientific validity prong of *Daubert*.

In terms of the first *Daubert* criterion, the plethysmograph can be, and has been, tested. Though given the lack of a standardized administration, it is not clear whether a study's results generalize to other situations. The plethysmograph clearly meets the second criterion in terms of it having been subjected to peer review and having had studies of its effectiveness published in the professional literature. It also meets the third criterion, general acceptance in the scientific community. Though there are strong and valid criticisms of the method, it is widely used in sexual offender treatment programs and, rightly or wrongly, has achieved a broad acceptance. The weaknesses of the plethysmograph are apparent in the fourth *Daubert* criterion. There is little information about the error rate of the instrument, or on how non-sex offenders perform on this test; and there is no widely used standardized administration.

The Hare Psychopathy Checklist-Revised (PCL-R)
The Hare Psychopathy Checklist-Revised (Hare, 1991), PCL-R, is a rating scale for the assessment of psychopathy. The twenty items on the scale tap a variety of behaviors and traits that relate to the construct of psychopathy. The assessment procedure involves both an interview and a review of collateral documents. With adequately trained raters, the reliability of the scoring is very high. The bulk of the research on the PCL-R has examined its effectiveness in predicting general recidivism as well as violent recidivism. It has consistently been shown to be a highly valid measure with moderate to moderately high predictive value. The PCL-R

has also been used to predict the likelihood of sexual offenders re-offending.

The admissibility of the PCL-R, in terms of predicting a sexual offender's risk to reoffend, has been challenged in California (A. Phenix, personal communication, July 19, 1999). The trial court, operating under *Kelly-Frye* "general acceptance" standards, ruled that it was admissible. In terms of the first *Daubert* criterion, not only can the PCL-R be tested, but the hypothesized relationship between elevated scores on the PCL-R and increased risk of sexual offending has been tested (i.e., Rice et al., 1990; Rice & Harris, 1997). It also meets the second criterion – peer review of the method in professional journals. Even restricting the focus only to studies of sexual offenders and the PCL-R, there have been over a dozen articles published between 1996 and 1998. The third *Daubert* criterion refers to general acceptance of the theory and technique within the scientific community. The PCL-R meets this criterion. Not only was it developed using a well accepted methodology, but as a review in *The Twelfth Mental Measurements Yearbook* (Fulero, 1995) described it, it is "the state of the art (p. 454)" in terms of risk assessment. The fourth *Daubert* criterion requires that an instrument have a known error rate and that there be standards to control the administration of the instrument. The PCL-R meets both parts of this criterion. Not only is there a known standard error of measurement for the test, but there is a growing body of research which details the strength of the relationship between the PCL-R and risk of sexual reoffending. The research suggests that the PCL-R is a moderately strong predictor. In terms of standardized administration, the PCL-R manual provides detailed information on scoring the instrument, and a certification process has been established (Robert Hare, personal communication, January 10, 1999) where an examiner's reliability in administration and scoring can be assessed and verified.

The Rapid Risk Assessment for Sexual Offense Recidivism (RRASOR)
The Rapid Risk Assessment for Sexual Offense Recidivism (Hanson, 1997), or RRASOR, is a brief actuarial risk scale. The author, R. Karl Hanson, drew upon an earlier meta-analysis (Hanson & Bussière, 1996) that he co-authored to identify variables associated with increased risk for sexual reoffending. He chose variables that were easily scored and applied them to seven different samples of sexual offenders. Using these samples, the author isolated four variables which were maximally predictive. These variables are weighted and summarized to provide an individual's RRASOR score. Hanson calculated the RRASOR scores of

the individuals in his seven samples, and in a postdictive study assessed the scale's ability to predict recidivism. The RRASOR demonstrated moderate predictive ability. He also applied the scale to an eighth sample to evaluate the scale's ability to predict recidivism; it performed at a similar level. It has been suggested (Boer, Hart, et al., 1997) that the RRASOR's accuracy is overestimated due to its use of multiple regression analyses and a postdictive design. Hanson acknowledges (Hanson, 1998) that a relative weakness of the RRASOR is that it ignores a number of dynamic factors as well as deviant sexual preference – a factor that has been highly correlated with sexual reoffending.

The admissibility of the RRASOR, in terms of its ability to predict whether a sexual offender will reoffend, has been repeatedly challenged in California (A. Phenix, personal communication, July 19, 1999). The trial courts, operating under *Kelly-Frye* "general acceptance" standards, have consistently ruled that it was admissible. In terms of the *Daubert* criteria, the RRASOR is readily testable. Hanson applied his scale to a sample independent of the one with which he developed the scale, and it performed at comparable levels. However, there has been no independent testing of the RRASOR on other samples, and questions remain as to whether it would perform as well with other samples. This deficiency is relevant to the second criterion: whether the test has been subject to peer review. The details of how the scale was constructed have appeared in the professional literature (Hanson, 1998), but there is no published research on the RRASOR's ability to predict sexual offending on independent samples. This deficiency may be rectified when recently completed studies of the RRASOR are published (e.g., Dempster, 1999). As regards the third criterion, general acceptance, the RRASOR fares better. It is being used by clinicians in the field and it is being taught as part of the training program at forensic institutes (e.g., Institute of Law, Psychiatry and Public Policy, Charlottesville, VA). Though it can be argued that this acceptance is premature, it does appear to have a significant level of acceptance. The RRASOR, to a degree, appears to meet the fourth criterion of *Daubert*. Its error rate from the initial sample is known, though, as previously mentioned, it is unclear if that rate would be reproduced with other samples. The administration of the RRASOR is fairly straightforward.

TOWARD A SCIENTIFIC FOUNDATION

In summary, this review of instruments for assessing risk of sexual reoffending finds that many meet the relatively low threshold of admissibility in terms of the *Daubert* criteria. However, this review also finds that many have significant weaknesses that would likely limit the weight they would be accorded in court. Some problems may be solved as further development occurs. Hanson (personal communication by e-mail, July 14, 1999) is currently working on an improved instrument, the Static99, which he hoped to have later in 1999. Rice (personal communication by e-mail, June 2, 1999) reported she and her colleagues are developing an improved instrument that may also be available for release in 1999. Abel (personal communication, June 23 1999) describes his assessment method as "a work in progress." Given the state of the art of sex offender risk assessment, it makes sense to use a multi-method approach, analyze all available data in each case, and carefully weigh relevant hypotheses, as well as the strength of the ultimate determination of risk level. The following guidelines are offered to clinicians as a means toward increasing the scientific foundation, the likelihood of admissibility, and the credibility of sex offender risk assessment results offered in a court of law:

1. Be aware of variables identified in the literature that are associated with reoffending and which increase the accuracy of your evaluation's predictions. Some variables are intuitively relevant, such as psychopathy and sexual deviance. Other variables that may seem intuitively relevant, such as depression and low self-esteem, may not be.

2. Generate several hypotheses to be tested, taking into account the context of the assessment – pre-trial or pre-sentencing, pre-commitment (civil), pre-treatment, or post-treatment. Additionally, consider whether the person you are evaluating has any known history of sexual offending, or whether they have no known history of offenses prior to the current accusation.

3. Gather as much evidence as possible, but withhold forming an opinion during all data collection. Evidence of early bias discredits the final opinion.

4. Follow acceptable procedures for each portion of the assessment and be prepared to testify to the validity and relevance of each.

5. Follow all ethical guidelines, particularly the Specialty Guidelines for Forensic Psychologists (Committee on Ethical Guidelines for Forensic Psychologists, 1991). When testifying, include references to relevant portions of the guidelines when defending your procedures.

6. Adhere to all relevant professional standards, such as the Standards for Educational and Psychological Testing (Committee to Develop Standards for Educational and Psychological Testing of the American

Educational Research Association, et al., 1985), and any procedures required by applicable law.

7. Weigh each hypothesis according to the evidence. Absolute truth is not an objective of science.

8. Present an opinion that is data-based; do not overstep the evidence. State your level of certainty and why (i.e., definite – 95% certainty or above, probable – 75% certainty or above, tentative – 50% certainty or above, speculative – 1% certainty or above, or no certainty at all; Rogers, 1986).

9. Do not feel responsible for the outcome of the case in court. Do not usurp the role of the trier of fact. Do not identify with either side's adversarial role.

10. Provide honest testimony and then forget about it.

REFERENCES

Annon, J. S. (1988). Reliability and validity of penile plethysmography in rape and child molestation cases. *American Journal of Forensic Psychology, 6,* 11–26.

Abel, G. G. (1997, September/October). "New relapse." *The Abel Screening News.* Atlanta, GA: Author.

Abel, G. G., Huffman, J., Warberg, B., & Holland, C. L. (1998). Visual reaction time and plethysmography as measures of sexual interest in child molesters. *Sexual Abuse, 10,* 81–95.

Abel, G. G., Lawry, S. S., Karlstrom, E. M., Osborn, C. A., & Gillespie, C. F. (1994). Screening tests for pedophilia. *Criminal Justice and Behavior, 21,* 115–131.

American Psychiatric Association (1999). *Dangerous sex offenders: A task force report.* Washington, DC: Author.

Berthiaume v. Caron, 142 F.3d. 12 (1st Cir. 1998).

Boer, D. P., Hart, S. D., Kropp, P. R., & Webster, C. D. (1997). *Manual for the Sexual Violence Risk-20: Professional guidelines for assessing risk of sexual violence.* Vancouver and Burnaby, British Columbia, Canada: (co-published) British Columbia Institute Against Family Violence and Simon Fraser University, The Mental Health, Law, & Policy Institute.

Boer, D. P., Wilson, R. J., Gauthier, C. M., & Hart, S. D. (1997). Assessing risk of sexual violence: Guidelines for clinical practice. In C. D. Webster & M. A. Jackson (Eds.), *Impulsivity: Theory, assessment, and treatment* (pp. 326–342). New York: Guilford.

Committee on Ethical Guidelines for Forensic Psychologists (1991). Specialty guidelines for forensic psychologists. *Law and Human Behavior, 15,* 655–665.

Committee to Develop Standards for Educational and Psychological Testing of the American Educational Research Association, the American Psychological Association, and the National Council on Measurement in Education (1985). *Standards for educational and psychological testing.* Washington, DC: American Psychological Association.

Daubert v. Merrell Dow Pharmaceuticals, Inc., 113 S. Ct. 2786 (1993).

Dempster, R. (1999, July) *Prediction of sexually violent recidivism: A comparison of risk assessment instruments.* Paper presented at the Psychology and Law, International Conference, Dublin, Ireland.

Freund, K. (1991) Reflections on the development of the phallometric method of assessing erotic preferences. *Annals of Sex Research, 4,* 221–228.

Fulero, S. M. (1995). Review of the Hare Psychopathy Checklist-Revised. In J. C. Conoley & J. C. Impara (Eds.), *Twelfth mental measurements yearbook* (pp. 453–454). Lincoln, NE: Buros Institute.

Hanson, R. K. (1997). *The development of a brief actuarial risk scale for sexual offender recidivism (User report No. 1997–04).* Ottawa, Ontario, Canada: Department of the Solicitor General of Canada.

Hanson, R. K. (1998). What do we know about sex offender risk assessment? *Psychology, Public Policy, and Law*, 4, 50–72.

Hanson, R. K., & Bussière, M. T. (1996). *Predictors of sexual offender recidivism: A meta-analysis (User report No. 96–04).* Ottawa, Ontario, Canada: Department of the Solicitor General of Canada.

Hanson, R. K., & Bussière, M. T. (1998). Predicting relapse: A meta-analysis of sexual offender recidivism studies. *Journal of Consulting and Clinical Psychology*, 66, 348–362.

Hare, R. D. (1991). *The Hare Psychopathy Checklist-Revised: Manual.* Toronto, Canada: Multi-Health Systems, Inc.

Harris, G. T., & Rice, M. E. (1996). The science in phallometric measurement of male sexual interest. *American Psychological Society*, 5, 156–160.

Harris, G. T., Rice, M. R., & Quinsey, V. L. (1993). Violent recidivism of mentally disordered offenders: The development of a statistical prediction instrument. *Criminal Justice and Behavior*, 20, 315–335.

Harris, G. T., Rice, M. E., & Quinsey, V. L. (1998). Appraisal and management of risk in sexual aggressors: Implications for criminal justice policy. *Psychology, Public Policy, and Law*, 4, 73–115.

Haywood, T. W., Grossman, L. S., & Cavanaugh, J. L. (1990). Subjective versus objective measurements of deviant sexual arousal in clinical evaluations of alleged child molesters. *Psychological Assessment: A Journal of Consulting and Clinical Psychology*, 2, 269–275.

Hubbart v. Superior Court, 969 P.2d 584 (Cal. 1999).

Howes, R. J. (1998). Plethysmographic assessment of incarcerated nonsexual offenders: A comparison with rapists. *Sexual Abuse*, 10, 183–194.

Kansas v. Hendricks, 117 S. Ct. 2106 (1997).

La Fond, J. Q., & Winick, B. J. (1998). Sex offenders and the law. *Psychology, Public policy and Law*, 4, 3–24.

Looman, J., Abracen, J., Maillet, G., & DiFazio, R. (1998). Phallometric nonresponding in sexual offenders. *Sexual Abuse*, 10, 325–336.

Malcolm, P. B., Andrews, D. A., & Quinsey, V. L. (1993). Discriminant and predictive validity of phallometrically measured sexual age and gender preference. *Journal of Interpersonal Violence*, 8, 486–501.

McAnulty, R. D., & Adams, H. E. (1991). Voluntary control of penile tumescence: Effects of an incentive and a signal detection task. *Journal of Sex Research*, 28, 557–577.

Meehl, P. E. (1954). *Clinical vs. statistical prediction.* Minneapolis: University of Minnesota Press.

Mossman, D. (1994) Assessing predictions of violence: Being accurate about accuracy. *Journal of Consulting and Clinical Psychology*, 62, 783–792.

Parker v. Dodgion, 971 P.2d. 496 (Utah 1998).

Quinsey, V. L., Harris, G. T., Rice, M. E., & Cormier, C. A. (1998). *Violent offenders: Appraising and managing risks.* Washington, DC: American Psychological Association.

Quinsey, V. L., Rice, M. E., & Harris, G. T. (1995). The actuarial prediction of sexual recidivism. *Journal of Interpersonal Violence*, 10, 85–105.

Rice, M. E. (1997). Violent offender research and implications for the criminal justice system. *American Psychologist*, 52, 414–423.

Rice, M. E., & Harris, G. T. (1995). Violent recidivism: Assessing predictive validity. *Journal of Consulting and Clinical Psychology*, 63, 737–748.

Rice, M. E., & Harris, G. T. (1997). Cross validation and extension of the Violence Risk Appraisal Guide for child molesters and rapists. *Law and Human Behavior, 21,* 231–241.

Rice, M. E., Harris, G. T., & Quinsey, V. L. (1990). A follow-up of rapists assessed in a maximum-security psychiatric facility. *Journal of Interpersonal Violence, 5,* 435–448.

Rice, M. E., Quinsey, V. L., & Harris, G. T. (1991). Sexual recidivism among child molesters released from a maximum security psychiatric institution. *Journal of Consulting and Clinical Psychology, 59,* 381–386.

Rogers, R. (1986). *Conducting insanity evaluations.* NY: Van Nostrand Reinhold.

Ruedrich, S. L., & Wilkinson, L. (1992). Deviant sexual responsiveness on penile plethysmography using visual stimuli: Alleged child molesters vs. normal control subjects. *Journal of Nervous and Mental Disease, 180,* 207–208.

Sewell, K. W., & Salekin, R. T. (1997). Understanding and detecting dissimulation in sex offenders. In R. Rodgers (ed.), *Clinical assessment of malingering and deception, 2nd ed.,* NY: Guilford

Simon, W. T., & Schouten, P. G. W. (1991). Plethysmography in the assessment and treatment of sexual deviance: An overview. *Archives of Sexual Behavior, 20,* 75–91.

United States v. Powers, 59 F.3d 1460 (4th Cir. 1995).

Walsh, E. R., & Cohen, F. (1998). *Sex offender registration and community notification: "Megan's Law" source book.* Kingston, NJ: Civic Research Institute.

Chapter 3

CLINICAL PRACTICE AND VIOLENCE RISK ASSESSMENT: AVAILABILITY OF MACARTHUR RISK CUES IN PSYCHIATRIC SETTINGS

Eric B. Elbogen, Cynthia Mercado, Alan J. Tomkins and Mario J. Scalora

Over the past three decades, assessments of risk of violence have become "a required professional ability" for mental health professionals working in psychiatric settings (Grisso & Tomkins, 1996, p. 928). Although clinicians regularly assess patients' risk of violence in practice, serious doubts have been raised over the years as to whether mental health professionals can in fact make judgments of dangerousness accurately (Monahan, 1981). In the wake of this assessment, a "second generation" of research studies has emerged seeking to establish empirically validated correlates of violent behavior (Borum, 1996; McNeil, 1998; Otto, 1992). The MacArthur Risk Assessment Study has summarized a number of risk factors found in the scientific literature to be associated with violence (Monahan & Steadman, 1994). Several research reports from the MacArthur Risk Assessment Study have already been published showing the potential value of actuarial devices to assess violence risk in psychiatric populations (e.g., Silver, Mulvey, & Monahan, 1999; Steadman et al., 2000).

As a theoretical/methodological model for understanding violence risk assessment, the MacArthur Risk Assessment Study has recommended the utilization of Social Judgment Theory (SJT) (see Steadman et al., 1994). SJT has long been used to understand complex decisionmaking (see generally Hammond, 1955; Hammond, Hursch, & Todd, 1964; Hammond, Stewart, Brehmer, & Steinmann, 1975). The first step of the model involves the identification of the array of informational "cues" available to decisionmakers in the specific decisionmaking context that is being examined (Hammond, 1994; Lamiell, 1979). Afterwards, the set of cues used in a decisionmaking environment is determined, permitting the relationship between these cues, the prediction, and the outcome to be analyzed (Hammond, McClelland, & Mumpower, 1980). Applied to help understand and improve decisionmaking in a number of different fields (see Hammond, Hamm, Grasia, & Pearson, 1997), SJT has also framed psycho-legal research in both criminal and juvenile arenas (see, e.g., Grisso, 1996; Grisso, Tomkins, & Casey, 1988; Tomkins, 1990).

The MacArthur Risk Assessment Study has proposed four specific domains within which to categorize risk cues (Steadman et al., 1994). First, *dispositional* cues refer to demographic, cognitive, and personality variables, the latter two of which are obtained through testing batteries. Second, *historical* factors include general social history and specific violence history information. Third, the *contextual* domain connotes aspects of an individual's situation that might either contribute to violence risk (e.g., access to weapons) or buffer against it (e.g., supportive social network). Fourth, *clinical* factors considered are those that enhance risk of violence, such as substance abuse or personality disorder. These four domains represent a comprehensive array of the type of risk cues that could be selected for actuarial formulas, which, if used, could potentially improve violence risk assessment in practice.

Most of the "second generation" of risk assessment research has focused on either the relationships between risk factors and occurrence of violent behaviors or the relationships between risk judgments and occurrence of violence behaviors (Grisso, 1996). In the past decade, only a few empirical studies have examined clinical decisionmaking of violence risk assessment and the relationship between risk factors and risk judgments (e.g., Menzies & Webster, 1995). One reason for this imbalance might be that clinical judgments have been shown to underperform actuarial instruments in general and with respect to violence prediction (Quinsey, Harris, Rice, & Cormier, 1998).

Given the complexity of decisionmaking when assessing violence risk, it would seem that studying clinical models and the relationship between risk factors and risk judgments is critical to supplement the development of actuarial tools. In particular, this type of research could help bridge the gap between science and practice in violence risk assessment, a gap some have lamented as being quite vast (Borum, 1996; Webster & Cox, 1997; Webster, Eaves, Douglas, & Winthrop, 1995). By obtaining a picture of how violence risk assessment occurs in practice, efforts can be made to ensure that actuarial models "mirror" the constraints of actual clinical practice (Mulvey & Lidz, 1995). This way, decisionmaking models can be developed that have both empirical validation *and* clinical utility. As a result, such research could assist in the transfer of actuarial technology.

One obstacle that faces incorporating risk assessment research in clinical practice is the fact that certain risk information, although predictive of violence, might not always be available for violence risk assessment. SJT points out that the availability of cues in decisionmaking environments defines the set of risk factors that can enter into risk judgments and actuarial formulas. Because of differing organizational constraints in psychiatric settings (see Borum, 1996), the four domains proposed in the MacArthur Risk Assessment Study probably differ in availability across contexts. Gardner, Lidz, Mulvey and Shaw (1996) observe that valuable historical cues – for example, past violent behavior – are often unavailable to clinicians in psychiatric settings that engender time pressures, such as in psychiatric emergency rooms or crisis centers. Although demographic dispositional cues are readily available in all clinical settings, personality and cognitive dispositional cues rely on testing administration, which may not be viable to conduct because of logistical, financial, or training reasons. Grisso (1996) notes that contextual factors, such as a patient's access to weapons, may be statistically correlated with violence but not feasible to obtain information in clinical practice. For these reasons, there are probably circumstances in which violence risk assessment "must be made with limited information" (McNeil, Sandberg, & Binder, 1998, p. 664; see also Jackson, 1988).

Grisso (1996) therefore recommends it is important to investigate "[w]hat domain of cues is usually available to the examiner in the specific type of setting and population for which assessments of future endangering behavior must be made?" (p. 128). In this study, we address this question and examine clinical documentation and perceived availability of violence risk factors, specifically those listed in the four cue domains prescribed in the MacArthur Risk Assessment Study. This study is aimed to assist in the development and implementation of actuarial devices by describing similarities and differences between clinical contexts on risk information availability. Although this study does not capture actual availability, examining documentation of risk cues at least provides a baseline for actual availability. Further, by eliciting clinicians' perceptions of cue availability, analyses can be conducted on the interrelationships among perceived availability, clinical documentation, and perceived relevance of MacArthur risk cues in different psychiatric settings. Because of a lack of previous research in this area, this study takes a preliminary step toward understanding the availability of risk factors in clinical practice.

METHOD

This study involved four inpatient psychiatric settings in the state of Nebraska: acute, chronic, crisis, and forensic. The acute, chronic, and forensic hospitals are located at a 240-bed state-operated psychiatric facility that serves most of the severely mentally-ill patients in the state as well as surrounding states. Half of the facility's beds are housed in the forensic hospital providing evaluation and treatment services for adults found Not Responsible by Reason of Insanity and Incompetent to Stand Trial as well as civilly-committed sex offenders. Non-forensic adult patients who are civilly committed are first treated in the 40-bed acute hospital for stabilization (average length of stay is 68 days). Those non-forensic adult patients requiring more intensive care are treated at the 40-bed chronic care hospital, which offers extensive psychosocial rehabilitation for long-term patients. The county crisis center is located within the local community mental center and is a 15-bed facility that serves as the initial gateway for longer-term inpatient mental health services. Patients in crisis, either at risk to harm themselves or others, are brought to the crisis center in order to evaluate the appropriateness of civil commitment. The crisis center receives over 50 admissions per month with an average length of stay of 12 days. Patients are discharged to the community or transferred to other inpatient facilities, typically the state hospital.

In this study, two independent procedures were employed to approximate availability of risk information. The first procedure involved retrospectively summarizing documented information routinely collected in patient charts during the provision of clinical care. Although it could not be assured that all the information available for a given patient would be included within patient charts, it was assumed that most of the information available would be reflected in the main reports written on the patient and at least provide a baseline for actual availability. For this reason, cue availability was defined broadly and dichotomously. A cue was rated as documented if any mention of the cue was made in the main reports in patient charts.

There were specific considerations in rating the documentation of certain factors from the MacArthur study. Dispositional factors included personality and cognitive cues (e.g., psychopathy, IQ) and were operationalized for this study as the documentation of personality or cognitive testing results. Information about job perceptions was rated under employment because of the difficulty in establishing consistent criteria distinguishing the two cues. For similar reasons, information about family upbringing fell under the rubric of family history rather than child rearing. Demographic cues were not coded because there is no question regarding whether such cues (e.g., gender, race) are available; demographic information always was available in the charts. Patient charts ($n=283$) were coded for documentation of MacArthur risk cues in the four psychiatric settings by six research assistants. Two research assistants coded charts at the state hospital facility, two at the crisis center, and two at both locations.

At the state hospital facility, 130 charts were randomly selected from a list of patients discharged between January 1994 and January 1998 from the acute ($n=65$), chronic ($n=32$), and forensic ($n=33$) hospitals. Patient chart ratings at the state hospital facility were made by four research assistants who achieved an interrater reliability of kappa=.77 before starting the chart reviews. Research assistants examined clinical staff reports in patients' medical records, which are those records typically available in charts to staff while the patient is being treated in the facility. Staff reports included psychiatrists' admission and discharge summaries, discharge information sheets, social work reports, nursing assessments, and psychological reports.

At the county crisis center, 153 charts were randomly selected from a list of patients discharged from the crisis center between January 1994 and January 1998. Patient charts at the crisis center were rated by four research assistants who achieved an interrater reliability of kappa=.87 before starting the chart reviews. Crisis center charts contained psychiatrists' admission and discharge reports and nursing assessments. The same chart coding procedures and operationalization of cue availability were employed as at the state hospital.

Two of the research assistants rated charts at both the state hospital and the crisis center in order to ensure that interrater reliability reflected actual presence of information in medical charts rather than potential individual differences between the research assistants coding at the two locations. The two research assistants who coded patient charts at both settings had an interrater reliability for crisis center documentation of kappa=.81 and for state hospital documentation of kappa=.69, indicating levels of agreement generally consistent with those described above. This suggests that differences found were not due to differences in the coders. The higher interrater reliability for the crisis center was most likely due to the fact that crisis center charts were easier to rate than the lengthier state hospital charts.

The second procedure in this study involved surveying mental health professionals at the four psychiatric settings about the availability and relevance of risk cues listed in the MacArthur Risk Assessment Study. Surveys, with informed consent forms attached, were provided for clinicians. In total, 134 mental health professionals (out of 210 requested; 64% response rate) completed and returned the surveys to the primary investigators (forensic=37%, chronic=24%, acute=22%, crisis=17%). Participants included professional staff (n=68) – nurses (43%), psychiatrists (5%), clinical psychologists (19%), and master's level social workers or psychologists (33%) – and paraprofessional staff (n=67).

Clinicians rated on a Likert Scale each risk cue for perceived availability (0=never available to 10=always available) and for perceived relevance for assessing violence risk (0=not relevant to 10=extremely important). Because of potential differences in violence risk assessment due to decisionmaking context (Heilbrun, 1997; McNeil & Binder, 1994), half of the participants received instructions to consider availability and relevance at the time of hospital admission (defined as the first week of hospitalization) and half were requested to rate availability in the context of discharge. Participants were randomly assigned to the admission versus discharge conditions.

RESULTS

Table 1 presents findings on the clinical documentation of MacArthur risk cues in patient charts from the crisis center, the acute hospital, the forensic hospital, and the chronic hospital. A MANOVA showed that documentation of MacArthur risk cues was significantly different across the four psychiatric settings [F (5, 276)=72.018, p<.001]. Although the *total number* of risk cues documented at the three state hospital settings was not significantly different [F(2, 127)=12.245, p=.160], *clinical documentation* of the MacArthur risk cues was significantly different across these three settings, as well [F (5, 124)=13.794, p<.001]. Follow-up analyses of variance indicated that each of the four settings differed from the other on documentation of the 30 MacArthur risk cues, with the greatest differences found between the crisis center and each of the state hospital settings.

Dispositional cues, specifically personality and cognitive testing, were documented least frequently in patient charts. For example, 63.8% of crisis center charts had the results of personality testing, which was more

Table 1: Percentage of Clinical Charts Documenting MacArthur Risk Factors

Risk Factors	Crisis	Acute	Forensic	Chronic	F	p
Dispositional Factors						
Personality Tests	63.8	12.0	40.6	20.6	24.71	.001
Anger	0.0	25.8	12.5	14.7	14.53	.001
Impulsiveness	0.7	4.5	3.1	0.0	1.61	.188
Psychopathy	0.0	0.0	0.0	0.0	—	—
IQ	2.7	20.9	53.1	23.5	23.57	.001
NeuroPsych Testing	0.0	46.3	6.3	94.1	134.38	.001
Mean	11.2	18.2	19.3	25.5		
Historical Factors						
Social History						
Family History	76.5	100.0	96.9	100.0	12.21	.001
Child Abuse	81.2	65.2	53.1	41.2	9.85	.001
Family Deviance	65.1	70.2	75.0	61.8	0.63	.599
Work History	84.6	97.0	90.6	97.1	3.47	.017
Educational History	64.4	95.5	93.8	94.1	14.69	.001
Prior Hospitalizations	86.6	100.0	93.8	97.1	4.43	.005
Treatment Compliance	20.1	80.6	40.6	91.2	51.63	.001
History of Violence						
Arrests	36.2	86.6	96.9	67.7	32.31	.001
Incarcerations	22.8	68.7	90.6	55.9	32.48	.001
Self-reported Violence	12.1	79.1	75.0	47.1	15.88	.001
Violence Toward Self	92.0	92.5	93.8	94.1	0.09	.967
Violence Toward Others	28.2	92.5	100.0	91.2	75.52	.001
Mean	55.8	85.7	83.3	78.2		
Contextual Factors						
Perceived Stress	83.9	80.6	53.1	70.6	5.54	.001
Activities of Daily Living	71.8	64.2	65.6	91.2	2.98	.032
Perceived Support	49.0	80.6	65.6	88.2	11.39	.001
Social Networks	44.3	98.5	96.9	97.1	46.89	.001
Means for Violence, i.e. Access to Weapons	6.1	19.4	37.5	8.8	9.46	.001
Mean	51.0	68.7	63.8	71.2		
Clinical Factors						
Axis I Diagnosis	95.3	98.5	100.0	100.0	1.41	.239
Delusions	94.0	88.1	87.5	97.1	1.45	.229
Hallucinations	93.3	89.6	81.3	94.1	1.78	.152
Violent Fantasies	12.8	14.9	40.6	3.0	7.32	.001
Symptom Severity	94.6	95.5	78.1	97.1	4.64	.004
Axis II Diagnosis	95.3	98.5	100.0	100.0	1.41	.239
Substance Abuse	85.0	100.0	100.0	93.6	5.99	.001
Mean	83.2	83.6	83.9	83.5		

Note. N=283

than charts at the three state hospital settings. However, with other testing results, charts from these three different settings showed higher frequencies of documentation than the crisis center; for example, documentation of intelligence testing was higher at the chronic hospital (94.1%) than the crisis center (2.7%). Psychopathy testing results were not found in any chart.

Charts from the state hospital settings documented more historical information than crisis charts. Only 28.2% of crisis center charts contained information regarding history of violence to others whereas at the state hospital history of violence was documented in over 90% of charts. Child abuse was documented more often at the crisis center than the acute, forensic, and chronic hospitals, mainly reflecting the fact that crisis center staff were asked to indicate this information in charts, whereas the state hospital staff were not. Previous hospitalizations (range 86.6%–100%) and work history (range 84.6%–97.1%) were the most commonly documented historical factors across all four settings.

Contextual factors were, on average, documented less frequently than historical factors but more often than testing cues (see Figure 1). Information about means for violence, such as access to weapons, was documented most frequently at the forensic hospital (37.5%), but only 6.0% of the time at the crisis center and 8.9% of the time at the chronic hospital. Clinical factors, on the other hand, were on average documented more frequently than all other risk cue domains. This varied slightly across different settings, specifically with information about substance abuse, symptom severity, and violent fantasies. Violent fantasies, however, were documented less frequently in charts at all four settings.

Clinicians' perceptions from the discharge condition were considered for statistical comparison with documentation of risk cues. Table 2 shows rank orders of cue domains based on the means of documentation, perceived availability, and perceived relevance of MacArthur risk factors. Clinicians' perceptions of the availability of risk cues at discharge were ranked. Clinical cues on average were ranked the highest, just as they were for clinical documentation. Historical cues were generally perceived as the next most available information, followed by contextual cues, and then testing.

The pattern was somewhat different for the perceived relevance of risk factors in the discharge condition. At the crisis center and on the acute hospital, testing factors were seen as the most relevant, followed by clinical factors. For clinicians working on the forensic and chronic hospitals, clinical cues were seen as the most relevant, with contextual

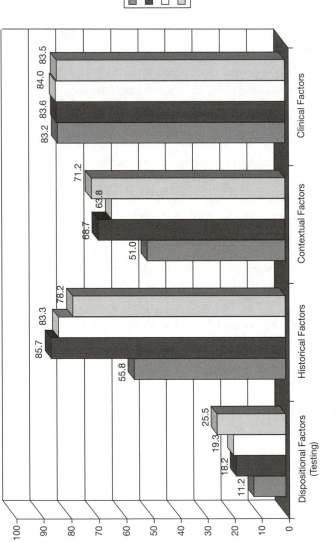

Crisis
Acute
Forensic
Chronic

FIGURE 1: MEAN PERCENTAGE OF DOCUMENTATION BY RISK DOMAIN AND PSYCHIATRIC FACILITY

Table 2: Rank Order of Risk Domains by Context

Documentation:

Crisis:	Clinical (83.2)	>	Historical (55.8)	>	Contextual (51.0)	>	Testing (11.2)
Acute:	Historical (85.7)	>	Clinical (83.6)	>	Contextual (68.7)	>	Testing (18.2)
Forensic:	Clinical (84.0)	>	Historical (83.3)	>	Contextual (63.8)	>	Testing (19.3)
Chronic:	Clinical (83.5)	>	Historical (78.2)	>	Contextual (71.2)	>	Testing (25.5)

Perceived Availability:

Crisis:	Clinical (8.40)	>	Contextual (6.76)	>	Historical (6.62)	>	Testing (5.67)
Acute:	Clinical (8.67)	>	Historical (7.59)	>	Testing (6.69)	>	Contextual (5.56)
Forensic:	Clinical (8.78)	>	Historical (8.48)	>	Contextual (7.46)	>	Testing (6.30)
Chronic:	Clinical (9.23)	>	Historical (7.92)	>	Contextual (6.69)	>	Testing (6.37)

Perceived Relevance:

Crisis:	Testing (8.73)	>	Clinical (8.53)	>	Contextual (7.92)	>	Historical (7.74)
Acute:	Testing (8.23)	>	Clinical (8.19)	>	Historical (8.06)	>	Contextual (6.94)
Forensic:	Clinical (9.11)	>	Testing (8.48)	>	Contextual (8.41)	>	Historical (8.37)
Chronic:	Clinical (8.71)	>	Contextual (8.64)	>	Testing (8.35)	>	Historical (8.15)

Note. For documentation, parentheses denote the mean percentage of clinical charts documenting risk cues in that domain. For perceived availability and perceived relevance, parentheses denote the mean ratings by clinicians in the discharge condition of risk cues in that domain on a scale from 0–10.

and testing cues perceived the next most relevant (in different orders for the two hospitals). Historical factors were seen as the least relevant in both the forensic and chronic settings. Despite these contextual differences, there was a very small range on clinicians' ratings of relevance in each setting (e.g., highest 8.73 to lowest 7.74 at the crisis center). Additionally, most MacArthur risk cues were rated as relevant by clinicians at all four settings.

The MacArthur risk cues were ranked according to clinical documentation, perceived relevance, and perceived availability on each setting. Pearson's correlations of rank order are recommended in order to analyze the relationships between rankings that originate from different data sets (Howell, 1997). Table 3 shows that rank-order correlations between clinical documentation and perceived availability were significant at each of the clinical settings in this study (e.g., at the forensic hospital, $r=.81$, $p<.001$). Clinicians' perceptions of the MacArthur risk cues that are typically available (or unavailable) were closely related to the clinical documentation of risk information. Conversely, there was no significant correlation between perceived relevance and clinical documentation or between perceived relevance and perceived availability. There were negative correlations between clinical documentation and perceived relevance on all four settings, though these correlations were not significant.

Table 3: Pearson's Correlations between Clinical Documentation, Perceived Availability, and Perceived Relevance of MacArthur Risk Cues

Rank Order Correlation	Crisis	Acute	Forensic	Chronic
Clinical Documentation and Perceived Availability	.80 **	.54 *	.81 **	.72 **
Clinical Documentation and Perceived Relevance	−.26	−.29	−.06	−.16
Perceived Availability and Perceived Relevance	.13	.03	.07	−.09

Note.
* $p<.01$ ** $p<.001$

DISCUSSION

Overall, the findings suggest that most of the MacArthur cues were documented and perceived as available at the three state hospital settings (acute, forensic, chronic). The majority of historical variables were on average represented in charts more than 80% of the time in these settings.

There were few differences on the total documentation of risk factors across the three state hospital settings, as well. The results were less conclusive about the availability of risk factors at the crisis center as MacArthur risk cues were generally documented less often than at the state hospital settings. Although not specifically measured in this study, demographic risk cues were readily available in all four settings. Clinical factors were also documented and perceived as typically available regardless of setting whereas testing results were documented least often and clinicians perceived these cues to be least available.

The results from this study have several implications for understanding how risk assessment occurs in clinical practice. Relevant risk information on testing results did not systematically get documented into patient charts at the crisis center and the state hospital settings. In the case of testing information, though, clinical documentation may be a poor indicator of actual availability. Personality testing results were documented in more than half of the crisis center charts and in less than half of the state hospital charts, however, the majority of patients at the state hospital were, at some point, processed through the crisis center. This finding suggests that testing results were not unavailable so much as they were not included in clinical documentation (see note on page 55). Consequently, the data on the documentation of testing results probably speaks more to the communication (or lack of communication) of potentially valuable risk information to clinical staff in psychiatric facilities. Indeed, the state hospital required an entire battery of assessment measures to be conducted on each patient and, therefore, results were in fact available for treatment planning and risk assessment. Despite this fact, clinical staff overall did not perceive these testing results to be readily available.

There may be a number of reasons why testing results were not documented, including fears by psychologists that non-psychologists may misinterpret results, no strict policy guidelines for documenting testing findings, and ethical limitations on entering court reports in treatment charts. Psychologists do not, of course, wish to include raw data in progress reports read by non-psychologists, but it seems important to impart these testing results to other clinical staff in a "user-friendly" manner. Such considerations may not bear directly on the actual availability of risk cues or the selection of risk factors for actuarial instruments per se, but do have important implications for how critical risk information and actuarial results themselves should be communicated to clinical staff. If clinical staff at psychiatric hospitals perceived testing in general to be less available to them, then testing results may factor into their clinical decisionmaking less often than other *more readily available* factors. It will therefore be important to stress that clinicians conducting actuarial risk assessments document and communicate findings to staff in a way that is clear and understandable. If this risk communication occurs unsystematically, then efforts to transfer actuarial technology to clinical practice may be hampered.

The data indicated that historical risk information was usually available at the state hospital settings but was inconclusive about the availability of this information at the crisis center. History of violence was documented in approximately 28% of the charts at the crisis center. Other research corroborates that historical variables are not always documented in clinical practice. For example, Malone, Szanto, Corbitt, and Mann (1995) found that clinical reports in psychiatric settings sometimes failed to document history of suicide attempts. It should be noted that, in our study, violence history was not only documented when a patient was violent; there were instances in which information indicated a patient had *no* history of violence. Furthermore, although the presence or absence of history of violence information in charts was examined, the accuracy of the history of violence information was not coded. Historical information may be unreliable if not gathered from multiple sources (Mulvey & Lidz, 1993).

It would appear from the findings in this study that clinicians working in psychiatric emergency settings who are time pressured to make decisions may have less predictive historical information at their disposal compared to their counterparts in longer-term inpatient settings (see Gardner et al., 1996a). Contextual information may be correspondingly difficult to obtain because of logistical constraints of the crisis center, because clients may be too psychotic to provide accurate information, or because clients refuse to sign releases of information when confronted with possible civil commitment. Research has already started to develop actuarial models for crisis screening (Gardner et al., 1996b; McNeil & Binder, 1994), some of which do not rely upon historical or contextual information. On the other hand, the results from this study also suggest that it may be worthwhile for clinicians to increase efforts to obtain and document accurate risk information, to the extent possible. It is probable that increasing availability and accuracy of research risk factors in clinical practice would help to improve risk assessments and enhance risk management of potentially violent patients.

The findings also have implications for the development and implementation of actuarial instruments. Even though most historical factors were available at the state hospital settings, it is important to note that outside of the forensic hospital, histories of incarcerations and arrests were on average less typically available. As Cooke, Michie, Hart, and Hare (1999) note, the possibility that criminal records are often unavailable in non-forensic settings has important implications for the construction and implementation of actuarial devices. Administration of instruments such as the PCL-R (Hare, 1991), the HCR-20 (Webster et al., 1995), and the VRAG (Quinsey et al., 1998) all depend, in part, on access to detailed case history information including a criminal record. As the findings in this study indicate, civil psychiatric settings appear to possess such records less often. Given the nature of the mental health system in the United States, forensic clinicians are likely to have more contact with the criminal justice system than their counterparts working at civil facilities (Melton et al., 1997). As clinicians in civil settings may need to take more time and make more effort to obtain this type of information, there may be more resistance to employing actuarial measures in non-forensic settings that rely on detailed criminal records. As a result, availability of this specific type of historical information may be relevant to transferring actuarial technology into non-forensic psychiatric settings.

Clinical and contextual cues were generally available across all four settings with two notable exceptions. First, clinical documentation frequency was low regarding means for violence and access to weapons. Most staff thought that this was an important risk factor to consider (it was ranked in the top ten of perceived relevance on all four settings), but as Grisso (1996) hypothesized, this information was apparently not feasible to obtain. Given the logistical difficulties in getting accurate information on this cue, researchers may wish to use caution before selecting this risk factor for an actuarial device, even if it shows high predictive validity. The findings from this study suggest this item has potential to be omitted from an actuarial formula when used in practice. Second, violent fantasies did not get documented as frequently as other clinical cues. Although patients may intentionally keep such fantasies private (and thereby make information about violent fanstasies "less available"), it is also possible that clinicians are not making efforts to ask about these. This may therefore speak more to clinical training issues than to cue availability. Thus, clinicians may need training on how to assess risk factors such as violent fantasies, particularly in non-forensic settings (see Borum, 1996; Webster & Cox, 1997). Regarding the availability of this particular risk factor, the findings remain unclear.

There were some limitations in this study that are important to keep in mind. First, cue availability was not directly measured in this study.

Findings may be dependent, in part, upon the methodology used to capture cue availability. Multiple sites were examined in this study because documentation of information in charts might reflect policies and procedures of particular sites rather than clinical practice. Because documentation might also reflect clinicians' preferences for risk cues, mental health professionals' perceptions of availability were obtained (i.e., if perceptions of *availability* matched documentation – which they did – then there would be more confidence that availability is being measured). By eliciting ratings on clinicians' perceptions of relevance, it also could be determined to what extent documentation and perceived availability did, or did not, merely reflect clinicians' cue utilization preferences. Instead, direct observation of the clinical process may have provided more objective measurements of cue availability (see generally, Mulvey & Lidz, 1985, 1995).

A second limitation of this study concerns its use of one site for each psychiatric setting. It is possible that findings rely upon procedures specific to the particular crisis center and state hospital settings investigated in this study. Thus, the generalizability of these results come into question, and more research will need to be conducted to determine if the same pattern of documentation emerges in different jurisdictions. Similarly, more work will be needed with comparable clinician cohorts to assess whether the perceptions of cue availability and relevance are unique to the sample of mental health professionals who participated in this study. In sum, in order to get a clearer picture of risk information availability, future research will need to occur at different research sites, perhaps using additional and more direct methodology.

Future research should examine information management issues surrounding violence risk assessment and attempt to connect findings of cue availability with utilization and development of actuarial measures. Both the quantity and quality of risk information available bear on the accuracy of actuarial results (Quinsey et al., 1998), and, as Social Judgment Theory suggests, efforts should be made to match the environmental constraints of cue availability with the construction of actuarial decisionmaking devices (Mulvey & Lidz, 1995). Findings also indicated that availability of risk information may be related to issues of risk communication (see generally Monahan & Steadman, 1996; Schopp, 1996), and future work should explore strategies for disseminating actuarial results to mental health professionals.

Other research should examine whether increasing availability of relevant risk factors, or increasing the reliability of information, helps to improve the accuracy of predictions of dangerousness. By identifying which predictive risk cues are unavailable in particular settings, risk assessment policies and procedures that are in need of improvement can be pinpointed. For example, consider the results concerning the documentation and perceived availability of history of violence information at the crisis center. If there were some formalized effort to cull additional information about history of violence, then perhaps more accurate risk assessments could be made in practice (McNeil, 1998).

Finally, future research should explore to what extent research risk factors, such as those listed in the MacArthur study, are being incorporated into regular clinical assessments of violent behavior. As Webster et al. (1995) note, the domains of research and practice may scarcely overlap with respect to violence risk assessment. Findings from this study indicated that mental health professionals do generally perceive MacArthur risk cues to be relevant for assessing violence risk. Further analysis is needed to clarify whether clinicians use research risk factors in practice. Such empirical studies would provide important information about how effective research efforts have been at changing and improving actual practice of violence risk assessment.

ACKNOWLEDGEMENTS

The first author was supported as a predoctoral fellow by an NIMH Training grant, "Training in Mental Health and Justice Systems Research" (5T32MH16156) during the preparation of this manuscript. We would like to acknowledge the helpful comments of Thomas Grisso, Randy Otto, Steve Penrod, and Robert Schopp on a prior draft of this manuscript.

REFERENCES

Borum, R. (1996). Improving the clinical practice of violence risk assessment. *American Psychologist, 51,* 945–956.

Cooke, D. J., Michie, C., Hart, S. D., & Hare, R. D. (1999). Evaluating the screening version of the Hare Psychopathy Checklist-Revised (PCL:SV): An item response theory analysis. *Psychological Assessment, 11,* 3–13.

Gardner, W., Lidz, C. W., Mulvey, E.P., & Shaw, E. C. (1996). Clinical versus actuarial predictions of violence in patients with mental illnesses. *Journal of Consulting and Clinical Psychology, 64,* 602–609.

Grisso, T. (1996). Clinical assessments for legal decisionmaking in criminal cases: Research recommendations. In B. D. Sales & S. Shah (Eds)., *Mental health and Law: Research, Policy, and Services.* (pp. 109–140). Durham, North Carolina: Carolina Academic Press.

Grisso, T., & Tomkins, A. (1996). Communicating violence risk assessments. *American Psychologist, 51*, 928–930.

Grisso, T., Tomkins, A., & Casey, P. (1988). Psychosocial concepts in juvenile law. *Law and Human Behavior, 12*, 403–437.

Hammond, K. R. (1955). Probabilistic functioning and the clinical method. *Psychological Review, 62*, 255–262.

Hammond, K. R. (1994). Naturalistic decision making from a Brunswikian viewpoint: Its past, present, future. In G. A. Klein, J. Orasanu, R. Calderwood, & C. E. Zsambok, (Eds.), *Decision making in action: Models and methods* (pp. 205–227). New Jersey: Ablex Publishing Corporation.

Hammond, K. R., Hamm, R. M., Grassia, J., & Pearson, T. (1997). Direct comparison of the efficacy of intuitive and analytical cognition in expert judgment. In W. M. Goldstein & R. M. Hogarth (Eds.), *Research on judgment and decision making* (pp. 144–180). New York: Cambridge University Press.

Hammond, K. R., Hursch, C. J., & Todd, F. J. (1964). Analyzing the comments of clinical inference. *Psychological Review, 71*, 438–456.

Hammond, K. R., McClelland, G. H., & Mumpower, J. (1980). *Human judgment and decision making: Theories, methods, and procedures*. New York: Praeger.

Hammond, K. R., Stewart, T. R., Brehmer, B., & Steinmann, D. O. (1975). Social judgment theory. In M. F. Kaplan & S. Schwartz (Eds.), *Human judgment and decision processes* (pp. 271–312). New York: Academic Press.

Hare, R. (1991). *The Hare Psychopathy Checklist-Revised*. Toronto, Ontario, Canada: Multi-Health Systems.

Heilbrun, K. (1997). Prediction versus management models relevant to risk assessment: The importance of legal decision-making context. *Law and Human Behavior, 21*, 347–359.

Howell, D. C. (1997). *Statistical methods for psychology* (4th Ed). New York: Duxbury Press.

Jackson, M. (1989). The clinical assessment and prediction of violent behavior. *Criminal Justice and Behavior, 16*, 114–131.

Lamiell, J. T. (1979). Discretion in juvenile justice: A framework for systematic study. *Criminal Justice and Behavior, 6*, 76–101.

Malone, K. M., Szanto, K., Corbitt, E. M., & Mann, J. J. (1995). Clinical assessment versus research methods in the assessment of suicidal behavior. *American Journal of Psychiatry, 152*, 1601–1607.

McNeil, D. E. (1998). Empirically based clinical evaluation and management of the potentially violent patient. In P.M. Kleespies (Ed.), *Emergencies in mental health practice: Evaluation and management* (pp. 95–116). New York: Guilford Press.

McNeil, D. E., & Binder, R. L. (1994). Screening for risk of inpatient violence: Validation of an actuarial tool. *Law and Human Behavior, 18*, 579–586.

McNeil, D. E., Sandberg, D. A., & Binder, R. L. (1998). The relationship between confidence and accuracy in clinical assessment of psychiatric patients' potential for violence. *Law and Human Behavior, 22*, 655–667.

Melton, G., Petrila, J., Poythress, N., & Slobogin, C. (1997). *Psychological evaluations for the courts: A handbook for mental health professionals and lawyers* (2nd ed.). New York: Guilford Press.

Menzies, R., & Webster, C. D. (1995). Construction and validation of risk assessments in a six-year follow-up of forensic patients: A tridimensional analysis. *Journal of Consulting and Clinical Psychology, 63*, 766–778.

Monahan, J. (1981). *The clinical prediction of violent behavior*. Rockville, MD: National Institute of Mental Health.

Monahan, J., & Steadman, H. (1994). *Violence and mental disorder: Developments in risk assessment*. Chicago: University of Chicago Press.

Monahan, J., & Steadman, H. (1996). Violent storms and violent people: How meteorology can inform risk communication in mental health law. *American Psychologist, 51,* 931–938.

Mulvey, E., & Lidz, C. (1985). Back to basics: A critical analysis of dangerousness research in a new legal environment. *Law and Human Behavior, 9,* 209–18.

Mulvey, E., & Lidz, C. (1993). Measuring patient violence in dangerousness research. *Law and Human Behavior, 17,* 277–288.

Mulvey, E., & Lidz, C. (1995). Conditional prediction: A model for research on dangerousness to others in a new era. *International Journal of Law and Psychiatry, 18,* 129–143.

Otto, R. (1992). The prediction of dangerous behavior: A review and analysis of "second generation" research. *Forensic Reports, 5,* 103–133.

Quinsey, V. L., Harris, G. T., Rice, M. E., & Cormier, C. A. (1998). *Violent offenders: Appraising and managing risk.* Washington, D. C: American Psychological Association.

Silver, E., Mulvey, E. P., & Monahan, J. (1999). Assessing violence risk among discharged psychiatric patients: Toward an ecological approach. *Law and Human Behavior, 23,* 237–255.

Schopp, R. F. (1996). Communicating risk assessments: Accuracy, efficacy, and responsibility. *American Psychologist, 51,* 939–944.

Steadman, H., Monahan, J., Appelbaum, P., Grisso, T., Mulvey, E., Roth, L., Robbins, P., & Kalssen, D. (1994). Designing a new generation of risk assessment research. In J. Monahan & H. Steadman (Eds.), *Violence and mental disorder: Developments in risk assessment* (pp. 297–318). Chicago: University of Chicago Press.

Steadman, H., Mulvey, E., Monahan, J., Clark-Robbins, P., Appelbaum, P., Grisso, T., Roth, L., & Silver, E. (1998). Violence by people discharged from acute psychiatric inpatient facilities and by others in the same neighborhoods. *Archives of General Psychiatry, 55,* 393–402.

Steadman, H., Silver, E., Monahan, J., Applebaum, P. S., Robbins, P., Mulvey, E. P., Grisso, T., Roth, L. H., & Banks, S. (2000) A classification tree approach to the development of actuarial violence risk assessment tools. *Law and Human Behavior,* 24, 83–100.

Tomkins, A. J. (1990). Dispositional decisionmaking in the juvenile justice system: An empirical study of the use of offense and offender information. *Nebraska Law Review,* 69, 298–345.

Webster, C. D., & Cox, D. (1997). Integration of nomothetic and ideographic positions in risk assessment: Implications for practice and the education of psychologists and other mental health professionals. *American Psychologist, 52,* 1245–1246.

Webster, C. D., Eaves, D., Douglas, K., & Winthrop, A. (1995). *The HCR-20 Scheme: The assessment of dangerousness and risk.* Burnaby, British Columbia, Canada: Simon Fraser University and Forensic Psychiatric Services Commission of British Columbia.

NOTE

It is possible that a subset of crisis patients, who were unable to complete testing, were the very group of patients transferred to the state hospitals. There would be some evidence for this since probably the most acute patients would require further hospitalization and have the greatest difficulty completing (or agreeing to complete) psychological testing. More empirical investigation tracking particular patient's charts as they are transferred through the mental health system would elucidate on this phenomenon.

Chapter 4

THE "RISKY" BUSINESS OF CHILD ABUSE ASSESSMENT IN BRITISH COLUMBIA

Margaret A. Jackson

In this chapter, I want first to situate the Child Abuse Assessment process in British Columbia (B.C.) in a historical and contemporary context to assist in understanding the current policies and procedures we have. I will then discuss how well those policies are working. The method I use is an examination of the relevant policies, the risk assessment model itself, a recent evaluation of the implementation of the model conducted by the Ministry of Children and Families, and interviews with child protection personnel. My primary interest is in trying to understand the process as it unfolded in the province. The paper concludes with comments about the implications of the model for human rights issues.

I will argue that it is because certain events came together at a particular point in time in British Columbia we now have the risk assessment model approach we do. The process was triggered by tragic events that caused public concern at a time when considerations of risk were widely being used for assessing potential risk for spousal assault, violence, and criminal behaviour. We do essentially now live in a "risk" society in which the management of risk assumes a high priority (Ericson and Haggerty, 1997). It gets characterized institutionally in the continual refinement of how risk is controlled for security purposes (Ibid.:9). The risk assessment instrument which came to be employed by the province of British Columbia for child abuse decisions emerged from this context of first, a highly profiled child abuse tragedy, and second, the existing environmental legitimacy given to the risk assessment approach. The third factor of influence was the uncertain policy environment – which continues even today – in the province. The policy question remains for child protection decision makers, which interests do have the most priority in these cases, the best interests of the child, the best interests of the family or the best interests of society?

The tragic event took place in B.C. in 1995, to five and a half year old Matthew Vaudreuil, who died at the hands of his mother from extreme abuse and neglect. The case highlighted existing problems with the child protection procedures in the province. I will only briefly describe that case which rocked the region and the rest of the country and resulted in widespread and continuing changes in policy and procedure for child protection. An excerpt taken from the report of the Inquiry Commission into his death details the case: Matthew, at almost six, weighed only 36 pounds. His face, arms, legs and back were covered in bruises, as if he had been bound. His buttocks were covered in bruises and welts. He had a fractured arm, 11 fractured ribs, and what looked like the imprint of a foot on his back. He had been tortured and deprived of food before he was killed of asphyxiation (the mother had held her hand over his mouth because he had been crying).

It was a stunning case, not only because of the manner of Matthew's death but because of all the things that seemed to have gone wrong within the system to handle it. The mother had come into the Ministry of Social Services' care when she was eight years old because she herself had been abused. She was assessed as having borderline intelligence and of being unable to be financially independent. Social services identified her as having difficulties with her parenting and consequently did direct multiple services to her care over a number of years. But despite reports of parenting problems, filthy living conditions, abuse to Matthew, and the fact that the mother begged to have the Ministry place Matthew into a foster home, the ministry made the error of leaving him in her care. They felt she was trying to abuse the system. I argue that they also did so in part because of the unresolved policy issues referenced earlier. That is, the policy question was, and remains, whose best interests are to be given priority in these types of cases in policy and practice? When the directing policy does not clearly establish priority, confusion can result for those who must work with it, and, consistent with decision-making theory tenets, they may fall back upon personal beliefs and heuristics to determine priority (Kahneman, Slovic, and Tversky 1982). In the case of Matthew, it was felt that the best interests of the family, such as it was, should receive priority in decision making.

The Inquiry Report, called the Gove Commission Report, that examined the case was quite damning of the system overall. The Commission subsequently reviewed 264 additional files of children's deaths in the province and concluded that the system was at fault because first, it did not have clear policies about how to handle the cases nor did it have a systematic record collection and management system – and second, there were inaccurate assessments of risk of family situations being made. The report recommended that a new Ministry of Children and Families replace the existing provincial agencies dealing with children's care. That over-arching Ministry was created and is still in the process of determining the scope of its own mandate. It has assumed authority over children's welfare from many other existing ministries, such as the Attorney General. That transition alone created chaotic confusion as social workers in one ministry who had been dealing with child abuse problems were assumed under the new ministry.[1]

In June of 1995, the government introduced two amendment acts which firmly articulated a provincial policy shift to a "best interests of the child" orientation in these types of cases. As well, it directed that risk factors in the family environment had to be more systematically examined. Thus there was a focus on changes in both policy and procedure. In September 1995, the development of a standardized risk assessment model was identified as a number one priority. The employment of this model was to assist in the assessment of a child's immediate safety needs, an exercise traditionally undertaken by the social workers, as well as to estimate the risk of any future harm to a child – the latter assessment was structured through the development of a new risk assessment tool. It was not intended to replace clinical judgment that focuses on the assessment of mental and emotional, i.e., psychological states.

An examination of existing risk assessment tools in the area was conducted by the province in 1995, with the adaptation of a New York state model for the province as the result – a first draft appearing in March 1996 – a very quick turn-around. Another province, Ontario, uses a version of the same New York model that British Columbia has implemented. U.S. models are adapted elsewhere as well, with the Hong Kong Child Protection Services Unit employing an adapted instrument from California. Its assessment matrix uses a low, intermediate and high risk scoring as opposed to the B.C. model which has a combination four point scaling and checklist approach. Overall, the B.C. model process has nine risk decision points, each having a detailed articulation of the criteria to guide each decision point. Clear overlap exists between the traditional decision points the social worker was previously required to undertake prior to the model's implementation.

The first six form the primary or core decision points (see Figure 1): the first decision remains the same as it had been previously, that is, to decide to investigate or not. The second is determining the response time to a report. The third decision is a major one – the assessment of the child's immediate safety. The fourth is the determination of the child's

Risk Assessment and Case Management Flow Chart

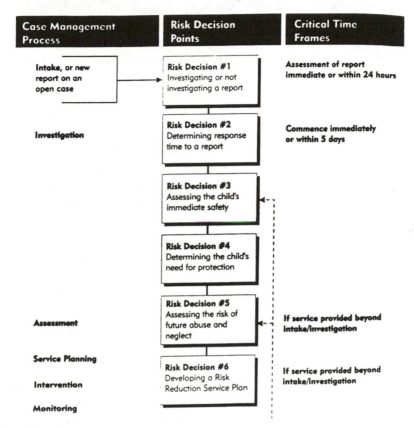

FIGURE 1: RISK ASSESSMENT AND CASE MANAGEMENT FLOW CHART
(Taken from: The Risk Assessment Model for Child Protection in British Columbia (1996).
Victoria: Ministry of Children and Families, p. 16)

need for protection; decision point five is the assessment of the risk of future abuse and neglect – this decision lies at the heart of the new risk assessment process. It considers 23 risk factors in five areas of influence to assess: parental, child, family, abuse/neglect, and intervention, and concludes with general risk considerations. This is followed by risk decision six, the development of a risk reduction plan – the area for which we will see there has been little training to date.

According to Sullivan, who actually conducted the evaluation of the implementation of the B.C. model, and who was also one of its creators, the experience in other jurisdictions setting up such models has been that success hinges on the implementation process itself (1997:2). A three stage evaluation of the process was proposed for the B.C. implementation which envisioned field training by line staff and supervisors which was to be followed by a staggered process of actual implementation throughout the province (Ibid.:2). The process was to be staggered in part because it was felt that the system could only handle a given number of changes in one period of time. It was feared that the new Ministry had reached a saturation point with the simultaneous introduction of new legislation, a new computerized information system, a large number of new and inexperienced staff, new training programs, major reorganization, plus the implementation of the new risk assessment model (Sullivan, 1997:3).

Problems began to emerge with the implementation process for the assessment instrument almost immediately, first of all because of a lack of resources and lack of time to undertake the training properly. This process occurred during a time of notable staffing problems and, as observed by Sullivan, the introduction of such models into the policy environment often "accompanies reductions in federal/provincial transfer payments and reduced social spending generally" (1998:1). It is almost as if the government, in putting into place a "reliable and valid tool of assessment" for predicting future abuse, feels justified in then cutting back on the human and other resources needed to support it. In essence, the human decisionmaker is not seen as necessary or effective as the structured instrument.

The reduction in sufficient resource support actually meant that social workers, many of whom were new and inexperienced, with increased caseloads, had less time to spend with clients to gather important information for decision making which in turn reduced the potential for the risk assessment model to contribute to careful decision making and service planning to an "objectified calculation of risk factors. Calculation replaces relationship as the medium through which uncertainty is addressed" (Sullivan, 1998:21). Basically then, while making judgements under uncertainty is integral to the human aspect of the problem of child abuse assessment and the Risk Assessment model is a potentially useful technology to introduce into this area of uncertainty, the technology can not take the place of the traditional social worker relationship with the family that can only build over some measure of time (Sullivan, 1998:21). In other words, the risk assessment process itself, as construed by the model, and most specifically by the instrument, may prove to be as risky to the best interests for the child as the initiating problem of abuse, in that it may leave the child more, not less, vulnerable.

It is true that almost all decisions concerning a child's welfare involve judgments concerning risk. Practitioners, though, have traditionally argued that skilled workers, making multiple observations, can assess risk through determining the unique characteristics of individual clients. Researchers, on the other hand, argue that statistical methods are the best approach to determine risk, and those methods have been empirically shown to be superior (Reid et al., 1995:5). In the end, the B.C. model attempts to reconcile the "realities of practice with rigorous research", in the hope that they can be mutually supportive. For example, although the risk assessment instrument does have ratings to make, there are no cutoff points provided to determine specific decisions, such as removal of the child, for the individual worker – it remains a subjective final judgment.

The employment of the risk assessment model is, however, not without perceived benefits. The Gove Commission Report had recommended the systematic tracking of cases in order that cases such as Matthew Vaudreuill's would be less likely to recur. Establishing a database through the documenting of the risk assessment outcomes can facilitate that kind of tracking. As well, the process is clearly set out for the decision makers, with definitions and steps detailed. The procedure also assures that all-important issues are considered, since they must be rated.

Apart from the policy environment concerns, that is, unclear policies about best interests, priorities and the negative impact of the government's fiscal policies, the actual data from the evaluation of the implementation pinpointed problem areas in the translation of the model to operational reality. The findings confirmed that some of the central elements of the instrument are open to "differing interpretations, subject to unreliability, and achieve greater accuracy only through multiple observations" (Sullivan, 1998:21). As in the case with other similar approaches, the risk assessment can improve the quality of decision making within the context of the traditional relationship between the social worker and the client. But, if there is less time available for the relationship of trust to develop and that relationship is in essence reduced to a calculation, then the role and accountability of the social worker is reduced to a type of audit exercise.

The reality check evaluation of the implementation involved a sampling of training tests from 1526 staff across the province, including 258 supervisors and acting supervisors, in May 1997 (Sullivan, 1997:7). For those participants who finished the entire three days of training (many did not because of other work priorities), a test was provided in which they had to complete both a safety assessment and a comprehensive risk assessment on either a written scenario or a video-taped case scenario – the latter of which was considered less complex (Ibid.:7). The results for the comprehensive risk assessment component will be focused upon briefly here, since that decision lies at the heart of the new assessment procedure. A sample of 158 comprehensive risk assessments were completed on both cases.

The frequency distributions of the responses to the written vignette were examined, as well as the inter-rater reliabilities, using both the full range of responses as well as the distribution after collapsing the response categories from 4 to 2. The latter exercise allowed a determination of whether participants were scoring the elements in the right direction. In looking at the results for the more complex vignette in the area of parental influence, the assessment of parents' mental/emotional ability to care for the child proved difficult for the workers and no acceptable level of consistency amongst them was achieved. Also, in the decision requiring the understanding of the risk assessment criteria for child influences, workers had the greatest difficulty in the assessment of the child's response to parents, the child's behaviour and the child's mental health and development. Again, consistency levels in the assessment of these elements were too low to assume acceptable inter-rater acceptability. In relation to abuse/neglect influences, this case vignette provided more information and a higher level of consistency was achieved, except for the assessment of intent and acknowledgement of responsibility. Overall, the collapsed categories indicated decisions were made in the right direction, but when the full range of ratings were used, a lack of precision emerged in the discrimination between the more discrete levels of risk.

In summary, to the extent the risk assessment instrument follows traditional assessment considerations, as seemed true for the immediate safety assessment exercise, it appears to be a viable tool, but problems do arise when: interpretations are not consistent; there is not sufficient time to both complete the instrument and to conduct multiple observations of the child and parents to establish a relationship; and when families feel threatened by the process of information gathering as also being a process that may result in their children being taken away from them. In the latter case, the process can change the kind of information gathered in a session, especially when the required follow-up risk reduction plan associated with the model does not get created because of lack of time and training.

Admittedly, the whole process of implementation and training of the new process in B.C. was skewed by the political climate of public outrage at the deaths of children. "Implementation plans were altered and training was fast-tracked on orders from the Deputy Minister in the wake of the negative publicity following the deaths of children known to the Ministry in the winter of 1996 and spring 1997" (Sullivan, 1998:1). One year had also passed since the release of the Gove Commission Report and pressure mounted to have the model in place. That meant however, as noted, that supervisors often did not get the full three days of training on the model, but were only given a one or two day introduction to it. The model was also intended to produce risk reduction service plans, but since many responsible for carrying out the plans were not sufficiently familiar with the model, that component of the approach has been compromised.

To return to the plight of the Ministry risk assessment model, as part of the triangulation exercise, part of my assessment of the process also included interviews with key representatives – both regional administrators and front-line workers. They provide a cross-reference for the information determined from the written evaluation conducted by Richard Sullivan. The interviewees did confirm that the training for the case management part of the model had for the most part not occurred because of time and resource constraints. The best interests of the child considerations, therefore, appeared to have fallen in between a best interests of the family and best interests of the public divide. And as well, it was argued by the interviewees, as Sullivan himself argues, that the "(r)isk assessment, risk management, the monitoring of risk and risk-taking" can become the key concerns for child protection workers and the public, rather than the welfare of the individual children per se (1998:21). It is true that, in Canada, the concept of risk has become entrenched – risk for insurance, risk in finance, risk to health. And that holds true organizationally as well. This is especially true in the criminal justice system with the determination of risk to reoffend, risk of danger to the public, but also now in other organizational mandates for the delivery of services and relationships with clients.

To return to the opening point, the concern in the risk assessment process of child abuse in British Columbia has to lie not only with the instrument itself and its validity and inter-rater reliability, or with the problems of implementation, but with the very policies which direct such procedures. While the policy guidelines for the Risk Assessment Model clearly set out the social values of import about child protection, that is, "the safety and well-being of children are paramount considerations; and children are entitled to be protected from abuse, neglect, and harm or threat of harm" (RAMCPBC: 11), the associated first guiding principle introduces the old confusion by stating that risk assessment should be both child-centred and family-focused. Therefore the earlier tensions once again are structured into the process without accompanying clarification of what either child-centred or family-focused means, or which has priority over the other, or how they even relate.[2]

By comparison, the Hong Kong model of risk assessment of child abuse sets out very clearly that it is the welfare of the child which is the priority – there is no reference to a competing family focus. The governing principle begins in bold with the statement, "(t)he *paramount* concern is the welfare of the child" (emphasis in original), and continues in the following sentence with, "(t)he procedural guidelines contained in this Guide are formulated to serve the best interest of the child . . .".

Article 3(1) of the UN Convention on the Rights of the Child (Canada ratified the Convention on January 12, 1992), clearly states that "(i)n all actions concerning children, whether undertaken by public or private social welfare institutions, courts of law, administrative authorities or legislative bodies, the best interests of the child shall be a primary consideration" (Convention on the Rights of the Child:2–3). The question still remains of course as to what constitutes the best interests of the child, but, in any case, in the Hong Kong model, there is no mention of a conflicting priority to be given to the best interests of the family. The point is that if the procedure of assessing risk to the child is already distorted by public outrage and pressure for action, a lack of resources, lack of training, and all of the other problems already discussed, then the lack of clarity in the directing policy itself adds a layer of ambiguity which further distorts a best interests of the child outcome.

Where does this leave us? As far as British Columbia, Phase III of the evaluation of the risk assessment model has yet to take place. It will assess the consistency of application over time and "whether resultant service plans effectively reduce risks in specified areas" (Sullivan, 1997:4) – the latter evaluation obviously can not take place until those plans are regularly and systematically being carried out. This more complete evaluation will require tracking individual cases over a long term.

In addition, as far as the human rights implications of the process, a 1999 review is now under way to determine how well Canada is adhering to the U.N. Convention on the Rights of the Child. In fact, for British Columbia, this will be the third such exercise. In the second review, an advocacy group called the Society for Children and Youth engaged in the process with an assessment of their own to provide input in 1998 (the first 1994 review did not have non-governmental sources providing reviews). One finding released was that our own provincial Human Rights Code (R.S.B.C. 1996, c.210) provides only a "fair" compliance with the Convention and only a "poor" compliance with regard to the views of a child. It is ironic since this is the Code that serves as a watchdog to the adherence of others with regard to human rights issues, and it might prove quite problematic when it comes to the assessment of child protection efforts afforded children under the risk assessment model in British Columbia.

In any event, it is hoped that the Stage III evaluation of the risk assessment procedure, in which it will be determined whether the model is applied consistently over time and whether it does effectively reduce risks, will be able to provide helpful feedback to the Ministry. Attention must be ultimately paid, however, in the wider longer term assessments, to not only the model's effectiveness for B.C. child abuse assessments at the operational level but at the higher policy level as well – for accountability reasons. It is the policy context which will ultimately determine whether a clear "best interests of the child" policy is being translated into "best interests of the child" outcomes.

NOTES

1 In fact, little seems to have changed since that time. The B.C. Child Advocate recently stated that the province's child protection system is "really dysfunctional". Calls to her office from children and families have "skyrocketed" in recent months, reflecting "rampant frustration. . . . The ministry has been writing policy like mad but the capacity of social workers to do it is lacking at the local level. That's where the disconnect occurs" (Tait, 2000: A19).

2 Another problem appears to be that the instrument is not as culturally sensitive as it should be, with Aboriginal communities being the most affected by such a limitation. It has been argued that one problem is that there is no accounting of collective care-giving in the risk assessment process, which often occurs in Aboriginal communities. One example is what happens at certain times of year in Aboriginal communities when both parents leave the reserve or family home to go on trips, such as for berry picking. They may not take their children along with them, but will organize to have a relative or a band member care for them. Thus, the employment of the risk assessment tool might not capture that kind of cultural behaviour which influences the care of children.

REFERENCES

Basic Issues Concerning the Assessment of Risk in Child Welfare Work (1995). Winnipeg, Manitoba: Faculty of Social Work/Faculty of Medicine, University of Manitoba.

Convention on the Rights of the Child (entry into force, 2 September 1990). Geneva, Switzerland: Office of the United Nations High Commissioner for Human Rights.

Cruickshank, D. (1998). "The UN Convention on the Rights of the Child: Does Domestic Legislation Measure Up?" Vancouver: The Society for Children and Youth of British Columbia.

Ericson, R. and Haggerty, K. (1997). *Policing the Risk Society*. Toronto: University of Toronto Press.

Kahneman, D., Slovic, P., and Tversky, A. (1982). *Judgment under Uncertainty: Heuristics and Biases*. Cambridge: Cambridge University Press.

Practice Standards for Child Protection (nd). Victoria: Ministry of Children and Families.

Procedures for Handling Child Sexual Abuse Cases (1996). Hong Kong: Family and Child Welfare Branch.

Report of the Gove Inquiry into Child Protection in British Columbia (1995). Victoria: Ministry of Social Services.

Sullivan, R. (1998). Implementing the B.C. Risk Assessment Model. In *Social Workers' Perspectives*, vol. 20, #2.

Sullivan, R., Stanley, D., and Groden, D. (1997). "Phase I Evaluation of the Implementation of the British Columbia Risk Assessment Model for Child Protection". Victoria: Ministry for Children and Families.

Tait, K. (2000). "Child-protection system 'dysfunctional'". *The Province*, Vancouver, British Columbia, p. A19.

The B.C. Handbook for Action on Child Abuse and Neglect (1998). Victoria: Ministry of Children and Families.

The Risk Assessment Model for Child Protection in British Columbia (1996). Victoria: Ministry for Children and Families.

Chapter 5

ASSESSING AND MANAGING RISK AMONG MENTALLY DISORDERED OFFENDERS IN NORTHERN IRELAND

Sinéad McGilloway and Michael Donnelly

'Jail diversion' programmes for mentally disordered offenders (MDOs) were implemented in the USA throughout the 1970s and 1980s. It has been UK government policy since 1990 to divert MDOs away from the criminal justice system into the care of health and social services (Home Office Circular 66/90). This policy was reiterated in a recent Home Office Circular (12/95) and in the Reed Report (1992). The current Regional Strategic Plan for health and social services in Northern Ireland (NI) also states that: *'comprehensive arrangements should be in place so that, where appropriate, people with mental illness can be diverted from the criminal justice system'* (DHSS (NI), 1996). An increasing range of mainly court-based diversion schemes has been developed in Great Britain, but whilst all share a common goal, there is variation with respect to, among other things, staffing, operating procedures and funding arrangements. However, relatively little is known about the appropriateness and effectiveness of these schemes which *'should be evaluated and tested as a priority and findings disseminated'* (James, 1996).

THE LOCAL SERVICE

A screening, assessment and referral service for offenders with mental health problems and/or learning disability (including substance abuse, personality disorder and acquired brain damage) was implemented in Northern Ireland (NI) in June 1998 in direct response to local and national recommendations. The scheme is based on the less common DAPA (Diversion At the Point of Arrest) model and also shares some features in common with Community Psychiatric Nurse (CPN) police liaison schemes, a number of which have been implemented in England. It was commissioned by the Eastern Health and Social Services Board (the largest of the four NI Boards) in collaboration with the Department of Health and Social Services (NI), the Northern Ireland Office, the Royal

Ulster Constabulary, the Probation Board for NI and other relevant statutory and voluntary agencies. The new service aims to provide a comprehensive mental health and risk assessment at the earliest point of contact with the criminal justice system plus a mechanism for referral, where appropriate, to health and social services.

The service is based in the busiest of four police stations in Belfast which operate under PACE legislation (Police and Criminal Evidence (PACE) NI Order (1989)) and which provide specialised settings for the treatment, questioning and identification of mentally disordered suspects. At the time of the study, the service was provided 7 days a week by two Community Mental Health Nurses (from 7.00 am to 3.00 pm daily and, twice weekly, from 12.00 pm to 8.00 pm) who receive an unspecified amount of support from forensic psychiatry. The CMHNs received a six-week 'induction training' period prior to the implementation of the scheme and have completed a two-year RCN accredited Diploma in Forensic Health Care. They liaise with the police, forensic medical officers (FMOs), probation officials and court representatives as well as health and social services professionals and voluntary agencies. The nurses provide more than a mental health and risk assessment in the sense that they act as co-ordinators of follow-up care – on occasion escorting clients to hospital – as well as providing ongoing advice and support. They are also required to advise the police and health care professionals about the management of MDOs.

The nurses screen the custody record forms of *everyone* detained in the police station against criteria developed for use in the Birmingham Court Diversion Scheme. These include evidence of: (1) a history of mental illness and/or learning disability; (2) an 'odd' crime; (3) a violent crime; and (4) unusual behaviour leading to referral by the police. The nurses also screen all those for whom an assessment is recommended by the FMO (or Resident Magistrate). This routine screening is designed to detect people who may have a mental disorder, but who have not been so identified by the custody sergeant and/or the FMO.

Everyone who meets *one or more* of the above criteria is approached by the nurse when in police custody or, occasionally, at the local Magistrates' Court, and asked if they would like to participate in an assessment. The nurses may also be required, on request, to assess remand prisoners. Following assessment, a brief psychiatric report is prepared which includes recommendations for appropriate follow-up treatment and support. This is made available to the court, arresting officer and the defendant's solicitor.

THE EVALUATION

This study was undertaken as part of a larger evaluation designed to assess the effectiveness of the new scheme and its impact on MDOs and existing services. Information is provided on: (1) the early performance of the scheme; (2) the characteristics of all those assessed by the scheme during its first six months; (3) the assessment of risk presented by violent offenders and/or those committing acts of self-harm; and (4) the symptomatology and functioning of offenders assessed during the period.

A formative-summative framework was chosen for the evaluation due to both the short timescale for implementation of the scheme and the lack of information about the most appropriate service response to MDOs. The summative phase will assess the impact of the scheme by means of, among other things, follow-up interviews with offenders and a survey of key 'stakeholders'. The evaluation is, to our knowldege, unique in that the researchers informed the practical implementation and day-to-day operation of the scheme during its first 6–9 months by: (a) appraising existing information sources; (b) introducing a system of performance indicators; (c) reviewing, adapting and testing screening and assessment measures; (d) identifying and recording 'stakeholder' views and multi-agency working; (e) providing ongoing formative feedback and advice to relevant agencies; (f) setting up and maintaining an anonymised database of all offenders; and (g) reviewing the progress and day-to-day operation of the scheme.

METHOD

An assessment 'pack' comprising the instruments described below was devised on the basis of a review of research and discussions with professionals in English court diversion services and with local 'stakeholders'. Instruments and procedures were piloted during the first six weeks of the scheme (see Figure 1). The 'mental health assessment pack' was designed with a view to enabling the nurses to undertake as comprehensive an assessment as possible within a relatively short period of time (30–40 minutes) as well as for the purpose of gathering research data. A series of in-built filters or 'gate' questions on most forms obviate the need to administer subsequent instruments (or parts thereof).

Profile Form (PF)

A *Profile Form* is completed for everyone who meets one or more of the inclusion criteria and who agrees to be assessed. The PF is based

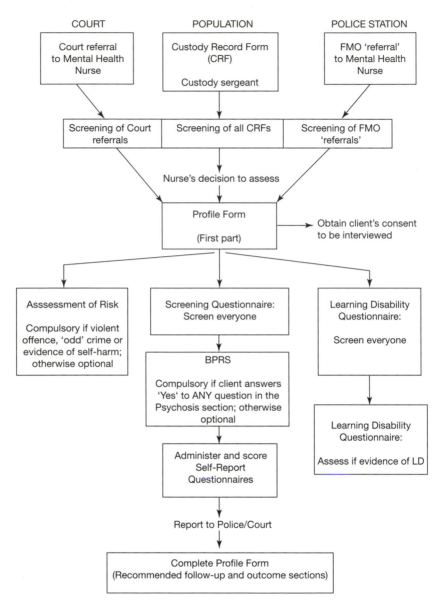

FIGURE 1: SCREENING AND ASSESSMENT SCHEMA

on an adapted version of the Case Register Form used in the Birmingham Court Diversion Service and includes information on: sociodemographic background; primary diagnosis; 'institutional' history; current and previous offence(s); police and court 'disposal'; and follow-up service(s).

Screening Questionnaire (SQ)

The SQ is administered to all respondents and comprises three sections including: (1) one question plus details about head injury (i.e. acquired brain damage); (2) a two-question case-finding instrument for depression on which a 'yes' reply to either question represents a positive test result (Whooley, Avins, Miranda and Browner, (1997); and (3) the *Psychosis Screening Questionnaire* (PSQ) (Bebbington and Nayani, 1995) comprising five 'introductory questions' on which a positive or uncertain response may be associated with psychosis and to which further 'key questions' are then required. Bebbington and Nayani report a sensitivity of 97% and specificity of 95% for the PSQ.

Learning Disability Questionnaire (LDQ)

Respondents are screened for learning disability using the four-item questionnaire devised by Lyall, Holland, Collins and Styles (1995). A positive response to *one or more* of the first three questions or attendance at a special school indicates a potential history of learning disability in which case an assessment of social interaction and behaviour problems – adapted from the *Disability Assessment Schedule* (Holmes, Shah and Wing, 1982) – is carried out. This assesses the extent to which the disability might present management problems pending imprisonment or release into the community.

Assessment of Risk Form (ARF)

Completion of the *ARF* is compulsory for offenders who have committed a violent offence, an 'odd' crime and/or where there is evidence of, or grounds for suspecting, self-harm. Information on previous incidents of violence is obtained from criminal records. The *ARF* comprises: (1) a checklist of selected items derived from the *Psychopathy Checklist* (Hare, 1980) and standard risk assessment guides; (2) 8 questions about the respondent's attitude to harming self and others (based on risk assessment guidelines); and (3) the *Dangerous Behaviour Checklist* adapted from the Problems Questionnaire (Clifford, 1987) in which five 'core' dangerous or risk-related behaviours are rated on a scale from 0 ('no problems') to 4 ('serious problems').

Brief Psychiatric Rating Scale (BPRS)

Each of the 18 items (or symptoms) on the *BPRS* (Overall and Gorham, 1962) is rated on the basis of observation and verbal report using a scale from 0 (not present) to 6 (extremely severe) to produce a maximum possible score of 108. A total score of 0–9 indicates 'not a (schizoaffective) case'; 10–20 'a possible (schizoaffective) case' and 21 or more, 'a definite (schizoaffective) case'. Joint rating sessions undertaken during the pilot study indicated good agreement between the nurses.

Self-report Questionnaires
Each respondent is asked to complete the *GHQ-12* (Goldberg, 1978) which provides a measure of psychiatric morbidity and on which a score above 4 (out of 12) indicates 'caseness'.

The *AUDIT* (Saunders, Aasland, Babor, De La Fuente and Grant, 1993) includes an opening 'gate' question followed by 9 questions which screen for hazardous and harmful alcohol consumption. Responses to 8 questions are scored from 0 (never) to 4 (4 times a week or more) in order of increasing severity while the last two are scored 0, 2 or 4 to produce a maximum possible score of 40. An overall score of 10 or more indicates a 'positive case' (i.e. alcohol dependency).

The *DAST (Short Form)* (Skinner, 1982) assesses problems associated with drug misuse and comprises 20 questions ('yes' scored 1; 'no' scored 0), two of which are 'gate' questions about the abuse of illegal and/or prescribed drugs. Scores above 4 indicate a drug abuse problem.

RESULTS

Administrative Outcomes: First Six Months
The nurses assessed 117 people during the period beginning 21 July 1998 and ending 8 January 1999. The nurses screened the custody record forms of all 1546 people detained in police custody during the above period, 15% (228) of whom met one or more of the assessment criteria. However, 96 people (42%) were not assessed either because the nurses were not on duty (83) or the defendant refused an assessment (13).

Fifteen people were assessed on two occasions and were excluded from the main analysis. The majority of defendants (82%, 96/117) were assessed within 24 hours of their arrest. Almost half of the potential MDOs (45%, 53/117) were identified from the routine screening of custody records by the nurse as opposed to a recommendation from the FMO (or magistrate).

Profile of Offenders
Defendants were typically single, unemployed males in their early thirties, the largest proportion of whom was living alone (26%, 31/117) (see Table 1). Sixteen per cent (19/117) were homeless – usually for less than

one year – while 11% (13/117) were living with friends or relatives. Approximately two-thirds (67%, 79/117) had an 'institutional' history, 47% (54/117) of whom had received psychiatric inpatient care. Almost half (42%, 48/117) had been in prison. Sixty-one per cent of those with a history of psychiatric hospitalisation (33/54) had at some stage committed a violent offence(s). Only two people had been in a mental handicap hospital. The most commonly recorded primary diagnoses were depression (44%, 51/117), alcohol/drug abuse problems (15%, 18/117), schizophrenia/paranoid psychosis (11%, 13/117) and anxiety state (11%, 13/117). The nurses indicated that a substantial proportion of people had a dual diagnosis involving alcohol. This is confirmed by the results of the standardised scales presented later. Two-thirds of defendants (78/117)

Table 1: Profile of Offenders (n=117)

Descriptor	Number	(%)[1]
Age (yrs)		
Mean	32	
Standard deviation	10.08	
Range	17–59	
Sex		
Males	93	(80)
Females	24	(20)
Marital Status		
Single	74	(63)
Married/co-habiting	18	(16)
Divorced/separated	23	(20)
Not known	2	(2)
Living situation		
Alone (in own/rented accommodation)	31	(26)
With parents	18	(15)
With spouse/partner	14	(12)
With spouse/partner and children	11	(9)
Lone parent	4	(3)
Homeless[2]	19	(16)
With friends/relatives	13	(11)
Other[3]	7	(6)
Employment Status		
Unemployed	103	(88)
Part-time employment	6	(5)
Full-time employment	6	(5)
Higher education	1	(1)
Not known	1	(1)

Notes: 1. Percentages may not sum to 100 due to rounding.
2. Eight people had been homeless for <6 months; 4 for 7–12 months; 3 for <3 yrs; and 1 for >5 yrs. (not known = 3)
3. 'Other' includes hospital (1); YOC (2) and shared accommodation (3).

were taking mental health medication and most of those for whom information on previous (or current) contact with mental health services was available had seen a psychiatrist (73/78).

Criminal History

Seventy-five per cent (52/69) of people for whom information on criminal history was available had *one or more* previous convictions. Almost two-thirds of current and previous offence(s) were of an 'acquisitive' (e.g. theft) or 'miscellaneous' nature (e.g. alcohol/drug related), while 23% (43/187) involved an offence against another person. Three-quarters of defendants (87/117) displayed *one or more* problem behaviour(s) prior to their referral to the service including physical and/or verbal aggression (39%, 34/87) and self-harm (14%, 12/87).

Follow-up Services

The follow-up services to which people were 'referred' included primarily GPs (53%, 62/117) – either by means of formal contact from the nurse or suggested 'self-referral', Community Addiction Services (28%, 33/117), the Community Mental Health Team (CMHT) (13%, 15/117) and/or psychiatric outpatient clinic (13%, 15/117). Eleven per cent (13/117) were recommended either for admission to, or assessment in, psychiatric hospital whilst 12% (14/117) were currently in contact with mental health services (Table 2).

Table 2: Recommended Follow-up Service(s)

Type of service(s)	Number	%[1]
Educational advice and support	58	49
Formal referral to GP	44	38
Referral to community addiction services	33	28
Suggest 'self-refer' to GP	18	15
Referral to CMHT	15	13
Continue with existing services	14	12
Voluntary attendance at weekly forensic clinic	8	7
Voluntary outpatient treatment	7	6
Other	6	5
No recommendation	6	5
Referral to/assess in hospital	5	4
Not known/missing	5	4
If remanded in prison, urgent psychiatric assessment	4	3
Client refused assistance for help/was indifferent to suggestions	4	3
Compulsory admission to (psychiatric) hospital	3	3
Referral to psychology services	1	1
Informal admission to (psychiatric) hospital	1	1

Note: 1. 79 people (67%) were referred to *more than one* service. Therefore, percentages do not sum to 100.

Early Outcomes

The majority of offenders were remanded on bail either to the community or in custody while only four were admitted to a psychiatric hospital. The police considered 'diversion' as a result of the nurses' report in 12 cases (10%), only one of which led to a release from custody to the care of health and social services.

Preliminary Screening and Assessment

The screening of defendants indicated that 30% (35/117) had sustained a head injury, but there was insufficient information in all cases to determine the extent, if any, of acquired brain damage. Three-quarters of respondents (88/117) had experienced depression during the previous month. Responses to the PSQ suggested the need for a BPRS assessment in all but six cases.

The *Learning Disability Questionnaire* identified 8 people who experienced difficulty in reading and writing at school and/or in learning, five of whom had attended a Special Needs school. However, only two people had a formal diagnosis of learning disability, both of whom were rated as having moderate behaviour problems related to impaired social interaction and physical aggression. Four people with a possible learning disability had a history of violence.

Assessment of Risk or Dangerousness

Sizeable proportions of people showed evidence – on the *ARF* – of psychopathic traits and characteristics (e.g. substance abuse) predictive of potentially dangerous behaviour (Table 3). More than half had a history of harming others (62/117) and/or self (58/117), many of whom indicated that they did *not* intend to stop this behaviour in the future. Fewer than half, in each case, admitted to feelings of guilt/remorse or showed any insight into the disorder that may have caused their behaviour. There were highly statistically significant associations between a history of self-harm (but not harm to others) and both current receipt of mental health medication ($\chi^2 = 20.98$, df=4, p<0.001) and institutional history ($\chi^2 = 25.78$, df=8, p$\leq$0.001). Furthermore, there was a statistically significant association between self-harm and harm to others ($\chi^2 = 28.25$, df=4, p<0.001) with 30 per cent (56/117) of the group presenting with a history of both.

Approximately half of the group (57/117) were judged, at the time of the assessment, to have violent tendencies, albeit of a mainly minor or mild nature (38/57). Similarly, more than a third were considered to have

Table 3: Assessment of Risk: Selected Items (n=114)

Item	Number who showed evidence of behaviour	%
Verbal abuse/threats	58	51
Glaring eye contact	36	32
Substance abuse	69	60
Lack of affect/emotional depth	36	32
Callousness/lack of empathy	26	23
Other psychopathic traits	32	28
History of hurting others[1]	62	54
(Intend to avoid harming others in future)	(22)	(35)
History of self-harm[1]	58	51
(Intend to avoid harming self in future)	(17)	(29)

Note: 1. Based on current offence and previous criminal history.

problems with suicidal preoccupations and self-harm (Table 4). Global ratings of dangerousness showed that 20 defendants (17%) posed a 'significant' (15/117), 'serious' (2/117) or 'very serious' (3/117) risk to themselves or others. *Urgent* professional intervention was considered necessary in 14 cases.

Mental Health Status

Almost three-quarters (71%, 75/105) of defendants who agreed to complete a GHQ-12 reported levels of psychological distress during the previous month to warrant formal mental health service intervention (Table 5). Forty-two per cent (44/105) obtained a maximum score of 12. Fifty-eight per cent (64/111) of those for whom a *BPRS* was completed scored above the clinical threshold indicating a 'possible' or 'definite schizoaffective case'. Consistent with the findings described above, the association between 'caseness' and history of self-harm was statistically significant ($\chi^2 = 11.92$, df=4, p<0.05). Fifty-nine per cent of 'cases' (38/64) also had a history of violence toward others.

Table 4: Dangerous Behaviour: Ratings on Selected Items

Item	Rating of severity (number (%))				Total	
	Minor problems	Mild problems	Moderate problems	Serious problems		
Tendency to violence	22 (19)	16 (14)	16 (14)	3 (3)	57 (49)
Self-harm	23 (20)	15 (13)	4 (3)	2 (2)	44 (38)
Suicidal preoccupations	18 (15)	16 (14)	4 (3)	2 (2)	40 (34)
Sexual assault	1 (1)	—	1 (1)	1 (1)	3 (3)

Alcohol and Drug Abuse

Three-quarters of the group (74%, 79/106) reported harmful or hazardous levels of alcohol consumption, 57% of whom (45/79) had a history of harming others (see Table 5 for summary scores). Comparatively fewer people reported problems related to drug abuse, although 46% (49/106) attained *DAST* scores above the cut-off of four (Table 5). Forty-eight people (45%) indicated that they had used (or were using) illegal drugs while a similar number (40%, 42/106) had abused (or were abusing) prescribed drugs. Those who reported harmful alcohol consumption were also more likely to be abusing drugs (χ^2=6.00, df=1, p<0.05) and 42 people (36%) were identified as positive cases on *both* instruments.

Table 5: Summary Scores on BPRS and Self-report Measures

Instrument	Mean score	Sd	Range	Number (%) scoring above cut-off
BPRS (n=111)	12.61	9.31	0–57	44 (40) – lower 20 (18) – upper
GHQ (n=105)	7.19	4.46	0–12	75 (71)
AUDIT (n=106)	20–28	12.37	0–40	79 (74)
DAST (n=106)	5.64	6.05	0–18	49 (46)

DISCUSSION

This study describes the development and formative evaluation of a new screening, assessment and referral service for MDOs in Northern Ireland. The findings suggest that the scheme is detecting and assessing most if not all offenders with mental disorders, a large proportion of whom may require specialist health and social services intervention. Only one person was diverted at the point of arrest and the police were perhaps more cautious in this respect than originally anticipated. However, it is important to note that, according to stakeholders, the scheme's raison d'être is the assessment and meeting of health and social care needs rather than diversion *per se*. To date, the scheme has achieved a 100 per cent screening rate (i.e. *all* custody records), has been received well by the various agencies involved, particularly the police, and is able to provide, within an inter-agency context, a comprehensive mental health and risk assessment as well as a referral service for offenders usually within 24 hours or less of their arrest and detainment. However, the findings should be interpreted mindful of the fact that the study covered only the first six months (approximately) of the scheme during which time it had to reach a 'steady state' in terms of its practical implementation and development of (still incomplete) inter-agency links.

The offenders were broadly similar to people assessed by court-based schemes in England (e.g. James and Hamilton, 1991; Greenhalgh, Wylie, Rix and Tamlyn, 1996; Shaw, Creed, Price, Huxley and Tomenson, 1999). However, there were fewer detainees aged under 30 (45%) in our study when compared to schemes elsewhere (e.g. 58% reported by Greenhalgh et al. (1996) in Leeds, Manchester and London) and considerably more of the local group had depression. It would appear, however, that the nature and distribution of diagnoses among offenders vary widely across studies, although most authors report, as in the present study, a consistently low incidence (around 2%) of learning disability (e.g. Joseph and Potter, 1993; Brabbins and Travers, 1994; Greenhalgh et al., 1996). Our data also indicate a high level of social deprivation and a significant homeless sub-group also seen (but to a greater extent) in schemes described elsewhere (e.g. James and Hamilton, 1991; Joseph and Potter, 1993).

Almost half of the MDOs in our study were identified from the routine screening of custody records as opposed to a recommendation from the FMO. This supports evidence suggesting that GPs fail to detect up to half of mental disorders in routine practice (e.g. Goldberg and Bridges, 1987). The detection rate in a criminal justice setting, however, may be particularly low due to the high incidence of alcohol and drug abuse (which may conceal a mental illness) and the frequent clinical presentation of sadness or depression in this population (Rice and Harris, 1997). It is also possible that the methods of identification employed by police officers are insufficiently thorough. This is an important finding because it suggests that a significant proportion of MDOs may pass, perhaps continuously, through the criminal justice system without receiving proper health and social care.

The high self-reported levels of hazardous alcohol consumption in this study and, in particular, the statistically significant association between AUDIT 'caseness' and history of harming others, supports the well-known relationship between alcohol abuse and crimes against the person (e.g. Lindqvist, 1986) as well as other violent or antisocial behaviours (Hore, 1990; Pihl and Peterson, 1995). The large numbers of offenders with significant alcohol and/or drug problems are not subject to the Mental Health (NI) Order (1986), nor are they considered to be psychiatric cases by the court, despite the well-documented social and psychological effects of prolonged abuse. Swanson, Holzer, Ganju and Jono (1990) reported that people with a dual diagnosis of mental illness and alcohol abuse – similar to most of those assessed in our study – were much more likely to engage in violent behaviour than MDOs without a history of alcohol abuse.

According to the nurses, those with a dual diagnosis may often not receive appropriate care due to a constant shift in the locus of responsibility between (demarcated) psychiatric and addiction service providers. The nurses also indicated that they were unable to refer most people *formally* to Community Addiction Services due to possible saturation of the service. Undoubtedly, this group presents particular management problems both within and without the criminal justice system not least because they tend to be violent, difficult to engage and typically non-compliant. The service response to this sub-group requires careful consideration as do the attendant training needs of the service providers. Brabbins and Travers (1994) suggest interventions ranging from a minimal educational package to more structured in- and outpatient treatment, but there is clearly a need for further research to identify how psychiatric services may be successfully delivered to this group.

The high incidence of self-harm in this study – in contrast to recent evidence reported by Fiander and Bartlett (1997) – was *not* associated with alcohol or drug abuse. It is consistent, though, with findings of increased deliberate self-harm in the UK prison (especially remand) population when compared to the general population (Dooley, 1990). Clearly, this group merits special attention in the context both of their increased suicide risk and their treatment within the criminal justice system.

The re-presenting rate (13%) – similar to the 12% reported in the first year of the North Humberside Diversion Project in England (Straite, 1995) – and the well-established criminal histories of most of the group, underline the importance of early intervention. Effective service delivery at an early stage may help to reduce recidivism rates particularly in the, albeit small, sub-group of vulnerable 'revolving door' detainees (i.e. who were assessed twice), more than half of whom appeared to have serious levels of psychiatric disability and/or alcohol or drug abuse problems. All but three had a history of violence.

The relatively small number of people considered suitable for referral to psychiatric hospital suggests that the scheme is unlikely, at least in the short term, to contribute significantly to the pressure on acute psychiatric beds. However, more than two-thirds of the entire group had previously been hospitalised, a significant proportion of whom might benefit, therefore, from care in a specialist mental health setting, particularly the 17% considered to present a risk to themselves or others. It is difficult to gauge the likely long-term impact of this new service on existing mental health provision, particularly in the absence of an integrated forensic psychiatric service in Northern Ireland. It is important, however, that the service is seen as a conduit to, rather than a substitute for, mainstream services and that a bedrock of flexible and co-ordinated community-based services is in place to address the often complex and largely unmet needs of this group. For example, the recently proposed establishment of a medium secure unit in NI would provide an invaluable complement to the new scheme as well as strengthening the underdeveloped forensic infrastructure.

The new service is evolving over time and has a pivotal role to play in, amongst other things, facilitating a closer liaison between psychiatric services and the criminal justice system and promoting a better understanding of crime (violent or otherwise), and its prevention. However, interviews with key stakeholders have identified several areas of concern which have important implications for the eventual success of this (and similar) scheme(s). These include: the level and degree of inter-agency partnership and joint working and, in turn, the development of a sense of collective ownership of the scheme; the need for more sharing of information and responsibility between (and within) health and social care professionals and criminal justice agencies; the lack of a support network of community-based forensic psychiatric and other follow-up services; and access to 'appropriate adults'.

Links with the court(s) and probation service are less well established than originally anticipated due, in large part, to a lack of awareness and understanding of the role of the scheme coupled with logistical difficulties at the court. However, a co-operative working relationship between the nurses and the probation service has recently been initiated. Furthermore, there is a firm commitment from all agencies involved to address the above issues and to undertake further work (e.g. an Awareness Training session for court personnel) in order that the full potential of the scheme may be realised. Nonetheless, without changes in general mental health service provision and a concomitant shift in attitudes, a significant proportion of MDOs – including a sizeable group of violent offenders and those committing acts of self-harm – are likely to remain indefinitely and perhaps unnecessarily within the criminal justice system without receiving the health and social care to which they are entitled.

ACKNOWLEDGEMENTS

The researchers would like to thank the Northern Ireland Office for funding this study and the two nurses, Brenda Scullion and Noel McDonald, for their help and co-operation.

REFERENCES

Bebbington, P. and Nayani, T. (1995) The Psychosis Screening Questionnaire. *International Journal of Methods in Psychiatric Research*, 5, 11–19.

Brabbins, C.J. and Travers, R.F. (1994) Mental disorder amongst defendants in Liverpool Magistrate's Court. *Medicine, Science and the Law*, 34, 279–283.

Clifford, P. (1987) The Problems Questionnaire. London: Research and Development for Psychiatry (RDP).

Department of Health and Social Services. (1996) *Health and well-being: into the next millennium: regional strategy for health and social well-being.* Belfast: Department of Health and Social Services (NI).

Dooley, E. (1990) Prison suicide in England and Wales 1972–1987. *British Journal of Psychiatry*, 156, 40–45.

Fiander, M. and Bartlett, A.E.A. (1997) Missed 'psychiatric' cases? The effectiveness of a court diversion scheme. *Alcohol and Alcoholism*, 32, 715–723.

Greenhalgh, N.M., Wylie, K., Rix, K.J.B. and Tamlyn, D. (1996) Pilot mental health assessment and diversion scheme for an English metropolitan petty sessional division. *Medicine, Science and the Law* 36, 52–58.

Goldberg, D. (1978) *Manual of the general health questionnaire.* Windsor: NFER-Nelson.

Goldberg, D. and Bridges, K. (1987) Screening for psychiatric illness in general practice *Journal of the Royal College of General Practitioners*, 37, 15–18.

Hare, R.D. (1980) A research scale for the assessment of psychopathy in criminal populations. *Personality and Individual Differences*, 1, 111–119.

Holmes, N., Shah, A. and Wing, L. (1982) The Disability Assessment Schedule: a brief screening device for use with the mentally retarded. *Psychological Medicine*, 12, 879–890.

Hore, B. (1990) Alcohol and crime. In R. Bluglass and P. Bowden (Eds) *Principles and practice of forensic psychiatry* (pp. 873–880). Edinburgh: Churchill Livingstone.

James, D.V. and Hamilton, L.W. (1991) The Clerkenwell Scheme: assessing efficacy and cost of a psychiatric liaison service to a magistrate's court. *BMJ*, 303, 282–285.

James, A. (1996) *Life on the Edge: Diversion and the mentally disordered offender.* London: Mental Health Foundation.

Joseph, P. and Potter, P. (1993) Diversion from custody I: effect on hospital and prison resources. *British Journal of Psychiatry*, 162, 325–330.

Lindqvist, P. (1986) Criminal homicide in Northern Sweden, 1970–1981: alcohol intoxication, alcohol abuse and mental disease. *International Journal of Law and Psychiatry*, 8, 19–37.

Lyall, I., Holland, A.J., Collins, S. and Styles, P. (1995) Incidence of persons with a learning disability detained in police custody: a needs assessment for service development. *Medicine, Science and the Law*, 35, 61–71.

Overall, J.E. and Gorham, D. (1962) Brief Psychiatric Rating Scale. *Psychological Reports*, 10, 799–812.

Pihl, R.O. and Peterson, J. (1995) Drugs and aggression: correlations, crime and human manipulative studies and some proposed mechanisms. *Journal of Psychiatric Neuroscience*, 20, 141–149.

Reed, J. (1992) *Review of health and social services for mentally disordered offenders and others requiring similar services.* London: HMSO.

Rice, M.E. and Harris, G.T. (1997) The treatment of mentally disordered offenders. *Psychology, Public Policy and the Law*, 3, 126–183.

Saunders, J.B., Aasland, O.G., Babor, T.F., De La Fuente, J. and Grant, M. (1993) Development of the Alcohol Use Disorders Identification Test (AUDIT): WHO collaborative project on early detection of persons with harmful alcohol consumption. *Addiction*, 88, 791–804.

Shaw, J., Creed, F., Price, J., Huxley, P. and Tomenson, B. (1999) Prevalence and detection of serious psychiatric disorder in defendants attending court. *The Lancet*, 353, 1053–1056.

Skinner, H.A. (1982) The Drug Abuse Screening Test. *Addictive Behaviours*, 7, 363–371.

Straite, C. (1995) Diversion from custody for mentally disordered offenders. *Prison Service Journal*, September.

Swanson, J.W., Holzer, C.E., Ganju, V.K. and Jono, R.T. (1990) Violence and psychiatric disorder in the community: evidence from epidemiologic catchment area surveys. *Hospital and Community Psychiatry*, 41, 761–770.

Whooley, M.A., Avins, A.L., Miranda, J. and Browner, W.S. (1997) Case-finding instruments for depression. Two questions are as good as many. *Journal of General Internal Medicine*, 12, 439–445.

Chapter 6

IMPLEMENTING RISK ASSESSMENT PROCEDURES IN A FORENSIC PSYCHIATRIC SETTING: CLINICAL JUDGEMENT REVISITED

Mats Dernevik, Mikael Falkheim, Rolf Holmqvist and Rolf Sandell

The practice of risk assessment and management with mentally disordered offenders has been a highly controversial issue in the past. The predictive validity of risk assessments has been riddled with methodological problems (Monahan 1984, 1988) and negative findings (Ennis & Litwack 1974).

In recent years there has, however, been a growing optimism about the possibility of accurate risk predictions for violent behaviour (Harris & Rice 1997; Mossman 1994; Rice 1997). There have been a growing number of studies on issues specifically related to violence and other types of criminal behaviour. These issues have typically been base-rates of violent behaviour (Monahan 1981, 1984; Monahan et al. 2000), associations with other concepts such as personality and mental health (Hodgins 1993; Lidz, Mulvey & Gardner 1993) and antecedents of violence (Blackburn 1993).

One instrument to attract attention has been the Historical-Clinical-Risk scheme (HCR-20), developed by Webster and Eaves (1995). The HCR-20 has been validated on various populations of disordered offenders (Belfrage 1998; Dernevik 1998; Douglas & Webster 1999; Strand, Belfrage, Fransson & Levander 1999). The reliability and validity of the HCR-20 makes it a promising tool for the forensic psychiatric practice. There are, however, a number of issues in the process of implementing an assessment procedure, such as the HCR-20 which need investigating. One such question concerns "clinical ecology". Many of the studies have been made in a research context, i.e. independent researchers have carried out risk assessments and measured outcomes in the setting of care administration, over which they have no influence nor are influenced by. In an "ecological" setting, however, the assessments are likely to be performed by a professional, involved in diagnosis and treatment issues for the particular client. This implies that issues, that are indeed central to the area of clinical judgement and the dubious task of predicting human behaviour in general, become relevant in turn to the area of risk assessment. There have been concerns about the lack of reliability and validity of clinical judgement in general psychological practice (Dawes 1994) as well as in expert forensic practice (Faust & Sizkin 1988). These concerns point to some problematic questions in the forensic field. What person is best qualified as an expert? Who should make the assessment and what information should be considered? What training is most appropriate? Given the limitations of clinical judgement, how can the assessment be validated? What influences the assessment, in terms of heuristics and biases in the decision-making process?

The present chapter aims at describing some of these limitations and questions and to empirically point to the role of irrational influences on clinicians carrying out risk assessments.

It also focuses on the task of implementing risk assessment procedures, using the HCR-20 scheme, in an ecological setting. In this setting the assessment is typically not done by a researcher or an academic, but by the clinician involved with the patient. The clinician is involved in various decisions regarding the patient and is subject to the "ups and downs" of the relationship to the patient in the forensic psychiatric setting. He or she will also be relying on information, observations and judgements made by other care-staff. In addition, the risk assessment will also need to be done continuously during the incarceration of the patient rather than on one occasion.

CLINICAL JUDGEMENT

A problem constantly facing clinical psychology and psychiatry is that of clinical judgement. Already in the 1950s Meehl (1954) examined the issue of clinical versus statistical prediction. Reviews of clinical judgement since then have often concluded that clinical and counselling psychologists are inaccurate in making important judgements such as diagnosis, formulation, prognosis and assessment of outcome (Gough 1963; Elstein and Bordage 1979; Kleinmuntz 1984). In an influential article in *Science*, Faust and Ziskin (1988) concluded that judgements made by mental health professionals are not reliable or valid and that clinical judges are no more correct than laypersons. Their conclusion was that allowing psychological expert testimony in court, despite the poor scientific base for clinical judgement, might undermine the credibility of clinicians and thus be counterproductive to the development of useful clinical knowledge and methods. More than ten years ago Faust and Ziskin ended their review on a hopeful note: "Psychological research should eventually yield more certain knowledge and methods that provide meaningful assistance to the trier of fact." (1988 p. 35). Maybe that time has come regarding risk assessments for violent offenders.

It would be of interest to discuss the reason for inaccuracy in clinical judgement. Nobody, or at least few people, would argue that the lack of validity is because clinicians generally have particularly poor judgement, insight or sensitivity. Instead there could be a number of possible reasons for the findings.

DIAGNOSIS

Clinical assessments and related judgement tasks, such as an adult's capacity to make decisions, or a risk assessment for violent behaviour, are very complex in nature. Quite often diagnostic categorisations are of little value for the prediction of behaviour. The broad diagnostic labels of the DSM –IV (APA 1995) and ICD-10 (WHO 1996) both refer to heterogeneous populations, and there might be great variations between individuals ascribed the same diagnostic label (Murphy and Clare 1995). The diagnosis of schizophrenia, for instance, has been found to have a negative correlation with violent recidivism in some studies (Quinsey et al. 1998; Monahan et al. 2000). However, recent studies have suggested that there are two distinct groups within the diagnostic group (Hodgins & Janson in press). The first group, "late-starters", is associated with low violent recidivism. This group is characterised by low psychopathy scores, substance abuse and a higher age at the first crime. The other group, "early starters", is associated with more criminality, substance abuse and psychopathy scores prior to onset of the mental disorder. Despite having the same diagnosis, the implications for risk and treatment are obviously quite different for the two groups.

The focus of diagnostic catalogues such as the DSM or the ICD schemes lies on taxonomy (Jablensky 1995). The very purpose of these schemes has been to enhance the validity of classification of mental illness. To some extent it could be said that they have done just this during the last decade even if some researchers are sceptical of such claims (Garb 1992). However, they still bring very little information on the prognosis or aetiology of the different categories that are described by lists of criteria. Consequently when a clinician is asked about a prediction of violent behaviour in a particular patient, the label of the disorder or the diagnosis is quite inadequate (Murphy & Clare 1995).

ECOLOGICAL VALIDITY

The claims of inaccuracy for clinical judgement may be exaggerated. Rock, Bransford, Maisto and Morey (1987) argued that the clinical judgement literature suffers from "an inadequate framework for understanding different types of judgements and different contexts within which judgements are made" (p. 645). When reviewing studies on clinical judgement such as Meehl (1954) and Gough (1963), Holt (1970) observed that clinicians generally are not permitted to use their accustomed procedures or materials. They often are asked to make judgements about phenomena such as school grades or future violent behaviour for which they have little training or experience. It is possible that the clinical judgement studies have low ecological validity from the point of view of the clinician (Rock et al. 1987). This would imply that clinicians are indeed capable of greater accuracy in risk prediction than previously argued. Recently Strand et al. (1999), in a study using the structured the HCR-20 risk assessment, found that clinical variables had a higher significance for the prediction of violent behaviour than most of the actuarial or historical variables. The study concerned only mentally disordered offenders, the traditional domain of psychological and psychiatric judgement, perhaps making clinical factors more appropriate predictors than in other correctional settings.

INFORMATION PROCESSING AND DECISION MAKING

Problems concerning information processing and decision making may also influence the accuracy of clinical judgement. Cognitive researchers in the area of decision making quite often differ in theoretical perspectives. Psychological models, both of the study of clinical judgement and the study of judges' and juries' decision making, seem to be both descriptive and prescriptive in nature. In the case of judges' and juries' decision making this mixture could derive from the nature of law itself (van Koppen 1995). In the case of clinical judgement the mixture appears to reflect the theoretical approach of the researcher. With the main focus on information processing, researchers seem to be interested in descriptions of cognitive processes rather than normative models of judgement.

A central issue is the limited or bounded rationality of people in general. Newell and Simon (1972) suggested that our relatively small capacity for short-term or working memory often influences accurate judgement. Findings from this perspective suggest that clinicians may make errors because they process information serially rather than in parallel and may rely too heavily on simple cues for generating hypothesises and evaluations (Kahneman and Tversky 1996). This theory might explain why statistical, actuarial and retrospective assessments of the risk of violence frequently fare better in concurrent validity than interview-based clinical assessments. The actuarial and highly structured Violence Risk Appraisal Guide (VRAG) has been shown to have a high validity (Harris and Rice 1997; Quinsey, Harris, Rice & Cormier 1998). Douglas and Webster (1999) found that the Historical items (H-10) in the HCR-20 were more strongly related to various indexes of past violence than the clinical items in the same assessment scheme. Grann, Belfrage and Tengström (1998) compared the VRAG and the H-10 in a sample of schizophrenic and personality disordered subjects. They found overall good predictive power for both schemes, although the H-10 showed a greater sensitivity for the schizophrenics. Both the Douglas and Webster study and the Grann, Belfrage & Tengström study were retrospective chart reviews, i.e. the assessors did not necessarily meet the subject and no interviews were done.

Less cognitively oriented researchers who are more interested in prediction of the criteria variables propose a social judgement model (Hoffman 1960). Methods of statistical regression are typically used to describe the judgement process and how accurate these methods are in predicting or classifying the criteria variables. The neural network approach to decision making might be seen as a recent and computerised development of the social judgement theory.

A third theoretical perspective on decision making is behavioural decision theory (Rorer and Dawes 1982). Emphasis is put on the development of methods for improving and evaluating the accuracy and efficiency of judgement. This approach could be relevant to decision making both in clinical and courtroom contexts (De la Fuente, Ortega, Martin & Trujillo 1997). The three approaches coincide on some of the following factors, all limiting judgement accuracy.

Biases

Tversky and Kahneman (1974) identified heuristics or shortcuts of information processing that affect judgement. One such heuristic is anchoring, or the tendency to stick to the initial assessment of clients whilst ignoring or adjusting information that is not in concordance, rather than reviewing and adjusting the conclusions of the assessment. They also observed *the conjunction fallacy*. This is the tendency to correlate information intuitively rather than by laws of probability. They argued that judgements about single cases or events might be skewed because of this. Chapman (1967) reported on *the illusory correlation* bias. This refers to the tendency to view unrelated events as correlated or overestimate the significance of a weak correlation. This bias has been shown in a wide range of clinical judgement tasks (Kurtz and Garfield 1978). One might also suspect that psychologists and other clinicians might have a tendency to attribute causal relationships in information about the client or patient. This might mean that information about, for instance, childhood events is viewed as the cause of behaviours later in the patient's life. This assumption might influence the "line of enquiry" and the questions asked in the clinical interview. This might lead to a "he who seeks shall find" strategy of the clinician, making him or her rely too heavily on simple cues for interpretation and evaluation.

It is obviously possible that all these biases play a role in the constantly low accuracy of unstructured risk assessments reported by Ennis and Litwack (1974).

Amount of information
Both clinical judgements and risk predictions typically require the clinician to handle vast amounts of information (Lueger and Petzel 1979). There may be information from case-history notes and documents, patient interviews, psychological tests (both cognitive and personality), behaviour observations, references from peers and family, and so on. The complexity of case-formulation makes it problematic to use a statistical approach to judgement and usually is more easily dealt with by a subjective clinical approach, even if there is substantial evidence that this approach is less accurate (Dawes 1979; 1994; Kleinmuntz 1984; Goldberg 1991). More than 40 years ago, Meehl (1957) stated that, "Mostly we will use our heads, because there just aren't any formulas" (p. 273). Reviews 40 years on still reinforce Meehl's conclusion (Kleinmuntz 1990; Phares and Trull 1997). Dawes (1994) also argued that an increasing amount of case related information might actually result in less accurate predictions than would be the case if the clinician had persisted with the available statistical formula.

Training and experience

There seems to be some controversy about who should be qualified to give expert judgement both in clinical and forensic psychology (Dawes 1994). In most countries it is the legal framework that defines the expert. In many legal frameworks, like the one in Sweden, profession rather than scientific or clinical merit determines the expert status. The empirical evidence does not generally support the position that increased experience leads to higher accuracy in judgement (Dawes 1994; Garb 1992). Faust (1986) noted that experts do not seem to outperform relative beginners. There could be a number of reasons for this sad state of affairs. One such reason could be a confusion over which questions require which kind of expert advice. A clinical training might be of little assistance when assessing the risk of future violent offending in a patient, rather like asking the plumber to look at your double-glazing. Another reason could be the lack of feedback on prediction. In risk prediction the true positives are often never heard of again, while the false negatives often are readmitted and reconvicted. This creates a negative feedback loop, the assessor is not able to adjust his or her methods or heuristics, thus the experience is rendered meaningless and sometimes even detrimental.

IRRATIONAL INFLUENCES

It is also possible that there could be irrelevant or irrational influences on clinical judgement and risk predictions. The perspective of the clinician is often idiographical (Phares & Trull 1997). He or she is interested in understanding the particular patient's thoughts, feelings and behaviour. In the endeavour to understand the individual the clinician might be inadvertently affected by, or consciously and systematically trying to utilise, his or her own feelings about the patient. There is a risk that these feelings are irrelevant or even irrational (Cohen 1983). They might also on the other hand contribute to the understanding of qualities of the individual that would otherwise go unnoticed. In the psychoanalytical tradition these phenomena are seen as one of the cornerstones of therapy (Holmqvist & Armelius 1996). The context of a forensic psychiatric unit is of an idiographic, clinical nature; the clinician is typically interested in being able to cure, or alleviate suffering of, the patient. At the same time the legal context, such as during risk or dangerousness assessments, also requires a nomothetical approach. Typically there are problems regarding representativeness when the two approaches need to be combined. How do risk factors, obtained from research on groups of offenders, apply to decisions about the particular patient? Sometimes the two approaches constitute a conflict for the clinician. The aim of the study described below was to look at the assessor's feelings towards the patient and how they affect his or her risk prediction, using one of the best validated schemes for this purpose; the Historical-Clinical-Risk assessment (HCR-20) (Webster, Douglas, Eaves & Hart 1997).

METHOD

Procedure

Eight patients were chosen from a high security hospital setting and asked to participate in the study. They were chosen from the criteria described under the "patients" below. They were asked to participate in the study and to be assessed by members of the ward-staff, as a part of staff training. All eight agreed to participate. Participation was not intrusive to the patients since they were in daily contact with the staff-raters, who had access to all relevant files on patients in their daily routine. The ethics committee of the county health authority had previously approved the present study as a part of the "Risk project in Vadstena".

In connection with this project, all patients had previously been assessed with the HCR-20 and Psychopathy checklist, Screening version (Hart, Cox & Hare 1995) by one (out of five) expert clinicians who were trained as described elsewhere (Dernevik 1998).

In the present study, each of the eight patients was assessed by, on average, five staff-raters, making it one assessment for each for the 40 staff-raters. Staff-raters were allocated a particular patient they knew well from their ward. They attended a day workshop as an introduction to the HCR-20, given by the first author. They were then asked to assess their patient during the following three weeks after which they were reassembled for a further day of training, containing feedback on their assessments and discussions of risk management. On this occasion the staff-raters were asked to rate their feelings towards their particular patient during the three weeks of assessment. This was done using the feeling word checklist described below.

The Patients

Eight patients were included in the study. Five inclusion criteria were used: (1) An index offence of a serious violent crime. (2) Being classified as suffering from a Severe Mental Disorder by a formal forensic psychiatric investigation as described by Kullgren, Grann and Holmberg (1996) and subsequently sentenced to forensic psychiatric care. (3) Having stayed a minimum of one month in the clinic and judged unlikely to be released within the next three months. (4) A diagnosed Personality disorder according to axis II in the DSM IV (American Psychiatric Association 1994). (5) Finally the patients had to agree to be assessed by staff as part of staff training.

The patients were all male and their mean age was 28 years with a range of 20 to 52 years. The mean length of hospital stay was 35 months with a range of four months to 10 years.

The index offences were: murder (n=3)(one double), Attempted murder (n=1), Manslaughter (n=1), Arson (n=2), Rape (n=1) and Serious assault (1). All patients but one had a criminal record before the index offence. Four of the eight patients had previously been admitted to psychiatric care. All men were single but two had been married and three had children.

Staff-Raters

Forty members of nursing staff working in a 40 bed forensic psychiatric, maximum secure clinic participated in the study. All were Registered Psychiatric Nurses and participated in a risk assessment and management training as part of their professional development while working on one of three wards in the clinic. There were 30 male and ten female nurses. Fourteen of the staff were key-nurses for their rated patient. Patients in the clinic are typically assigned to two key-nurses upon admission to hospital. The role of key-nurse entails introducing the patient to routines and assisting the patient with financial and practical matters as well as liaising between the patient and other clinicians and agencies.

The average age was 47.3 years and the mean time working in psychiatry was approaching 25 years. The high figures are probably representative of Swedish forensic and psychiatric nurses. In the last decade the number of hospital beds have declined and few new and young members of staff have been recruited, leaving the elder members of staff on the wards. The average time of working with the assessed patient is almost three years but the standard deviation is high as shown below (Table 1).

The Scales
Feeling Word Checklist
To map staff-raters' feelings about patients a Feeling Word Checklist (FWL) was used. Whyte, Constantopoulus and Bevans (1982) originally

Table 1: Number of years worked by nurses in forensic and general psychiatry and number of months worked with assessed patients prior to study

	Mean	Std Dev.	Min	Max	N
Years working in Psychiatry	24,6	6,8	9,0	36,0	40
Months of working with rated patient	33,5	28,9	1,0	120,0	40

constructed the checklist. Holmqvist and Armelius (1994, 1996, 2000) have described the measurement and statistical properties of the scale. The checklist contains 30 words for different feelings. The scores for each word were counted on a four-point scale (0–3). The nurses were asked to indicate to what extent they had the different feelings in relation to the rated patient during the period of risk assessment (3 weeks). The checklist is shown in Table 2. The 30 feeling words have been grouped into eight subscales of feelings in a circumplex model. Factor analysis supported the position of viewing the subscales as four continuous variables (Holmqvist & Armelius 1994).

The structure of the circumplex is based on four dimensions, *Helpfulness* versus *Unhelpfulness*, *Closeness* versus *Distance*, *Accepting* versus *Rejecting*, and *Autonomous* versus *Controlled*.

The total word scores in each subscale were added and then divided by the number of words on each subscale, thus making an average per subscale between 0 and 3. The eight subscales are arranged in a circumplex model (see Figure 1 below).

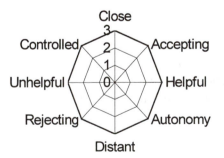

FIGURE 1: CIRCUMPLEX MODEL OF EIGHT FEELING SUBSCALES
Numbers 0–3 indicate the strength of the experienced feelings.
From Holmqvist & Armelius (1996). With permission.

Table 2: Feeling Word Checklist

When I think about....... I feel:

1	Helpful	16	Surprised
2	Happy	17	Tired
3	Angry	18	Threatened
4	Enthusiastic	19	Receptive
5	Anxious	20	Objective
6	Strong	21	Overwhelmed
7	Manipulated	22	Bored
8	Relaxed	23	Motherly
9	Cautious	24	Confused
10	Disappointed	25	Embarrassed
11	Indifferent	26	Interested
12	Affectionate	27	Aloof
13	Suspicious	28	Sad
14	Sympathetic	29	Inadequate
15	Disliked	30	Frustrated

The Historical Clinical-Risk assessment (HCR-20)

The HCR-20 (Webster and Eaves 1995) was designed as a systematic way of gathering and evaluating information about the individual relevant to dangerousness and risk. It breaks the task of risk assessment into three major components (Webster, Menzies & Hart 1995). The HCR-20 combines actuarial, historical information (10 items), clinical evaluations (5 items) and situational factors (5 items). It also includes the screening version of the Hare Psychopathy Checklist; PCL-SV (Hart, Cox and Hare 1995). Webster et al. (1997) have described a second version of the assessment. Reports indicate that the HCR-20 has a high inter-rater reliability (Dernevik 1998; Belfrage 1998) and predictive validity (Strand et al. 1999; Douglas & Webster 1999). The HCR-20 consists of 20 items, coded on a 0–2 scale, higher scores indicating higher risk of re-offending (maximum score 40).

RESULTS

The nurses rated the HCR-20 mean score for the eight patients at 26.3 points (SD 6.1). The expert assessors rated a significantly lower mean score at 22.7(SD 6.12) on a one sample, two tailed T-test. The scores for the PCL-SV were also significantly higher for the nurses with a mean score of 16.1 (SD 6.1). The experts had a mean score of 14.9 (SD 3.5). (See Table 3).

There was a reasonable overall coherence between the nurses and expert assessors. The HCR-20 had a correlation of 0.59. The historical items had a correlation of 0.62, the clinical items 0.56 and the situational risk items a lower correlation at 0.36 (Pearson's *r*) (see Table 4).

Table 3: HCR-20 and PCL-R Scores for Nurses and Expert Raters

	Experts (n=8)		Nurses (N=40)		
	Mean	SD	Mean	SD	p
HCR-20	22.7	6.5	26.3	6.1	,000
PCL-SV	14.9	3.5	16.1	6.1	,000

Table 4: Correlation Matrix for HCR-20 Ratings of Nurses and Experts

Scale		r	p
10	Historical items	, 62	, 000
5	Clinical items	, 56	, 001
5	Risk items	, 36	, 05
20	Full Scale	, 59	, 001

The results show the nurses' scores on the HCR-20 assessment to be influenced by their scores on the feeling word checklist. Using the HCR-20 score as the dependent variable for the feelings scores, the multiple regression was .659 and the R square was .433. This means that the scores on the four continuous variables on the feeling-word checklist explain 43% of the variance in the risk assessments. This is significant at F= 4.791. p =0.0052 (see Table 5). Whether the staff-rater was the appointed Key-nurse to the assessed patient or not, did not have a significant effect on risk scores. The R square was 0.10 (F= 3.42, p =0.075).

Table 5: Two-way Analysis of Variance of HCR-20 at FWL, Total Score

Source	SS	%	df	MS	F	p
All Feelings	613	43	7	24.6	4,79	.005

Not all subscales of feelings towards the patient were associated with the HCR-20 score. The Subscales *Rejecting* and *Control* had very small means (0.4 and 0.3). Maybe these negative feelings are seen not to be professional and hence censored in the FWL. Feeling *Close* and *Accepting* towards the patient is associated with a higher HCR-20 score, while feelings of *Helpfulness* and *Autonomy* are associated with a lower score (see Figure 2).

The feeling subscales were found to have a large variability between staff-raters, even when rating the same individual (see Figure 3).

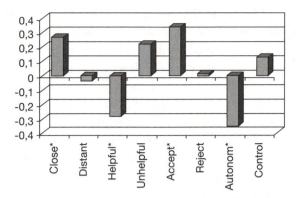

FIGURE 2: PEARSON'S *R* FOR THE EIGHT FEELINGS IN FWL AND HCR-20 SCORES
* $p<0.05$

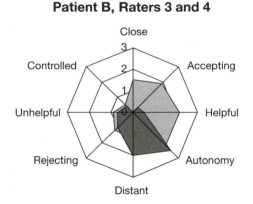

Patient B, Raters 3 and 4

FIGURE 3: GRAPHICAL REPRESENTATION OF SCORES ON THE SUBSCALES ON THE FEELING WORD CHECKLIST (FWL)
The same patient rated by two members of staff (No.3, gray area and No.4, black area).

DISCUSSION

The main finding of the present study was the strong link between feelings towards the patient and the risk assessment. The conclusion is that irrational influences, even on assessments with an instrument which has an actuarial structure like the HCR-20, can not be ignored or prescribed not to influence the assessor. In addition there is some controversy about whether feelings, as they are defined by the Feeling Word Checklist (FWL), should be regarded as irrational. Few people, especially psychologists, would argue that our perception and judgements of people are not influenced by our feelings towards them. The argument would be that feelings towards people influence all kinds of human information processing and can not be ignored even in the use of prescriptive and objective instruments like the HCR-20. It would also be wrong to see feelings only as biases, making risk predictions less accurate. Unfortunately there are no follow-up data on the eight patients available yet and this study includes no outcome measure of the predicted risk. The feelings towards patients might, perhaps, contribute to a more accurate prediction. In psychoanalytical terms this would be described as countertransference and is in this school of thinking regarded as providing important information about the patient (Kernberg 1975; Goldstein 1990; Holmqvist and Fogelstam 1996).

It is also interesting to note which feelings influence the risk assessment. Feelings of autonomy and helpfulness are associated with lower risk scores, feelings of closeness and acceptance with higher scores. Since the average total risk scores were higher for the nurses than the expert assessors it might be that feelings of autonomy and professional helpfulness are the most appropriate for appraising risk. Nursing staff are generally more exposed to patients (eight hours a day) than other clinicians and hence more likely to get more emotionally involved. On the other hand the risk score was not significantly influenced by whether the staff-rater was the key-nurse to the rated patient or not. It can be assumed that the key-nurse is more likely to be more emotionally involved with the patient. The finding that the nurses assess the average risk to be significantly higher than the experts could also be explained by the possibility that their assessments are more accurate than the experts are. They might have more information on items in the HCR-20 such as emotional stability and more insight into the patient. Only follow-up of the assessed patients will be able to determine if this might be the case.

It can also be argued that the nurse-assessors had a poor training for this kind of assessment. They only had a one-day workshop, which of course is not enough to make anybody an expert in risk assessment. All the assessors were nurses and had little previous formal training in clinical assessment or "researcher" approach to this task. On the other hand they had vast experience with mentally disordered offenders and information on how the assessed patients cope and interact on a daily base and in a variety of situations. They also had access to the same file-based information as the expert assessors. This kind of information is not unfamiliar to them although they may not have had the experience of other clinicians such as psychologists or psychiatrists. We would suggest that there are a number of points to be considered to assure a high quality of risk assessment procedures in a forensic psychiatric setting. Webster and Eaves (1995) suggested 20 considerations for improving prediction accuracy in the original HCR-20 manual. We would like to underline two of them from the findings of this study: Firstly: "*Overemphasis on the individual's personality and presentation can be misleading*" (p. 6). In our study the patient's personality probably greatly influences the feelings of the staff and thus the risk score. This does not mean that this is of relevance to the actual risk of violent behaviour. Secondly: "*Personal and professional biases should be eliminated to the fullest extent possible*" (p. 7). This study suggests a way to make the assessor aware of the possibility of hidden biases in their feelings towards the assessed patient. We would suggest that scales like the FWL could achieve this and contribute to more accurate predictions.

There needs to be a continuing process of undertaking validation procedures for the assessments. We think that group assessments, i.e. having experienced assessors monitoring each other's assessments, can achieve this. It is also desirable to limit the number of assessors in the workplace for practical reasons as well as for consistency. This study shows the need for continuous training of the assessors. In order to make this training efficient, feedback from all risk assessments carried out by the rater needs to be collected; in other words we need to keep tabs on the criteria outcome in order to improve accuracy. It may well be that the under-predicted patients come back if reconvicted, but others are not heard of. This might give an overly negative impression of the prediction accuracy.

We also think that this study shows that the relation between the assessor and the patient could be important. It is probably less appropriate that the assessment is made by somebody who is involved with the patient's treatment in other ways, such as by a medical officer or therapist. Apart from the irrational influences of feelings towards the patient one should also look out for more "rational" influences. A high-risk score might mean more frustration for the patient and cause trouble on the ward. Low risk might on the other hand mean removing patients who are destructive, threatening or generally a nuisance out of the ward.

By having a small group of trained assessors rating each other's patients this can be avoided. There is also an issue on the usefulness of risk assessment in the clinical context. In our experience a good risk assessment can help in clarifying goals for treatment. It is important that the patient is informed of the result of the assessment. In fact, it is sometimes therapeutically helpful, if carried out with a proper discussion of each item. The patient may of course not agree with all the results but the relative objectiveness of the scheme is facilitating in these discussions. The actuarial items in the scheme cannot be improved, but the clinical and risk items often can and they need to be in focus for treatment. A lowered risk score can be an incentive for change for the patient.

ACKNOWLEDGEMENTS

We are grateful to Mrs Ann-Marie Averland, Mr Jan Lövstedt, Mr Kenneth Rydenlund and Dr. Lars Naimell for their contribution to this study and also to Professor Ann Frodi for her helpful comments on the study.

This study was part of a risk management Research Programme supported by the Health Research Council in the SouthEast of Sweden.

REFERENCES

American Psychiatric Association. (1994). *Diagnostic and Statistical Manual of the Mental Disorders (4th edition)* Washington D.C.: Author.

Belfrage, H. (1998). Implementing the HCR-20 scheme for Risk Assessment in a Forensic Psychiatric Hospital: Integrating Research and Clinical Practice. *Journal of Forensic Psychiatry*, 9. pp. 328–338.

Blackburn, R. (1993). *The Psychology of Criminal Conduct*. Chichester: Wiley.

Chapman, L. (1967). Illusory correlation in observation report. *Journal of Verbal Learning and Verbal Behavior*, 6, pp. 193–217.

Cohen, L. (1983). The controversy about irrationality. *Behavioral and Brain Sciences*, 6, pp. 317–370.

Dawes, R. (1979) The robust beauty of improper linear models in decision making. *American Psychologist*, 34, pp. 571–582.

Dawes, R. (1994). *House of Cards: Psychology and psychotherapy built on myth*. New York: Free Press.

De la Fuente, I., Ortega, A., Martin, I & Trujillo, H. (1997). Formal Patterns in Jury Decision Making. In Redondo, S., Garrido, V., Perez, J. & Barbaret, R. (Eds.), *Advances in Psychology and Law*. Berlin: de Greuyter & Co.

Dernevik, M. (1998). Preliminary Findings on Reliability and Validity of the Historical-Clinical- Risk Assessment in a Forensic Psychiatric Setting. *Psychology, Crime & Law*, 4, pp. 127–137.

Douglas, K., & Webster, C. (1999). The HCR-20 Violence Risk Assessment Scheme. Concurrent Validity in a Sample of Incarcerated Offenders. *Criminal Justice and Behavior*, 26, pp. 3–19

Elstein, A. & Bordage, G. (1979). Psychology of clinical reasoning. In Stone. G., Cohen, F, & Adler, N. (Eds.), *Health Psychology – A Handbook*. San Francisco: Jossey-Bass.

Ennis, B. & Litwack, T. (1974). Psychiatry and the presumption of expertise: Flipping coins in the courtroom. *California Law review*, 62, 693–752.

Faust, D. (1986). Research on Human Judgement and its Application to Clinical Practice. *Professional Psychology: Research and Practice*, 17, pp. 420–430.

Faust, D., & Ziskin, J. (1988). The Expert Witness in Psychology and Psychiatry. *Science*, 241, pp. 31–35.

Garb, H. (1992). The trained Psychologist as Expert Witness. *Clinical Psychology Review*, 12, pp. 451–467.

Gough, H, (1963). Clinical versus statistical prediction in psychology. In Postman, L. (Ed.), *Psychology in the making*. New York: Knopf.

Goldberg, L. (1991). Human Mind Versus Regression Equation: Five contrasts. In Cicchetti & Grove (Eds.), *Thinking clearly about psychology*. 1, pp. 173–184. Minneapolis: University of Minnesota Press.

Goldstein, E. (1990). *Borderline disorders: clinical models and techniques*. New York: Guilford.

Grann, M., Belfrage, H. & Tengström, A. (1998). Actuarial assessment of risk for violence: Predictive validity of the VRAG and the historical part of the HCR-20. Manuscript, Stockholm: Karolinska Institute.

Harris, G., & Rice, M. (1997). Risk appraisal and management of violent behavior. *Psychiatric Sevices*, 48, pp. 1168–1176.

Hart, S., Cox, D. & Hare R. (1995). *Manual for the screening version of the Hare Psychopathy checklist-revised* (PCL-SV). Toronto, Canada: Multi-Health Systems.

Hodgins, S. (1993). The criminality of mentally disordered offenders. In Hodgins, S. (Ed.), *Mental Disorder and Crime*. Newbury Park. Sage.

Hodgins, S. & Janson, C.G. (in press). *Criminality and Violence Among the Mentally Disordered: The Stockholm Metropolitan Project*. Cambridge. Cambridge University Press.

Hoffman, P. (1960). The paramorphic representations of clinical judgement. *Psychological Bulletin*, 57, pp. 116–131.

Holmqvist, R. & Armelius, B. (1994). Emotional Reactions to Psychiatric Patients. *Acta Psychiatrica Scandinavica*, 90, pp. 204–209.

Holmqvist, R. (1996). Methods of Identifying Conspicuous Countertransference Reactions. *British Journal of Psychotherapy*, 12, pp. 487–500.

Holmqvist, R. & Armelius, B. (1996). The Patient's Contribution to the Therapist's Countertransference feelings. *Journal of Nervous and Mental Disease*, 184, pp. 660–666.

Holmqvist, R. & Fogelstam, H. (1996). Psychological climate and countertransference in psychiatric treatment homes. *Acta Psychiatrica Scandinavia*, 93, pp. 288–295.

Holmqvist, R. & Armelius, K. (2000). Countertransference Feelings and the Psychiatric Staff's Self-Image. *Journal of Clinical Psychology*, 56, pp. 475–490.

Jablensky, A. (1995). Kraepelins Legacy: Paradigm or pitfall for modern psychiatry? European Archives of Psychiatry. *Clinical Neuroscience*, 245, pp. 186–188.

Kahneman, D. & Tversky, A. (1996). On the reality of cognitive illusions. *Psychological Review*, 103, pp. 582–591.

Kernberg, O. (1975). *Borderline conditions and pathological narcissism*. New York: Jason Aronsson.

Kleinmuntz, B. (1984). The scientific study of clinical judgement in psychology and medicine. *Clinical Psychology Review*, 4, pp. 111–126.

Kleinmuntz, B. (1990). Why we still use our heads instead of formulas: Towards an integrative approach. *Psychological Bulletin*, 107, 296–310.

Kullgren, G., Grann, M., & Holmberg, G. (1996). The Swedish Forensic Concept of Severe Mental Disorder as Related to Personality Disorders. *International Journal of law and Psychiatry*, 19, No.2. pp. 191–200.

Kurtz, R. & Garfield, L. (1978). Illusory correlation: A further exploration of Chapman's paradigm. *Journal of Consulting and Clinical Psychology*, **46**, pp. 1009–1015.

Lidz, C., Mulvey, E. & Gardner, W. (1993). The accuracy of predictions of violence to others. *Journal of the American Medical Association*, **269**, pp. 1007–1111.

Lueger, R. & Petzel, T. (1979). Illusory correlation in clinical judgement: Effects of amount of information to be processed. *Journal of Consulting and Clinical Psychology*, **47**, pp. 1120–1121.

Meehl, P. (1954). *Clinical versus statistical prediction: A theoretical analysis and review of the evidence*. Minneapolis, MN: University of Minnesota Press.

Meehl, P. (1957). When shall we use our heads instead of the formula? *Journal of Consulting Psychology*, **4**, pp.268–273.

Monahan, J. (1981). *Predicting violent behavior: An assessment of clinical techniques*. Beverly Hills, CA: Sage.

Monahan, J. (1984). The prediction of violent behavior: Towards a second generation of theory and policy. *American Journal of Psychiatry*, **141**, 10–15.

Monahan, J. (1988). Risk Assessment of Violence among the mentally disordered: Generating useful knowledge. *International Journal of Law and Psychiatry*, **11**, pp. 249–257.

Monahan, J., Steadman, H.J., Appelbaum, P.S., Robbins, P.C., Mulvey, E.P., Silver, E., Roth, L.H. & Grisso, T. (2000). Developing a clinically useful tool for assessing violence risk. *British Journal of Psychiatry*, 176, pp. 312–319.

Mossman, D. (1994). Assessing predictions of violence: Being accurate about accuracy. Journal of Consulting and Clinical Psychology, 62, pp. 783–792.

Murphy, G., & Clare, I. (1995). Adults' Capacity to Make Decisions Affecting the Person: Psychologists' Contribution. In Bull, R. and Carson, D. (Eds), *Handbook of Psychology in Legal Contexts*. Chichester: Wiley, pp. 97–128.

Newell, A. & Simon, H. (1972). *Human problem solving*. Englewood Cliffs, NJ: Prenice-Hall.

Phares, J. & Trull, T. (1997). *Clinical Psychology* (5th ed.) Pacific Grove, CA: Brooks/ Cole, pp. 263–290.

Quinsey, V., Harris, G., Rice, M. & Cormier, C. (1998). *Violent Offenders: Appraising and Managing Risk*. Washington, DC. American Psychological Association.

Rice, M. (1997). Violent offender research and implications for the criminal justice system. *American Psychologist*, **52**, pp. 414–423.

Rock, D., Bransford, J. & Maisto, S. (1987). The Study of Clinical Judgement: An Ecological Approach. *Clinical Psychology Reveiw*, 7, pp. 645–661.

Rorer, L. & Dawes, R. (1982). A base-rate bootstrap. *Journal of Consulting and Clinical Psychology*, **50**, pp. 419–425.

Strand, S., Belfrage, H., Fransson, G., & Levander, S. (1999). Clinical and Risk Management Factors in Risk Prediction of Mentally Disordered Offenders – More Important than Historical Data? *Legal and Criminological Psychology*, **4**, pp. 67–76.

Tversky, A. & Kahneman, D. (1974). Judgement under uncertainty: Heuristics and Biases. *Science*, **185**, pp. 1124–1131.

Van Koppen, P. (1995). Judges' Decision-making. In Bull, R. and Carson, D. (Eds), *Handbook of Psychology in Legal Contexts*. Chichester: Wiley, pp. 581–610.

Webster, C., & Eaves, D. (1995). *The HCR-20 Scheme. The Assessment of Dangerousness and Risk*. British Columbia: Simon Fraser University.

Webster, C. D., Douglas, K. S., Eaves, D., & Hart, S. D. (1997). *HCR-20. Assessing risk for violence. Version 2*. Vancouver, Canada: Mental Health, Law and Policy Institute.

Webster, C., Menzies, R. & Hart, S. (1995). Dangerousness and Risk. In Bull, R. and Carson, D. (Eds), *Handbook of Psychology in Legal Contexts*. Chichester: John Wiley & Sons, pp. 465–479.

Whyte, C., Constantopoulos, C., & Bevans, H. (1982). Types of Countertransference identified by Q-analysis. *British Journal of Medical Psychology*, 55, pp. 187–201.

World Health Organisation (1996). *International Classification of Diseases*. Geneva: Author.

B

SEX OFFENDERS AND OFFENCES

Chapter 7

CLINICAL, LEGAL AND ETHICAL ISSUES FOR MENTAL HEALTH PROFESSIONALS IN IMPLEMENTING A SEXUAL PREDATOR LAW IN THE UNITED STATES

John Q. La Fond

During this past decade Americans have become enraged by sex offenders and the crimes they commit. As a result public policy has focused with a special intensity on how law can prevent convicted sex offenders from committing more sex crimes. States have enacted new laws designed to prevent such crimes including sex offender registration and community notification laws (Simon, 1998), chemical castration laws (Miller, 1998), and sexually violent predator commitment laws ("SVP laws") (Winick, 1998).

SVP laws allow the government to confine convicted sex offenders considered at high risk of reoffending who have served their full prison sentences and are about to be released from prison. They authorize confinement of dangerous sex offenders who can no longer be incarcerated in the criminal justice system or hospitalized in the general civil commitment system (Janus, 1998). The government must prove the individual suffers from a "personality disorder" or "mental abnormality" that makes the individual likely to commit a serious sex crime if released. Commitment is indefinite and the individual can be released only when his or her mental condition has improved so that he or she is safe to live in the community. (The Texas SVP law only authorizes outpatient commitment for sexual predators. Aggressive community monitoring and treatment rather than institutional confinement is used to prevent sex offense recidivism (Texas Sexually Violent Predators Act).)

In 1997 the Supreme Court in *Kansas v. Hendricks* upheld these statutes as a valid exercise of the state's civil commitment authority (*Kansas v. Hendricks*, 1997). At least fifteen states have enacted SVP laws and more states are likely to do so. Future litigation will focus on how these laws are implemented. Special scrutiny will be given to how Mental Health Professionals (MHPs) perform the roles required by these new laws with particular emphasis on how MHPS assess risk for future sexual offending (Hanson, 1998).

HOW THE SVP LAWS WORK

A state agency must review the records of sex offenders convicted of qualifying sex crimes nearing the end of their prison term to determine if individual offenders satisfy the statutory definition of a predator (Washington Sexually Violent Predators Act). The names and records of individuals selected by this process are then sent to a prosecuting authority. If this official decides to initiate commitment, he or she files a petition seeking commitment.

Probable cause hearing

A judicial "probable cause" hearing is then held. If a judge finds there is probable cause to believe the offender is a predator, the judge issues an order directing that the individual be evaluated. This evaluation may be conducted either in the prison where the offender is serving his or her prison term or the offender may be sent to a central state facility specializing in evaluation of predators.

Trial

The individual will usually resist commitment and a trial will be held to determine if he or she is an SVP (Kansas Sexually Violent Predators Act). Under SVP laws, individuals are entitled to an expert of his or her choice to conduct a separate evaluation, to assist their attorney, and to testify at trial.

Commitment & release

If committed, the state must provide treatment for SVPs. Staff must periodically review the progress of SVPs to determine if they can be released into a community transition program or, if they no longer qualify as an SVP, are entitled to be released outright.

ROLES FOR MENTAL HEALTH PROFESSIONALS

SVP laws require MHPs to play crucial roles in their implementation. These roles include participating in screening, evaluation, treatment, and release of sex offenders.

Screening

MHPs review records of sex offenders nearing the end of their prison terms to identify individual offenders who might qualify as SVPs under these laws.

Evaluation, reporting, and testifying

MHPs evaluate individual sex offenders to determine if they qualify for commitment under SVP laws. MHPs must prepare a written report stating and explaining their opinions. Finally, MHPs may have to testify, either for the prosecution or for the defense. These laws require MHPs both to diagnose and to make a risk assessment for each offender.

Treatment

MHPs provide treatment for individuals committed to institutional custody. Most laws provide committees with the right to treatment and courts will ensure that the state complies with its constitutional duty to provide treatment (*Turay v. Weston*, 1994).

Release

MHPs will evaluate and diagnose SVPs eligible for conditional release and for final release. They may also testify in a court hearing on whether the offender's condition has improved sufficiently to allow safe release.

Post-release treatment

MHPs will also provide treatment to offenders placed in a community transition placement.

LEGAL DEFINITION OF SEXUALLY VIOLENT PREDATOR

SVP laws vary from state to state. Most SVP laws define an SVP as a sex offender who has: (a) been convicted of a qualifying sex crime against a stranger or an individual with whom he or she has established a relationship for the purpose of victimization; (b) is about to be released from prison; and (c) suffers from a "mental abnormality" or a "personality disorder" which makes him or her "likely" to commit another serious sex crime (Washington Sexually Violent Predators Act).

Qualifying sex crimes and future offenses

Many SVP laws apply to offenders who have been convicted of a *single* qualifying crime. These laws usually exclude offenders who have committed sexual offenses against family members (thereby eliminating incest offenders) and against familiars (thereby eliminating "date rape" offenders). Some SVP laws require multiple victims (California Sexually Violent Predator Act). Other SVP laws include within the definition of qualifying offense crimes that, though not sexual in nature, were nonetheless "sexually motivated" (Washington Sexually Violent Predator Act). Thus, the clinician must be certain to know all the elements contained in the statutory definition of "sexually violent predator" or its equivalent term. This definition will be the operative legal road map for the evaluation.

Mental abnormality

Most SVP laws define "mental abnormality" as "a congenital or acquired condition affecting the emotional or volitional capacity which predisposes the person to the commission of criminal sexual acts in a degree constituting such person a menace to the health and safety of others" (Washington Sexually Violent Predator Act). This term has no recognized meaning in authoritative mental health texts such as the DSM IV (Diagnostic and Statistical Manual of Mental Disorders, APA, 1994) and is not limited to psychiatric or psychologically familiar terms.

It also calls for a normative judgment. The evaluator must determine if the individual suffers an emotional or volitional deficit; then, make a judgment as to whether that condition makes the offender a "menace" to the public. The clinician should be sensitive to this subjective element and be prepared to explain why they believe the offender poses such risk.

Because "mental abnormality" is not a recognized diagnosis, each MHP will have to construct their own operational definition for this key diagnostic concept. Each MPH will have to explain clearly to the court what they mean by this term when they are testifying. Consistent application of this key diagnostic term is problematic. It is quite possible that MHPs testifying for the government and for the defense will not be using the term with a shared meaning.

Some experts argue that "mental abnormality" is shorthand for mental disorders recognized in the DSM IV. Many MHPs may decide that the closest recognized diagnosis to satisfy this term will be the "paraphilias" contained in the DSM IV. DSM IV defines paraphilias as "recurrent, intense sexually arousing fantasies, sexual urges, or behaviors involving 1) nonhuman objects, 2) the suffering of humiliation of oneself or one's partner, or 3) children or other nonconsenting person that occur over a period of at least 6 months. "Pedophilia" is the recognized diagnosis most likely to fit sex offenders who commit sex crimes against children. It would most likely fit the case of individuals who become scoutmasters or obtain other positions of trust or authority over children in order to victimize them.

SVP laws are also used to commit rapists. There is no DSM IV diagnosis that is specific to rapists, unless the clinician resorts to a diagnosis of paraphilia based on the offender's arousal to the suffering of the victim. This diagnosis might not be appropriate unless there was strong evidence of inflicting exceptional pain and suffering on the victim.

Personality disorder

This term does have a recognized diagnostic meaning in the DSM IV. The most likely diagnosis to be used to satisfy this term is "antisocial personality disorder." DSM IV defines "antisocial personality disorder" as "disregard for, and violation of, the rights of others that begins in childhood or early adolescence and continues into adulthood." Caution is urged in the use of this diagnosis, however. As the American Psychiatric Association has noted, approximately one-quarter to one-half of all offenders presently incarcerated in the United States probably qualify for this diagnosis (APA Draft Report on Sexually Dangerous Offenders, 1996). Moreover, this diagnosis is not specific to sex offenders. Becker and Murphy conclude that the presence of an antisocial personality disorder is not sufficient by itself to commit someone as an SVP; they would also require a paraphilic diagnosis (Becker and Murphy, 1998).

A Constitutional requirement: substantial volitional impairment

In *Hendricks* the Supreme Court concluded that Kansas' SVP law was a constitutional form of civil commitment rather than unconstitutional preventive detention because the law did not allow the state to confine an individual based *solely* on dangerousness. Justice Thomas in the majority opinion concluded that the SVP law did require mental abnormality:

> These added statutory requirements serve to limit involuntary civil commitment to those who suffer from a *volitional impairment rendering them dangerous beyond their control*. . . . The precommitment requirement of a 'mental abnormality' or 'personality disorder' is consistent with the requirements of these other statues that we have upheld in that it narrows the class of persons eligible for confinement to those who are *unable to control their dangerousness*. (emphasis added.) (*Kansas v. Hendricks*, 1997).

Thus, the condition must severely diminish the individual's volitional ability to refrain from committing sex crimes. It would seem that abnormal sexual desires or arousal patterns would not, by themselves, establish this constitutionally required loss of self-control. Nor would a history, even an extensive history, of sexual reoffending by itself establish it. The evaluator must bear in mind that only those sex offenders who cannot control their behavior can be committed under predator laws. Offenders who have extremely powerful urges to commit sex crimes and act impulsively on them are likely candidates for commitment as SVPs.

But, Professor Bruce Winick cautions:

> There is nothing in the diagnostic criteria for pedophilia or any of the other paraphilias that suggests that individuals diagnosed with these disorders suffer from any cognitive impairment that affects their ability to understand the wrongfulness of their conduct or that renders them unable to control their actions. Such persons may have strong urges to gratify their aberrant sexual desire for children, but there is nothing in the clinical literature that suggests that sex offenders are unable to exercise self-control (Winick, 1998).

He observes that pedophiles do not commit crimes when police officers are around or when detection is highly likely. Winick concludes that pedophiles do not satisfy the lack of volition required by the Supreme Court in *Hendricks*. Becker and Murphy note: "Unfortunately, there is little research literature on this question of whether these sexual urges are irresistible impulses . . . or impulses not resisted" (Becker & Murphy, 1998).

This condition must also make the offender "likely to commit" another sexual offense. This statutory element necessarily requires the evaluator to make an assessment of dangerousness; i.e. what is the probability that the offender will commit another sexual offense if he is not committed. A diagnosis is not particularly useful for the risk assessment required by these laws.

Most SVP laws are silent on the question of how soon is the offender likely to reoffend if released. This lack of temporal specificity complicates the MPH's predictive task. Most recidivism studies of sex offenders tend to be limited to measurement periods of five years or less (Hanson, 1998). And, as a general proposition, the longer the period studied, the lower the "survival" rate of offenders; i.e. the more likely they are to reoffend. Though there is little legislative history or scholarly commentary on this question, it is likely that SVP laws should be limited in their application to sex offenders who, because of significant volitional impairment are at high risk of reoffending within a relatively short period of time of release unless committed. Otherwise, a plausible argument could be made that many offenders may reoffend sometime in their remaining lifetime. This approach would undoubtedly result in an exceptionally high number of false positives and increase significantly the SVP population at state mental health facilities.

Treatability not a Constitutional requirement

Sexual predator laws do not require that sex offenders be amenable to treatment before they can be committed. The primary purpose of these laws is to safeguard the public against mentally abnormal and dangerous sex offenders.

In *Hendricks* Justice Thomas said:

> While we have upheld state civil commitment statutes that aim to incapacitate and to treat, we have never held that the Constitution prevents a State from civilly detaining those for whom no treatment is available, but who nevertheless pose a danger to others . . . To conclude otherwise would obligate the state to release certain confined individuals who were both mentally ill and dangerous simply because they could not be successfully treated for their afflictions. (*Kansas v. Hendricks*, 1997)

Thus, clinicians, as part of their evaluation, do not have to determine whether a potential SVP has a mental condition that will benefit from treatment or whether the individual is willing to accept treatment.

SCREENING, EVALUATION, DIAGNOSIS & PREDICTION

Screening

MHPs who screen sex offenders currently in prison must ensure that the offender's records are complete. Researchers have noted that original records are often difficult to locate or have been destroyed (Hanson, 1998). They have also found out-of-state conviction records to be especially time-consuming and difficult to obtain. California had to hire staff to assemble these histories (La Fond, 1998). MHPs must be certain that the offender has been convicted of a qualifying offense. Moreover, the risk assessment required by the statute should be based largely on historical data that will have to be obtained from the offender's records.

Evaluation

Mental health professionals will be called on to evaluate sex offenders to assist courts in determining whether they are SVPs. In most states MHPs who screen offender records will not serve as evaluators. In some states, MHPs generally serve as evaluators exclusively for the government or for the state.

Clarification of role & warning of non-confidentiality

At the outset the clinician must make clear to the offender what role the clinician is performing. The clinician must tell the offender that he or she is not there to treat the offender as a patient. It must be made clear why the clinician is there; i.e. that the court, prosecutor, or defense counsel has asked the clinician to conduct this evaluation and that the clinician may be asked to render an opinion in court based, in part, on this evaluation. The clinician should also inform the individual that this evaluation may be used to commit the offender as an SVP.

The clinician must also make it clear that their communications are not covered by a doctor–patient privilege. In fact, the evaluator must inform the offender that everything the offender says may be (and, in some cases, *must* be) revealed to third parties, including the court and the prosecutor.

Evaluation instruments

California requires MHPs to evaluate sex offenders "in accordance with a standardized assessment protocol, developed and updated by the State Department of Mental Health to determine whether the person is a sexually violent predator . . ." (California Sexually Violent Predators Act). It requires an "assessment of diagnosable mental disorders, as well as various factors known to be associated with risk of reoffense among sex offenders. Risk factors to be considered include criminal and psychosexual history, type, degree, and duration of sexual deviance, and severity of mental disorder" (California Sexually Violent Predators Act). Other states allow evaluators more flexibility.

Complete and current history

Evaluators should have a complete and current clinical history and offense history for the individual. This history should include a complete record of charged and convicted offenses, medical and mental histories, and prison history. In addition, an evaluator should compile a detailed psychosocial and psychosexual history of the offender. Because many sex offenders deny their offenses, the Association for the Treatment of Sexual Abusers recommends that evaluators gather information from sources other than the offender (Becker & Murphy, 1998). These sources include victim statements, police reports, previous mental health and medical records, juvenile and adult criminal records, and probation and parole reports when available. Because SVP proceedings are initiated at the end of a prison sentence, however, this information may be difficult to obtain.

Statements of others

If the clinician consults with other individuals, he or she will have to be alert to possible bias on their part (La Coursiere, 1998). This may be especially true if a MHP consults with victims or family members of victims.

Cooperation by the offender

Most courts have ruled that SVP proceedings are civil, not criminal. Consequently, they have concluded that there is no 5th Amendment privilege against self-incrimination (*Allen v. Illinois*, 1986). Thus, an offender can be ordered to answer all questions related to the evaluation. Nonetheless, many offenders refuse to cooperate with government evaluators or will not answer questions candidly or completely. As a practical matter, then, evaluators often rely primarily on offense history as the primary basis for their opinions. This data may be stale, especially if they relate to offenses committed many years ago.

Recent evidence of dangerousness

Many general civil commitment laws or cases interpreting those laws require the government to introduce recent evidence of dangerousness (*Lessard v. Schmidt*, 1972). SVP laws do not require recent evidence of dangerousness because policy-makers have concluded that prison affords little or no opportunity for offenders to manifest their sexual dangerousness (*In re Young*, 1993). Nonetheless, MHPs should carefully review an offender's prison history to ascertain if there is any behavioral evidence indicating mental disorder, volitional impairment or sexual dangerousness.

Plethsymograph

Some evaluators consider the use of a plethysmograph helpful in forming their opinion. Not all facilities have them and suitable testing facilities available and not all offenders will cooperate. Of course, only MHPs trained in their use should use this device and they should be aware of its limits (Harris, Rice, and Quinsey, 1998).

Predictions of dangerousness

Perhaps the most important component of a clinician's opinion is the determination of how likely is it that this offender will commit another crime of sexual violence. A clinician must be knowledgeable about the current state of the art in predicting sexual dangerousness.

Risk assessment methods

There are several methods of risk assessment for sex offenders: pure actuarial (using a small number of variables with explicit rules for translating rankings on the individual variables into overall risk assessment), adjusted actuarial (using actuarial predictions adjusted for other compelling evidence), clinical, and guided clinical approach (Hanson, 1998). Hanson argues that the guided clinical approach appears to be the most appropriate for use under SVP laws. In this approach, MHPs "consider a wide range of empirically validated risk factors and then form an overall opinion concerning the offender's recidivism risk." The method of translating the identified risk factors into recidivism rates is not explicitly determined. Other experts argue that actuarial methods for appraisal of risk of sexual aggression should replace clinical methods (Harris, Rice, and Quinsey, 1998).

Hanson maintains that the expert must "provide credible answers to three questions: (a) What, in general, are the factors that predict recidivism? (b) How does the particular offender rate on the relevant factors? And (c) Given this combination of factors, what is the probability that the offender will commit a particular type of offense (sexual, violent, any) over a given time period (e.g. 1 month, 2 years, a lifetime)?" (Hanson, 1998).

Base rates

Hanson points out that "The starting point for all recidivism estimates should be the base rate expected for 'similar' offenders" (Hanson, 1998). Sex offenders as a group do not have an especially high recidivism rate. Based on a review of 61 follow-up studies Hanson concluded that sex offenders, as a group, have a recidivism rate of 13.4% during the 4 to 5 year follow-up period. Within that group rapists had a recidivism rate of 18.9% and child molesters had a rate of 12.7% (Hanson, 1998). Thus, the MHP is trying to determine if a particular offender has a significantly higher probability of reoffending than most sex offenders.

Predictors of sexual reoffense

Some of the most reliable predictors of sexual offense recidivism include those shown in Table 1.

Sexual recidivism is most closely associated with an established pattern of sexual deviancy, as measured by factors such as prior sexual offenses,

Table 1: Predictors of Sexual Offence Recidivism

Predictor	Average correlation ("r")
Sexual preference for children	.32
Any deviant sexual preference	.22
Prior sexual offenses	.19
Failure to complete treatment	.17
Antisocial personality disorder Or psychopathy	.14
Any prior offenses	.13
Age (young)	.13
Never married	.11
Any unrelated victims	.11
Any male child victims	.11

deviant sexual interests, and deviant victim choices. Historical factors are probably the most useful in calculating the risk each sex offender poses for committing another crime of sexual violence. Most of these factors are static; they do not change over time (though they can get worse). Other researchers have suggested that factors associated with future sexual recidivism include: number of prior sexual offenses; age at time of release; male victims; and unrelated victims (Hanson, 1998).

Dynamic risk factors

Dynamic risk factors—factors that can change over time—associated with sexual offense recidivism include negative social relationships, attitudes tolerant of sexual offending, and lack of self-management skills. Dynamic risk factors need to be used cautiously, however, because they are based primarily on interviews. Moreover, as Hanson notes, there is "no explicit method of translating combinations of individual risk factors into overall recidivism probabilities. None of the individual risk factors are sufficiently discriminating to justify use in isolation" (Hanson, 1998).

Hanson concludes that predictive approaches are available which "can be expected to reliably identify a small subgroup of offenders with an enduring propensity to reoffend. The rate at which this highest risk subgroup actually reoffends with another sexual reoffense could be conservatively estimated at 50% and could reasonably be estimated at 70% to 80%" (Hanson, 1998).

CAUTIONARY NOTES

Group v. individual risk

It should be noted that actuarial prediction tools only identify offenders who are members of a group that has these probabilities of committing another sex offense. They do not necessarily identify which individual members of the group will reoffend. Moreover, even if such accuracy is available in the numerous predictions that will be conducted under varying conditions, MHPs should recognize that predictions of reoffense are *incorrect* from 20% to 50% of the time. In addition, they do not identify the time period within which the individual can be expected to reoffend or identify which individuals could be managed through aggressive community monitoring.

Correlation v. causation

Even validated risk factors only establish correlations; they do not establish causation. The Supreme Court decision in *Hendricks* requires that the individual suffer a very significant volitional impairment over their sexual conduct. Thus, these factors may identify a group of individuals who may be at much greater risk of sexually reoffending. Most of them, however, do not shed much light on the behavioral dynamics of the offense. Put simply, they do not identify individuals who suffer from the type of volitional impairment constitutionally required for civil commitment. It will be the exceptional case in which the offender admits (as Hendricks seemingly did in his trial) that 'he cannot help himself' from committing sex offenses against children.

TREATMENT

Many mental health professionals will be required to treat this growing population. There are over 1000 individuals either committed as SVPs under these laws or in confinement awaiting evaluation or trials. Most state forensic staff are not trained or experienced in treating sex offenders (La Fond, 1998). Almost all states have had to train and retool virtually all staff who treat SVPs.

Treatment methods

There are a number of treatment modalities available to treat sex offenders. These include individual or group psychotherapy, behavioral and cognitive behavioral treatments, relapse prevention, medication, including sex-drive reducing hormonal treatment, and other approaches (Harris, Rice, and Quinsey, 1998). There are a number of issues to which MHPs need to be sensitive.

Treatment efficacy

There has been a fair amount of recent research and literature on the efficacy of treatment. Unfortunately, there is no persuasive evidence yet that treatment for sex offenders reduces sexual reoffense recidivism. This is not to say that treatment does not work or that there are no principles for adopting treatment. It simply means that we do not know if treatment reduces sexual offense recidivism (Harris, Rice, and Quinsey, 1998).

Right to treatment

The State is required under SVP laws to provide treatment for committed individuals. The Supreme Court itself in *Hendricks* has indicated that the state must provide treatment to predators, at least when the state considers such offenders amenable to treatment. One court has found a constitutional right to treatment. This mean that states must provide a humane and therapeutic environment, adequate numbers of professionally qualified staff, individual treatment plans, and programs consistent with current knowledge about sex offender treatment (*Turay v. Weston*, 1994). Without treatment, states will not be willing to release most SVPs.

Competence

MHPs should be competent to treat their patients. Preparation and training are essential for MHPs who have no prior training or experience in treating sex offenders. At the very least programs should have in positions of responsibility MHPs who are qualified to treat sex offenders. On-going training and supervision should be provided to staff who are becoming trained in such treatment techniques. Patients will quickly detect whether MHPs are qualified to treat them. Without confidence in the expertise of the mental health professional, it will be difficult to form the therapeutic alliance essential for effective treatment.

Confidentiality & warnings

SVP laws require staff to perform both treatment and evaluation functions. Thus, MHPs will treat these sex offenders and will also determine whether they are safe to be released into a community transition program or to be released outright. This dual obligation creates conflict problems.

MHPs must fully inform offenders that their communications are not confidential. They should also tell their patients what mandatory reporting obligations apply to MHPs. Some state laws require treatment providers to inform authorities of any sex offenses the offenders may have committed. This information may expose the patient to additional prosecution and punishment. Such a warning may well chill the free flow of information that is vital to effective therapy.

Anecdotal evidence suggests that some MHPs tell their patients that there is no need for them to be specific about the details of these undetected crimes, such as the date and the victim. General discussion about criminal histories will suffice. This allows MHPs to learn of the offender's history without providing sufficient information to trigger any requirement to report past crimes. The clinician can thus learn important information because past offense history is an extremely important variable in making an accurate risk assessment.

Coercion

It should be noted that treatment is being provided to patients on a coercive basis. The motivation of such patients is problematic. Winick cautions that clinicians should be alert to the possibility that they may "experience a high degree of frustration in working with [these] unmotivated patients" (Winick, 1998). Moreover, much of the research on treatment efficacy involved offenders who *voluntarily* chose treatment. Thus, it is not clear whether coercive treatment will be effective. Finally, clinicians must consider whether they are ethically and morally comfortable in serving what is primarily a social control function rather than a therapeutic function.

Chemical castration

A number of states have passed laws requiring sex offenders to take sex drive reducing drugs as a condition of probation. Studies have shown that these medications may be effective in reducing sex offense recidivism for some offenders (Dangerous Sex Offenders, 1999). These laws were not enacted as part of a sexual predator law. However, it is very possible that prosecutors might seek, or judges may order such compulsory medication as a condition of community placement or outright release of an SVP.

Dr. Robert Miller maintains that, when used to render sex offenders impotent, these laws are "morally repugnant" because "they violate offenders' constitutional rights to privacy, as well as physician's ethics because they permit nonphysicians to prescribe medications for medically inappropriate purposes" (Miller, 1998). Clinicians may have to decide whether they will participate in prescribing these medications.

Costs

Costs for implementing an SVP law are substantial. It costs approximately $100,000 per year to maintain an individual in these institutions. Some states are committing more SVPs and releasing fewer SVPs than they initially projected (La Fond, 1998).

Release

Most SVP laws make it difficult for offenders to be released unless the treatment staff concludes that the offender is safe to be released. This will require MHPs to undertake risk assessments to determine whether the individual still poses a significant risk of reoffending.

The decision to release is very difficult for several reasons. First, actuarial scales for measuring treatment outcome have not been established. Thus, it is difficult to determine whether treatment has succeeded. Second, factors related to predicting dangerousness at the time of release are dynamic; i.e. they change over time. Research has not yet established which validating factors are associated with low sexual recidivism. Finally, MHPs are biased in favor of safety (Hanson, 1998). The fierce political backlash that is predictable if (when) a released sex offender reoffends also increases the reluctance staff will have in concluding that an offender is safe to be released.

MHPs must accept their statutory responsibility for recommending release when, in their professional opinion, it is warranted. The state's authority to commit an individual is extinguished when the individual no longer satisfies the statutory terms for commitment. Without release for some predators, it is unreasonable to expect other sex offenders to participate in treatment. As a result, the populations at SVP institutions will grow beyond all reasonable projections, leading to increased litigation and the diversion of scarce public resources (La Fond, 1998).

Liability

Many SVP laws do not specifically address whether MHPs can be held liable either for concluding that a sex offender is not an SVP or for recommending community placement or outright release of an SVP. There does not appear to be any reported case law on this question. There are a number of cases in which crime victims or their families were allowed to sue department of corrections (*Washa v. Oregon Dept. of Corrections*, 1999), cities (*Hertog v. City of Seattle*, 1997), and residential treatment facilities (*Koellen v. Nexus Residential Treatment Facility*, 1993) for harm caused by released sex offenders.

It is not clear whether such causes of action will be allowed under SVP laws. Each state will have to determine this issue under applicable state law when the first case is filed. If states allow them, it is likely that staff will be more reluctant to recommend community placement or release lest the individual reoffend and thereby expose them to individual civil liability. By requiring the SVP to obtain a court ordered placement or release, MHPs may be able effectively to insulate themselves from liability. It would be extremely unfortunate if the threat of civil liability made placement or release even more unlikely. The hydraulic pressure of civil liability is powerful. A good case could be made either for granting MHPs absolute individual immunity for such liability or for setting the standard at recklessness rather than gross negligence.

Community placement

MHPs may also treat SVPs released on a community transition plan. These plans usually imposed very stringent conditions on the offender. These conditions are usually explicitly set forth in the court order imposing the conditions of community release and the order usually specifies that any breach of these conditions may result in revocation of the release. Some SVPs may miss scheduled treatment sessions with clinicians and MHPs may be required to notify public authorities

During therapy MHPs may learn that the offender is not complying with other conditions of his or her community placement. For example, the offender may disclose prohibited contacts or activities. Such behavior is often the precursor to reoffense. Failure to report such conditions may result in liability and licensure risks for MHPs. It is probably a wise course for MHPs to explicitly tell the offender what the treatment provider's responsibilities are in the event that the offender does not comply with the conditions of his or her community placement.

Duty to warn

Finally, MHPs may have to decide what, if any, preventive action they will take if the individual reports inappropriate sexual fantasies or other ideation that may indicate increased risk of reoffense. This area is more problematic because professional judgment as to the significance of such ideation is involved.

CONCLUSION

SVP laws are a unique and powerful use of involuntary civil commitment in the United States. They keep in confinement sex offenders who have served their full prison term and who suffer from a mental condition that so impairs their volitional control that they need to be confined and treated until they are safe to be released. These laws impose special responsibilities on MHPs. They must screen, evaluate, identify, predict, testify, treat, warn, prevent, and release. In a very real sense MHPs will be the primary gate-keepers "up front" and at the "back end." In addition, they will have primary responsibility for changing SVPs. Perhaps no other law in our history has imposed so much responsibility on MHPs to serve both a therapeutic and a social control function. It is an awesome responsibility.

REFERENCES

Allen v. Illinois, 478 U.S. 364, 106 S. Ct. 2988 (1986).

American Psychiatric Association *Draft report on sexually dangerous offenders, December 15, 1996.*

Becker, Judith V. and Murphy, William D. (1998). *What we know and do not know about assessing and treating sex offenders*, Psychology, Public Policy and Law, 4, 116–137,

California Sexually Violent Predator Act , Cal. Welf. & Inst. Code, §6600 et. seq. (1999)

Dangerous sex offenders: a task force report of the American Psychiatric Association (1999).

Diagnostic and statistical manual of Mental Disorders IV, American Psychiatric Association, 1994.

Hanson, R. Karl, (1998) *Appraisal and management of risk in sexual aggressors: implications for criminal justice policy*, Psychology, Public Policy and Law, 4, 50–72.

Harris, Grant T., Rice, Marnie E., and Quinsey, Vernon L, (1998). *Appraisal and management of risk in sexual aggressors*, Psychology, Public Policy and Law, 4, 73–115.

Hertog V. City of Seattle, 979 P.2d 400 (1999).

In re Young, 122 Wn. 2d 1, 857 P.2d 989 (1993).

Janus, Eric S. (1998). *Hendricks and the moral terrain of police power civil commitment*, Psychology, Public Policy and Law, 4, 297–322.

Kansas Commitment of Sexually Violent Predators Act, Kan. Stat. Ann. § 59–29a01 et. seq. (1999).

Kansas v. Hendricks, 521 U.S. 355, 117 S. Ct. 2106 (1997).

Koelln v. Nexus Residential Treatment Facility, 494 N.W. 2d 914 (1993).

La Fond, John Q. (1998). *The costs of enacting a sexual predator law*, Psychology, Public Policy and Law, 4, 468–504.

Lacoursiere, Roy (1998). *Evaluating sex offenders*, paper presented at annual meeting of the American Academy of Psychiatry and Law,

Lessard v. Schmidt, 349 F. Supp. 1078 (E. D. Wisc. 1972).

Miller, Robert D. (1998). *Forced administration of sex-drive reducing medications to sex offenders:treatment or punishment?* Psychology, Public Policy and Law, 4, 175–199.

Simon, Jonathan (1998). *Managing the monstrous: sex offenders and the new penology*, Psychology, Public Policy and Law, 4, 452–467.

Texas Civil Commitment of Sexually Violent Predators Act, Texas Statutes and Codes Ann. chapter 841 et. seq. (1999).

Turay v. Weston, No. C-91-664WD, U.S. Dist. Ct. W.D. Wash. June 3, 1994.

Washa v. Oregon Dept. of Corrections, 979 P.2d 273 (1999).

Washington Sexually Violent Predator Act, Wash. Rev. Code § 71.09.09 et. seq. 1999).

Winick, Bruce J. (1998). *Sex offender law in the 1990s: a therapeutic jurisprudence analysis*, Psychology, Public Policy and Law, 4, 505–570.

Chapter 8

SPECIAL LEGAL REQUIREMENTS FOR COMPETENT
FORENSIC ASSESSMENTS OF QUESTIONABLE "RECOVERED
MEMORIES" OF CHILDHOOD SEXUAL ABUSE IN
CRIMINAL TRIALS

Bryan Tully

THE CONCEPT OF "RECOVERED MEMORIES"

Since the early days of the debate over putative "Recovered Memories"
there has been a steady shift away from the language and definitions of
"massive repression", and recovery therefrom of memories of repeated,
extensive, traumatic childhood sexual abuse. There has been a considerable loosening and blurring of terminology. Currently such "Memories"
may be stated to have been recovered from amnesia, or simply "delayed",
"inhibited" or "cognitively avoided".

A number of writers have pointed out that many cases of recall
following a period of forgetting are everyday and natural and can be
accommodated within standard and non controversial theories of
human memory (Roediger et al. 1997, Schooler et al. 1997). There is great
potential to be misled by referring to these as "Recovered Memories",
pooling them with possible disputable cases and then claiming that some
of this overall pool have some corroboration. Andrews et al. (2000)
provide an example of such overinclusive methodology. Some people talk
in a colloquial way about memories having been completely "blocked
out" or "buried". Closely following their verbatim accounts sometimes
makes it clear that they are not actually claiming amnesia, simply some
relevant trigger which brought specific memories they had not thought of
for a long time, back to mind. There are many studies where people report
historical trauma and say quite directly that there was a time when they
had less memory than currently (when they are actively reflecting on the
past) or indeed no memory at all of these events (see Brown, Scheflin &
Hammond 1998, for a review of many). Unfortunately, these utterances
are not reliable pointers to post traumatic amnesia as Read and Lindsay
(2000) demonstrated when asking people to recall in a sustained way

ordinary autobiographical non traumatic events of, for example, summer camps. Similar proportions of subjects claimed less or lack of memory and indeed the more they reflected and recalled in current time, the more they biased their metamemorial judgement of their past state of memory.

Another type of case has been reported by Schooler et al. 1997. A woman claimed a "Recovered Memory" and it was presented as such in the professional literature, even though it was also documented that the woman concerned recalled these events several times in the past, but forgot she had done so. Some writers (e.g. Andrews et al. 2000) have collected retrospective opinions from psychotherapists through telephone surveys without making any differentiation as to the nature of claims of memory. There are in addition perhaps several hundred short case summaries published in the literature of claims of significant and true "Recovered Memories". Unfortunately many of these authors (e.g. Christiansen and Engleberg 1997, Schooler et al. 1997, Cheit 1998) have been unable to provide any further documentary evidence beyond their short published summaries. In many ways it is only when the issue of "Recovered Memories" comes to Court that any reasonable degree of scrutiny is possible. Psychological science may be called to serve the Court's purpose, but this paper argues that Court proceedings and the forensic examinations pursued in relation to those cases actually throw light on the scientific disputes extant in this controversial area.

This chapter deals with serious and controversial "Recovered Memory" phenomena such that either some theory of reversible repression or dissociative amnesia is required, or else the alternative conclusion is arguable, that the claims are such that ordinary mechanisms of memory would have to be stretched to breaking point to accommodate them, as Schooler et al. (1997) have put it. The "Memories" are questionable. Initial capitals are used to denote this more strictly defined use of the term and to differentiate them from theoretically non disputable forms of forgetting and remembering.

In all the following four cases there is arguably *some* corroborative evidence. They provide a foundation for the purpose of this chapter, which is to argue for special legal requirements so that satisfactory forensic psychological assessments can assist the Court.

FOUR CASES OF QUESTIONABLE "RECOVERED MEMORIES"
OF CHILDHOOD ABUSE LEADING TO CRIMINAL PROCEEDINGS
IN ENGLAND

Case 1. Yes he raped me, no he didn't
An adult daughter *A*, with psychological problems, heard news that a
man *B*, connected with a youth club she used to attend, had been
convicted for extensive sexual abuse of children. She wondered if another
worker there *C*, whom she had disliked, might have also been involved
and mentioned this thought to her mother *D*. Her mother went to police
who arranged two interviews with *A*, but nothing was forthcoming. Police
referred her to a psychotherapist who diagnosed trauma without taking
a history, and "Recovered Memories" began to emerge over a period of
months. Accounts mushroomed to include multiple group organised
sexual abuse often preceded by administration of hypnotic drugs. Mother
took *A* to locations identified in the conviction of *B*, and showed photos
from old papers. Statements taken at this time documented there was
no recognition. Each set of new memories were recorded and dated
by the psychotherapist, and decanted into half a dozen police statements
within a week or so of each therapy session. *C* was arrested and indicted.
Inconsistencies in respect as to whether *A* was raped by *C* or *B* appeared
over the course of statements. The psychotherapist explained this as
arising from residual attachment of *A* to the accused and that she needed
to defend her conscious ego from the unbearable pain of his allowing
her to be raped by someone else. With therapy, *A* was able to determine
finally that it had been *B* who raped her, with the now accused *C* assisting.
Then *A* began to recall that when she had seen a photo of *B* from newspaper photos, she had recognised him immediately as part of the sexually
abusive group she had been subjected to. Complainant *A* was not available for psychological assessment. The Crown Prosecution decided not
to proceed with the case after considering this author's report setting
out the above.

Comment: *This case exhibits a vast staggered mushrooming of memories,
typical of some kinds of "Recovered Memories" cases. Changes and
instability were identified in not only the content of the remote
"Recovered Memories", but also in the recent process by which the
Memories came to mind. What was "remembered" to have been recently
recognised (in this case from newspaper photos) was also subject to
change. In this case, the extension retrospectively of how long it had been*

since A *claimed she had recognised an abuser looks like an example of what has been described as the "knew it all along phenomenon" (Fischoff 1982), a general tendency to misremember how long something has been known, when that is objectively not the case. In this case, the mother who had always thought there must be some reason why this daughter was not as successful as her other two, the police officer and the psychotherapist were all far more informed about the background case in relation to the conviction of* B *and provided an active and powerful co-operative triad of psychological midwives to the "Recovered Memories" of* A.

Case 2. Questionable "Recovered Memories" arising from credible non Recovered Memory

Sister A reported a long history of incestuous abuse by her father from her early teens to mid twenties. The account was coherent, detailed, and recognisable in respect of both victim and offender behaviour. There were no "Recovered Memories". Father, defendant B, had spent most of his time with A during her pre-teen and teen years, generally ignoring her sister, his other daughter C, who spent most of her time with mother D. Eventually the mother and daughter C and a brother, E, left the family home and emigrated to Canada. Mother and daughter C always suspected there was something unhealthy about A's relationship with her father. Contacts were maintained by phone and letter as the daughters grew up into young adulthood. One day A told her sister on the phone that her father had been sexually abusing her for many years since her early teens. She described how this had started. Father had come into the bathroom and explained she would need to have her vagina widened and he would help by using his fingers. Inexorably over time this initial assault led to everything else including full intercourse. Sister C in Canada and her mother immediately recognised this story. When C was a young teenager her mother had tried to assist her fit a tampon. Mother mentioned the difficulty to father. Father had come into the bathroom and used his fingers to help widen the vagina. C was uncomfortable about this, but reported mixed feelings since the fact her father was paying her any attention at all was unusual and was welcome for that reason. Once out of the bath, she was stood up against a wall and a further penetration took place, which was painful. Now she ran away crying and a further effort by father to follow up with her was completely rebuffed. Father never bothered her again. Sister C and mother then reported to the Canadian police and thence the police in Birmingham, England visited A and obtained a detailed statement from her. At this point there was no whiff of anything having been Recovered. Common complaint against the Defendant constituted a very strong case.

Then, for reasons which were never properly determined, but which seemed to entail a serious anxiety state, sister C in Canada began to undergo a serious psychological deterioration which was to interrupt her university studies. She turned for help to psychotherapists who considered this could all be attributed to her childhood sexual abuse and – as is not uncommon with psychotherapists – did not take a full history or make a formal psychological formulation before starting to "explore the issues". Working frequently as they did with putative victims of crime and in association with the legal and law enforcement services they made a point of writing how they "*never suggest, never lead*". Nonetheless, from their own records it was plain the therapy sessions were very long, 2–3 hours or 3–4 hours. Moreover they were mixed with additional group therapy sessions with many other survivors of sexual abuse, all sharing their histories. The psychotherapists stated they used the model of *Remembrance and Mourning* developed by Judith Herman (1992). This purposely requires a detailed reconstruction which transforms wordless and static traumatic memories into an integrated life story narrative. The role of therapy is to provide the music and words to snapshots or silent movie imagery. The uncovering (from repression) work is timed to remain bearable to the patient. Whatever the problems are in expressing, the therapist aids the patient to give a full and vivid description. As an illustration, Herman cites approvingly Jessica Wolfe's approach (in her case with combat veterans) "*We have them reel it off in great detail as if they were watching a movie, and with all the senses included. We ask them what they are seeing, what they are hearing, what they are smelling, what they are feeling, what they are thinking*".

C began to reel off in great detail a whole mushrooming of new sexually abusive experience both before and after the incident she had always recalled. This rapidly overtook her sister's experiences in extent and seriousness. They reached back in age-time further and further to include events when C would have been 2, 3 and 4 years of age. Sister A then wrote a short letter to the police "*I, A, will defend my father B against my sister C*". It was enough to make any prosecutor despair. The situation had been transformed from common complaint by witnesses presenting as joint victims and allies, to a form of victim sibling rivalry. Not only was this likely to undermine the Prosecution but to damage the relationships between A and the rest of her family and possibly therefore the rest of her life. The latest psychotherapy notes, which were delivered just before the trial was due, documented how the process of C Recovering what she believed to be Memories had now extended to include abusive activity *by* her sister A, and with her brother, frequently without father being present. As again is so often the case, even after the hundreds of hours of therapy, C's psychological state was hardly restored. In the end the Prosecution dropped proceedings in respect of C, and the Defence pleaded to an indictment of incest in respect of A. Neither complainant had been available for direct assessment.

Comment: *The first problem with C's mushrooming of memories during the Remembrance and Mourning procedure is that this was simply inconsistent with the schismatic lifestyle the family had developed and was confirmed by all members of the family. Secondly, as the process evolved it reached further back in time into the period of childhood amnesia, where it is not possible to recall detailed individual events in the way they were in fact described. The process of therapy described has many features in common with circumstances where vulnerable people become highly suggestible and will recount false confessions of matters which they are led to think might have happened and involved them (see Gudjonsson 1992, Ofshe & Watters 1994). If C's extended "Recovered Memories" had been essentially true, then her repression / dissociation / inhibition of memory must have operated perfectly for all memories and coping reactions prior to the events she did recall, and immediately afterwards. Her actual long term memory would have to have been an oasis in a desert of amnesia. Additionally, either her brother E and sister A must have been lying in failing to corroborate her memories of their involvement, or both have suffered perfect repression / dissociation / inhibition of memories of childhood sexual abuse. This is a very important case if it is accepted that it is reasonable to consider C's later "Recovered Memories" as questionable and probably false. It shows that dubious "Recovered Memories" may arise in the context of non dubious stable long term, always remembered, normal, memory. There is of course no good reason or principle of psychological theory as to why this should not happen sometimes. The forensic assessor can usually be more confident when questionable "Recovered Memories" arise entirely and completely from nothing at all of long term memory, but the possibility of a mix of true and false cannot be discounted in many cases, nor a line drawn between them with the same confidence as in this exceptional case.*

Case 3. "Recovered Memories" à deux

A teenager *A* told her psychiatrist (Notes 1) she had been sexually abused by maternal grandparents, the Defendants *B* and *C*. She could give little detail, but her mother *D*, although sceptical at first, began to recover memories of her own sexual abuse by her parents viz. *B* and *C*. *A* was admitted to an inpatient unit (Notes unavailable) and started various therapies including family therapy with her mother. Before and arising out of family therapy came new material for both complainants and each made two statements to police. A policy was made by the family therapy team at the in-patient unit to treat all reports as true because mother and daughter corroborated each other. The second of each statement incorporated significant material from the other's first statement, producing a converging memorial leapfrogging. For example *A* first stated her grandparents never physically hurt her; she just felt she was expected to co-operate in their abusive activity. In her next statement she stated had been subjected to substantial physical abuse including near drowning in the bath, just as her mother had only recently said happened to her. Both women "Recovered Memories" of *D*'s sister *E* (*A*'s aunt) being involved, which *E* proclaimed no knowledge of, nor indeed any other abuse. Later *A* Recovered a Memory that her first step-father (*D*'s first husband) had sexually abused her. *D* Recovered a Memory of her sister *E* being seen in bed 7 years ago with father *B*, who was then 68 years old. *E* claimed this was nonsense. That had prompted no memory of any thoughts by *D* *at that time* that this was odd or that her children might be at risk from her father. Both complainants *A* and her mother *D* had substantial mental health histories. *D* had recalled some years previously when she was suffering panic disorder (Notes 2) that when she was 4 years old she had been locked in a cellar by her parents *B* and *C*. That was a childhood panic inducing experience, but there was no way of telling from documents if this was a Memory Recovered for the first time then. In the weeks prior to giving a statement to police regarding childhood sexual abuse, she Recovered a Memory of *why* she was locked up. She now recalled watching an uproar in her parents' bedroom and what appeared to be a bloody abortion procured on her mother *C*. Then the bloody bundle was taken out and buried in the garden with a shiny spade. Claimed recollections of actual words spoken were recorded in police officer's notebook, but were not included in drafted statement. Subsequently both complainants reported believing the Defendants (a retired postman and his wife in their 70s, living hundreds of miles away in Scotland) had agents out looking to assassinate them. Subsequent psychiatric notes (Notes 3) indicated *D* was reporting that babies had been buried in the garden of more than one home. None of this was entered in the statements. The family therapy team refused to hand over individual therapy notes, but wrote summaries. These did not include full clinical histories or reviews of psychological treatments and assessments to date. Other healthcare notes (Notes 4) were later made available and included records of *A*'s admission to a hospital Accident & Emergency department, just prior to her first ever claim to have been sexually molested. She had been taken to hospital by ambulance after claiming (falsely as it turned out) she had taken an overdose of tablets at a party. A physician noted her strange rocking movement, but only when the doctor entered the room. Mother *D* at this point expressed extreme scepticism over any claim of sexual abuse, but nothing was actually described. The Accident and Emergency doctors documented mother's information that her daughter emulated a character on a Television soap, including reporting voices in the head, taking tablets and thinking of suicide. When the General Practitioner's notes (Notes 5) were reviewed it was found the G.P. had suggested to *A* just one week before, that her self laceration behaviour could be a sign of having been sexually abused. Prior to this incident, *A* had decided not to see her own Psychiatrist any further (Notes 6) but had been seeing him without her mother's knowledge as mother was anticipated to accuse her of "*craving attention for herself*". Later, when mother changed her scepticism about sexual abuse to reporting similar memories this was a surprise and a basis for some emotional family therapy work. The complainants refused to be available for psychological assessment by the Defence instructed experts (this author and a Professor of Psychiatry), but a few weeks before the trial began, the Crown Prosecution instructed a hospital psychiatrist to examine the two women. The report was limited but expressed reservations as to the converging statements. The Prosecution decided not to proceed and sought to leave charges on the file. The Judge ruled the two Defendants deserved the comfort of a Not Guilty verdict.

Comment: *This is a report of an extremely complex case. Hugely escalating "Recovered Memories" are evident. Where zealous clinicians and psychotherapists fixate on one hypothesis without a full and proper history being taken, that augurs badly for both clinical outcome and justice. The implications of possible personality disorder and delusional thinking were never considered in this case or explored as differential diagnoses. Once a serious police investigation was under way, it was wrong for a police officer to join a group therapy meeting where further* *testimony was being solicited from a vulnerable witness, and for the proceedings not to be written down verbatim and made available for those who were parties to the Court proceedings. Even without individual psychotherapy notes (needed to document the course of memorialisation, not to catch the psychotherapists out), this case had much which brought the complainants' accounts into question. Much of that was to be found in obscure corners of healthcare and hospital notes, especially of practitioners who were monitoring the complainants before and after the genesis of the questionable Recovered Material. This is a clear reason why this material should be disclosed and considered by police and prosecutors themselves in the first instance. Some of these more questionable aspects were absent from statements, which was itself misleading. Digging of a more literal sort is indicated if a woman is considered believable when reporting babies and aborted foetuses buried. Like a number of other contemporary "Recovered Memories" cases, panic disorder of some kind figures in relationship to a number of Memories of panic inducing experiences preceding "Recovered Memories" of childhood sexual abuse. There is no justifiable reason to bypass an expert instructed by the Defence if the Prosecution itself agrees that an expert opinion is useful. At the very least there should be permitted consultation prior to the examination. Clinical assessors seldom examine original notes from preceding professionals who have dealt with their patient. Forensic assessors should do so whenever possible.*

Case 4. Prosecution and Defence Experts co-operate

A disabled nursing student *A* presented with continuity of memory of serious and persistent physical and emotional abuse by stepfather *B*. Depressed, she underwent therapy, and "Recovered Memories" of childhood sexual abuse, although not arising during therapy time (apparently so; one therapist was credited by *A* with knowing what had happened before she did). For two years *A* had sought out specialist books on remembering abuse, toxic parents etc. Journals, diaries, and poetry were disclosed and she agreed to be assessed by two Psychologists, this writer and a colleague instructed by the Crown Prosecution. Assessment was able to trace provenance of many ideas and memories through specific activities recorded in the journals and other material, over a protracted period with many re-visualisations and re-writings of similar, evolving material. There was evidence of unusual imaginative capacity from religious experiences and going off on "imaginative journeys" with a friend. Much of the writing read like a novel with the subject referring to herself in the 3rd person or directly addressing "the child within". Apart from general "touching" on the bottom there were only a handful of more serious acts recalled, apparently attempted just the once each. Some scenes had been dreamed first and then embellished in writing. Feelings and flavours of abuse always came first. Experts' review of papers led to agreed reservations about memories arising simply from stable long term memory. The Prosecution then dropped their own expert witness. The Judge advised the Prosecution he was worried a sincere disabled and vulnerable witness might appear credible and the Jury needed to know if there were unusual psychological aspects outside their ordinary experience. This led to joint assessment of A by both Psychologists. The final report agreed that the assessment added clarification and detail to the doubts and reservations. After some delay, the Prosecution decided not to proceed after pleading to the Court they had always been a bit worried about this case!

Comment: *Many "Recovered Memories" in recent times now arise outside of therapy time. Whether or not from within therapy, they always require the active entertainment of an idea (even if doubted at first) by the complainant. Active "memory work" by the complainant is the common factor (Ceci & Loftus 1994). Critics of certain therapists for "planting" false memories use the horticultural metaphor in a misleading way. Many complainants' minds are fertile ground for seeds which may arise from anywhere. Psychotherapists may play a more or less contributory role in fertilising and husbanding the growth of such active generative processes. Without the personal journals and the brave co-operation with the assessment by this complainant, the fuller understanding of what had been happening to her would not have been manifest. Her police drafted statement only gave the most equivocal of clues that this was a complex case of questionable Recovered Memory. No-one, including the Crown Prosecution, thought her always remembered credible accounts of physical and emotional abuse required any response, until the issue of sex arose belatedly.*

[Identifying biographical details have been changed in the above cases.]

LEGAL PRINCIPLES AND FORENSIC PSYCHOLOGICAL ASSESSMENTS

The above cases illustrate why the first principle required to be understood by police investigators, prosecutors and the courts is that the problem of complainants' credibility is not ordinary in these cases; memory is a probative issue. In 1998 the Canadian Psychological Association issued the following public policy statement:

"The Canadian Psychological Association recognises the very serious concern of child abuse and child sexual abuse in our society. The Canadian Psychological Association also recognises that justice may not have been served in cases where people have been convicted of offences based solely on 'repressed' or 'recovered' memories of abuse, without further corroborative evidence that the abuse in fact occurred. Developments in the state of our knowledge about repressed or 'Recovered Memories' suggest that such memories, if they exist, may not be sufficiently reliable to serve as the sole basis for a criminal conviction. To the extent that some people may have been convicted of offences based solely upon the testimony of people's 'Recovered Memories', the Canadian Psychological Association urges the Minister of Justice to conduct a special inquiry into this category of convictions."

Many professional psychologists would agree with the statement of the Canadian Psychological Association as it stands. This still leaves open the issue of what counts as reliable corroborative evidence and how far that stands up against other evidence which may throw that testimony into a different light. Although most professional associations have warned that there is no reliable way for true "Recovered Memories" to be distinguished from false ones, some strong advocates who appear as expert witnesses in England have told courts that the current scientific position is that "Recovered Memories" are only likely to be false if they have emerged under the most extreme of sustained suggestive pressure. Contradictory or more sceptical views are said to be an invention by the False Memory Societies and their Advisers.

The legal principle of disclosure is key to the scientific adversarial settlement of these issues. Disclosure of all psychotherapy and healthcare notes, journals and letters is necessary. Police notebook and investigative logs have been found to contain significant evidence. In England many miscarriages of justice can be seen to be due to a single-minded drive to prove one obvious hypothesis. Without the preservation of the trail of development of memories, then reasonable conclusions as to the provenance of such are difficult and potentially misleading. There is a problem. In England the search for evidence which *might* assist a criminal defence case is often considered a "fishing expedition" and courts frown on efforts to discover otherwise private information. Direct attempts to obtain such from those who may be called by the Crown Prosecution as witnesses risk a charge of attempting to pervert the course of justice. Only police investigators are expected to "fish" for evidence. The danger in these cases is not that prosecutors don't disclose all they find (although that sometimes is so) but that they haven't searched hard enough before wrapping up the minimum evidence needed to present a prosecution case based on the single hypothesis. Legal subpoenas may be necessary to overcome reluctance of therapists and their supervisors to hand over their notes.

In English criminal proceedings there is no compulsion for complainants to be psychologically assessed or even interviewed independently of the prosecuting authorities. In cases where intimate physical samples are considered crucial to a prosecution, it is almost unthinkable that a complainant would refuse such an examination, and it would be very unlikely that a prosecution would go forward if that evidence which could prove guilt or innocence was not forthcoming. To date there is no principle to compel complainants to have "Recovered Memories" examined as a precondition to a criminal prosecution. However, a strong steer by a Court has been known to influence the Prosecution to persuade the complainant to co-operate. Examination of the complainant, although only undertaken in a handful of cases, has always led to a change of perspective, indeed an agreed one as between assessors, even if the assessors' overall views about the recovered memory debate may not be the same. In Scotland by some contrast, the interviewing of the other side's witnesses (including expert witnesses) is standard practice. The process is referred to as "precognition".

Confidentiality and privacy
Insofar as legal principles push towards disclosure, this challenges the rights of a complainant to confidentiality and privacy, especially with respect to matters he or she would not reasonably want disclosed to a defendant. The problem in English law is that disclosure usually means disclosure to the defence as a whole. A number of ad hoc arrangements have been tried out which suggest the kind of more formal legal principle required. Sometimes a judge reviews files and decides what material is relevant to the trial. Of course this entirely depends on the judge's appreciation of what is relevant. There can be no informed challenge. An alternative has been for this author to receive files and review them for the defence on the understanding that he will not reveal anything to those instructing him unless he judges it is material to his expert opinion. This depends on informal agreements which may be hard to find in some cases. A suggested compromise is that all confidential material is disclosed to

the experts in the case, and anything claimed to be relevant and disclosable at trial be put to the Judge, allowing arguments to be put if the experts and advocates don't agree. This would at least curtail breaching confidentiality beyond what appears necessary.

Admission of expert testimony
In England the Crown Prosecution cannot call any expert to bolster the credibility of any complainant. This tends to have the result that they do not consult any expert at the early stage of proceedings. Often the full novelty of "Recovered Memories" will not have been made clear through the carefully drafted complainant statements. Complainants, aware of the controversy and the doubts arising, have been known to strategically minimise the novel and Recovered nature of their "Memories". In the first documented criminal case in the U.S. a conviction based on a "Recovered Memory" was finally overturned, not only because doubts persisted about the sincere but arguably false memories from the complainant, Eileen Franklin, but also because she was shown to be making proven false statements in an effort to sustain the credibility of the process by which her putative "Recovered Memories" had arisen (Hansen 1996). As far as the Prosecution is concerned, a bit of "blocking out" seems very understandable. Ideally a complainant needs to be assessed in these circumstances. Otherwise the forensic assessor may be called upon to show why the evidence may be more suspect than it appears. This evidence is usually heard during pre-trial proceedings or "voir dires". Once this sort of evidence is admitted, then the Prosecution can bring in an expert to rebut the psychologist who has raised doubts as to credibility. In so doing, they will be re-bolstering credibility. Decisions on the admissibility of any of this evidence cannot be based on any general acceptance of views within the relevant scientific community since by definition they are disputed views. However, it has only been by hearing disputed views over the years that courts on both sides of the Atlantic have begun to appreciate what has been going on in the controversy as it affects expert evidence and the very phenomena of "Recovered Memories" at the core of the trial issue. A more relaxed attitude to the admissibility of expert evidence is required in this area, coupled with the safeguard of the trier of fact being completely aware that there is a "range of opinion". Although strictly speaking experts in England can give evidence as to research findings and should not comment on the credibility of the complainant per se (that being an exclusive issue for the Court), nevertheless since the whole issue is about credibility then certain questions which clearly are relevant

to that case need to be asked and Judges are moving understandably to a more relaxed attitude as to where they draw the line.

Co-operation of experts

"Recovered Memories" fall at a crossroads of our understanding of trauma, memory and child abuse, not to mention an appreciation of the impact of feminist and psychoanalytic theories on the debate which has powerful social and political ideological components fuelling the controversy. Even those who have regular experience of being instructed in such cases soon realise there are few standard patterns to learn from. Each case (to this author anyhow) has presented an atypical and eccentric challenge. There are few experts comfortable with this range of issues and are ready to construct assessments for these proceedings. It follows therefore that when there are more than one involved, co-operation should be expected and required. Assessments of complainants should be jointly undertaken and planned. Sometimes there are objections that an expert is a male. Even so, by joint planning and the use of video-links it is possible to overcome the special barriers which these cases present, if there is a will to do so, and the Courts make clear they expect it.

Coaching of counsel vs coaching of experts

Experts are required under English law to assist the court regardless of which party has instructed them. There is an expectation of impartiality and where that is clearly compromised, the courts have made their displeasure felt strongly. There has always been a tension between this expectation and the natural helpfulness obtained from an expert to the side who instructs and pays. Experts are trained these days to resist coaching by their own counsel and to avoid tactical traps set by cross examining counsel opposite. In "Recovered Memory" cases the coaching often flows the other way, especially if the complainant has refused to be psychologically assessed by the expert. Counsel will have one chance to conduct a revealing psychological examination by proxy during cross examination. This is not easy. If a tearful, shaking complainant enters the box, her demeanour will be granted as an allowance for her not answering counsel's questions fully. If counsel breaks into an "attack" mode this is likely to be counter productive and to alienate the sympathy of the jury. Here is the abuse being recapitulated in court. On the other hand where questions are gentle and exploratory and encourage the complainant to talk, even if it is not all exactly to the point, then material may be produced freely which actually is highly probative. In one case counsel elicited a completely new "Recovered Memory" from the complainant right there in the witness box. She Recovered what she had been *thinking* about a mark on her T shirt and what she thought her mother would think about that when she was just 3 years of age. Asked why she had never thought of this before, she stated that unless she was asked about something she wouldn't imagine herself back in the circumstances and see and hear what had happened. The jury's faces plainly expressed not their loss of sympathy for this complainant, but their unwillingness from this point to simply accept her whole story as an account of the defendant's villainy. They acquitted.

REFERENCES

Andrews, B., Brewin, C., Ochera, J., Morton, J., Bekerian, D., Davies, G. & Mollon, P. The timing, triggers, and qualities of recovered memories in therapy, *British Journal of Clinical Psychology*, 39, (1), 11–26.

Brown, D., Scheflin, A. and Hammond, D. (1998) *Memory, Trauma Treatment and the Law*, New York: W.W. Norton & Co.

Ceci, S. and Loftus, E. (1994) "Memory Work': A Royal Road to False Memories?'. In Grossman, L. and Pressley, M. (Eds.) Recovery of Memories of Childhood Sexual Abuse, Special issue. *Applied Cognitive Psychology*, 8: 351–64.

Cheit, R. (1998) Consider This, Skeptics of Recovered Memory, *Ethics and Behavior*, 8 (2), 141–160.

Christiansen, S-A and Engleberg, E. (1997) Remembering and forgetting traumatic experiences: a matter for survival. In Conway, M. (Ed) *Recovered Memories and False Memories*. Oxford: Oxford University Press.

Fischoff, B. (1982) 'For those condemned to study the past: heuristics and biases in hindsight'. In Kahneman, D., Slovic, P. and Tversky, A. (Eds.) *Judgement under Uncertainty: Heuristics and Biases*. New York: Cambridge University Press, pp. 335–51.

Gudjonsson, G. (1992) *The Psychology of Interrogations, Confessions, and Testimony*. Chichester U.K.: Wiley.

Hansen, M. (1996) Repressed memory case unravels. *The American Bar Association Journal*, 82, 40.

Herman, J.A. (1992) *Trauma and Recovery*. London: Harper Collins.

Ofshe, R. and Watters, E. (1994) *Making Monsters*. New York: Charles Scribner's Sons.

Read, D. and Lindsay, S. (2000) "Amnesia" for summer camps and high school graduation: Memory work increases reports of prior periods of remembering less. *Journal of Traumatic Stress*, 13 (1), 129–147.

Roediger H., McDermott K., and Goff L. (1997) 'Recovery of true and false memory; paradoxical effects of repeated testing'. In Conway M. (Ed.) *Recovered Memories and False Memories*. Oxford: Oxford University Press.

Schooler J.W., Bendiksen M., and Ambadar Z. (1997) 'Taking the middle line: can we accommodate both fabricated and recovered memories of sexual abuse'. In Conway M. (Ed.) *Recovered Memories and False Memories*. Oxford: Oxford University Press.

Chapter 9

DELAYS IN REPORTING CHILDHOOD SEXUAL ABUSE AND IMPLICATIONS FOR LEGAL PROCEEDINGS

Rosaleen McElvaney

UNDERREPORTING OF SEXUAL CRIMES

It is acknowledged that sexual crimes are underreported in our society. According to Torrey (1991) no more than 10% of the sexual asssaults which take place in the UK, the US and Canada are reported to the police. Edwards (1996) refers to low levels of reporting of rape in the UK, Canada, the US, Australia and New Zealand. Studies have shown that victims may be reluctant to report sexual violence for a variety of reasons (Temkin, 1987; Adler, 1987; Katz and Mazur, 1979). Edwards attributes women's reluctance to report to a combination of elements: fear of retaliation, shame, distrust of the reaction of family and friends, and lack of confidence in the police and the court process. Studies on rape have also shown a reluctance to report if the assailant is known to the victim (McColgan, 1996; Russell, 1984; Winkel and Vrij, 1993). Similarly, studies of adults who were sexually assaulted in childhood show a striking tendency on the part of child victims not to disclose their abuse experiences (Mendel, 1995; Russell, 1983). The same elements are understood to apply, in particular, fears of not wanting their experiences to become public knowledge (U.S. Dept. of Justice, 1994) and secondary victimisation (Holmstrom and Burgess, 1978).

Esselman, Tomz and McGillis (1997) outline the following ways in which victims may experience secondary distress as a consequence of their involvement in the legal process.

(i)   insensitive questioning by police
(ii) attitudes of scepticism or disbelief demonstrated by the police or by the prosecuting authorities
(iii) fear of reprisal by the defendant or his network
(iv) lack of information about the status of the case
(v)   frustration and inconvenience related to delays in court hearings

(vi)   anxiety about testifying in open court

(vii)   hostile questioning by the defence lawyer

In a comparative study of the laws and legal procedures relating to rape and their impact upon victims of rape in the fifteen member states of the European Union, conducted by the Dublin Rape Crisis Centre and the School of Law, Trinity College Dublin, researchers found that in Ireland, all the victims interviewed (n=15) felt less confident, were less articulate and experienced more stress about testifying in court than the interviewees in any other country. The authors suggest that this may be attributed to the adversarial mode of trial, and in particular the style of cross-examination used in adversarial courts. Defence lawyer strategies such as misinterpreting or manipulating the words of the victim, and minimising the effects of the rape upon the victim were experienced as very distressing. The victims felt that they were on trial (Dublin Rape Crisis Centre, 1998).

Some additional factors which can have an influence on victims' decisions to report include the severity of the assault that they experienced, the injuries they may have incurred, the degree of acquaintanceship with the assailant and the level of social support available to them (Greenberg and Ruback, 1992; Ruback, 1993). The social perception of 'classic' rape (stranger, dark alleyway etc.) is often reinforced by the media, and may partly explain why victims whose experiences do not fit the prescribed pattern fail not only to report but even to recognise these as rape. Moreover, societal presumptions and myths about rape may foster feelings of guilt and self-blame which inhibit victims from reporting. McColgan (1996) concludes that many women do not define their experience as rape, particularly if they know their attacker. Widely publicised rape acquittals in particular have a significant impact on women's perception of the criminal justice system, and thus the prospect of acquittal of an attacker will deter other women from reporting in the first place (Edwards, 1996).

Skelton & Buckhart's (1980) experiment in motivation to report on a group of female psychology students confirmed that willingness to report is stronger when more violence is used, and lower when the rapist is an acquaintance of the victim (Winkel and Vrij, 1993). This is particularly relevant to cases of child sexual abuse given that the majority of sexual abuse perpetrators are known to the victim and more often involve coercion rather than violence. Katz and Mazur (1979) cite a survey of rape victims who reported for the following reasons: wanting help for themselves; wanting to protect themselves or others; and feeling that the perpetrator should be punished for what he had done.

The victim is not always the one to take the decision to report the rape. Holmstrom and Burgess (1978) found that in more than half of the adult cases which they examined, someone other than the victim was involved in reporting the rape to the police, in many instances directly contacting the police while in others, persuading the victim to contact the authorities herself. Greenberg and Ruback (1992) found that often it was someone in the victim's social network, her family, partners or friends, who contacted the police.

Despite the growing trend in Ireland in reported sexual offences as noted in Gardai annual reports between 1988 and 1997, from 18% of reported indictable crimes against the person in 1988 to 56% in 1997, it is unclear whether there has been an increase in incidence rates or whether the reported increase reflects an increasing willingness to report such offences (Murphy, 1998).

Blau and McElvaney (1999) reported on the introduction of mandatory reporting to a statutory counselling service in Ireland and the impact of this on numbers attending the service. Following the introduction of reporting procedure, two-thirds of adult clients who had already sought counselling declined the offer when informed that their experiences of childhood sexual abuse would be reported to child protection services. Subsequent monitoring of phonecalls to the service revealed a significant proportion of clients who did not wish to make formal complaints in relation to sexual abuse. Drop-out rates from therapy have also been documented elsewhere. Watson and Levine (1989) reported a drop-out rate of approximately 25% following an actual report by a therapist. Steinberg (1994) surveyed Psychologists about reactions following a report and noted that about 27% of clients dropped out of treatment shortly after the report was made. According to Levine and Doueck (1995), the negative effects of reporting on the therapeutic relationship can be overcome in time but those who drop out when a report is made, or shortly afterwards, usually cannot be reclaimed. According to Blau and Hallahan (1996), family loyalties play a major role in adults' willingness to have their abuse reported to the authorities. Their report on the counselling service found that a significant shift occurred in the pattern of intrafamilial/extrafamilial abuse disclosed by clients attending the service. Women in particular who were willing to have their abuse reported were those who were sexually abused by someone outside the family.

LEGAL IMPLICATIONS OF NON-DISCLOSURE

In recent years, delays in reporting childhood sexual abuse are being highlighted in the increasing number of cases coming before the courts which involve adult complainants reporting childhood sexual abuse. Given the delay between the occurrence of the alleged abuse and the time of the formal complaint, this has presented a challenge to our legal system. The legal and constitutional position is that a person charged with a criminal offence is entitled, as part of their right to be tried in due course of law, to a trial with reasonable expedition (see Finlay C. J. in *State (O'Connell) v Fawsitt* (1985) 1 R 3762 at 378., Article 38. 1, Irish Constitution). The right to reasonable expedition needs to be evaluated in each individual case. Finlay (1994) relied on those as being length of delay, reason for the delay, the defendant's assertion of their right and the prejudice to the defendant by the delay. The defendant in criminal prosecution proceedings can therefore seek to have the decision to prosecute judicially reviewed by the High Court, claiming that the delay in the institution of criminal proceedings has irreparably prejudiced the prospect that the defendant would get a fair trial.

Delays in criminal proceedings can be very difficult for victims to endure. Ironically, although the accused has a Constitutional right to a speedy trial, it is a common defence strategy to delay the trial for as long as possible. This is because witnesses die or move away, memories fade, and the emotional impact of the crime diminishes. This delay strategy is described in an oft-cited adage of the defence bar: "a good defence, like a good wine, gets better with age".

The Report of the Inquiry into matters relating to child sexual abuse in swimming (Government of Ireland, 1998) noted that witnesses complained of the legal process whereby the prosecution of the accused was prohibited by the court largely because of the delay in making the complaint: "the test is whether there is a real risk the applicant by reason of the delay would not obtain a fair trial, that the trial would be unfair as a consequence of the delay." (p. 79). In the case *G v DPP and District Judge Kirby* (1994), it was noted that the Court might be satisfied and justified in reaching the conclusion that the extent to which the applicant had contributed to the delay in revealing offences and the subsequent reporting to the prosecution authorities meant that he should not be entitled to the order (i.e. prohibition of the trial proceeding).

Judge Denham of the Supreme Court in *B v DPP* (1997) cautioned that each case should be treated individually and that no definite time limit or exhaustive list of factors should determine the outcome of such cases. She noted that where dominion was exercised in family relations by the accused over the complainants, this prevented the complainants taking steps to proceed within a more usual time frame. She did not elaborate as to what the court would consider to be a more usual time frame in cases of sexual abuse. Another Supreme Court judgement, Keane in *C v DPP* (1998) broadened the definition of dominion in a case which involved a delay of 13 years. In this case, the accused, a coach driver, was according to Justice Keane in a position of trust in relation to his child passengers and given the disparity in age the question to be considered was whether the delay was referrable to the accused's own actions. Morris J. (1998) in *JOC v DPP* (unreported) reported a case where a potential alibi had since died and combined with understandable poor memory on the part of the accused acknowledged that even though the delay may have been attributable to the accused's conduct, the effect of such delay would result in the applicant being deprived of a fair trial. In concluding, the Judge referred to the poor health of the applicant and his limited capacity to defend himself. The judgement allowed the prohibition of the trial on the grounds that the applicant's constitutional rights would be breached by such a trial.

These cases understandably focus on legal arguments. However, there would appear to be a growing recognition of the psychological dynamics of child sexual abuse and how these dynamics interplay with a child's reluctance to report their experiences of sexual abuse. Keane, J. (1998) acknowledged that there are cases where disparity in age is such that the possibility arises that the failure to report the offence is explicable, "having regard to the reluctance of young children to accuse adults of improper behaviour and feelings of guilt and shame experienced by the child because of his or her participation, albeit unwillingly, in what he or she sees as wrongdoing; In addition, of course, in individual cases there may be threats, actual or implied, of punishment if the alleged offences are reported. . . ." The delay may also be more readily explicable "where (the person) occupies a particular role in relation to him or her – dominion by the alleged perpetrator over the child and a degree of trust on the part of the child may be more readily inferred" (p. 5). However, Justice Keane did not acknowledge that this reluctance may be inherent in the experience of sexual abuse: "clearly, the fact that the offence charged is of a sexual nature is not of itself a factor which would justify the Court in disregarding the delay, however inordinate, and allowing the trial to proceed". Rather, he placed the emphasis on "Whether the court is satisfied as a matter of probability that, assuming the complaint to be truthful, the delay in making it was referable to the accused's own actions." Thus it is the task of the prosecution to 'prove' that the delay was the fault of the accused. However, Justice Denham did acknowledge that it was the very nature of the offence of childhood sexual abuse which prevents early complaint (Denham, 1997).

CHILD SEXUAL ABUSE AS SYNDROME OF SECRECY

It is accepted among theorists and practitioners working in the field of child sexual abuse that the abuse experience is secretive in nature. Among clinicians, it is regarded as inherent in the nature of sexual abuse that a child often does not disclose the abuse and even as the child grows into adulthood a number of factors inhibit the individual from making this disclosure. These factors are associated to some extent with the individual and his or her own family circumstances, the abuse and its effects, societal responses to disclosures of sexual abuse and the nature of legal proceedings.

Furniss (1991) discusses child sexual abuse as a syndrome of secrecy for the child which is determined by external factors, by specific aspects of secrecy in the abusive interaction itself and by internal psychological factors. *External factors of secrecy* include the lack of forensic proof or medical evidence in the majority of cases; the reliance on the verbal accusation of the child or of another person on the child's behalf in the face of denial on the part of the abuser; the secrecy intrinsic to the experience – abused children are often told not to tell anyone and are sometimes threatened with violent consequences either to themselves or to family members. In many cases children have been threatened that they will be sent away, that the abuser may kill them or may kill themselves, that the marriage of the parents will break up and that the disclosure will lead to family disintegration. The full range of threats from the warning that nobody will believe the child anyway to the threat of murder constitutes a strong external factor for the child not to disclose. *Interactional aspects of secrecy* refer to the interaction between the abuser and the child. The abusive interaction is often carried out in a manner which in many respects denies the reality of what is taking place. Furniss describes how this occurs on three contextual levels. Firstly by the context in which the abuse takes place. Children often describe how the abuse would take place in silence or without any eye contact or in total darkness and with drawn curtains, even if nobody would have been able to look in from outside; the child often reports conflicting physiological sensations of both heightened anxiety and arousal or pain which leads to confusion. Secondly, by the change of the abuser into 'the other person'. Sexual abusers in states of sexual arousal often behave very differently from their usual self and this can be very frightening when someone familiar to the child turns into 'the other person' with changed gestures, unusual speaking pattern, altered tone of voice and strange physical behaviour. This does not allow the child to perceive reality as reality and to name the experience of the abuse as abuse. Thirdly, by a further interactional layer of denial through entrance and exit rituals: the entrance ritual serves to transform an ordinary father–child interaction into the 'other person'–child interaction without naming this transition. This process is reversed in the exit ritual. Abusers usually try to avoid any open recognition of what is happening. The time span and the experience can be cut out from their mutually recognised reality as if it had never existed.

Finally, Furniss discusses internal psychological factors as determining child sexual abuse as a syndrome of secrecy. Summit (1983) in describing the child sexual abuse accommodation syndrome referred to how secrecy and helplessness and possible unpredictability and threat to life are constantly reinforced in renewed invasions into the child's physical and mental integrity and autonomy. The child psychologically adapts to the sexual abuse and accommodates so that life is turned into a seemingly normal event allowing for psychological survival.

Anna Salter draws on her experience of working with both victims and offenders in describing the grooming process and highlighting the difficulties for the victim in disclosing child sexual abuse. According to Salter (1995) the nature of sexual abuse is usually secretive and furtive and specifically designed to reduce the possibility that the child will tell. If the disclosure is early enough, the offender often has not broken the law, or has broken it minimally. There is a high risk that the disclosure will be either disbelieved or dismissed. Later disclosures concern behaviour more difficult to minimise, but it produces more negative sequelae for survivors. Not disclosing at an early stage gives rise to difficulties in recognising where the responsibility for the abuse lies. Children often believe that because they did not disclose the abuse earlier they are in some way culpable (why didn't I say it earlier?, people will think I have something to hide; if I was innocent, I would have said it sooner). Salter notes that some offenders do not even discuss disclosure because they assume the child either will not tell or will not be credible. Particularly with young children, offenders may not discuss disclosure because they do not want the child to know there is anything inappropriate about the behaviour (Salter, 1995).

Research has indicated that those factors which may inhibit males to disclose their abuse experiences include (a) a belief that men are not victims and, if they are, that they are less traumatised by victimising experience than are females; (b) feelings of shame based on the perceived failure to protect oneself or to achieve appropriate revenge against the offender; (c) exaggerated efforts to reassert masculine identity in an attempt to compensate for the failure to protect oneself; (d) behaviour patterns with power/control dynamics due to attempts to overcompensate for the powerlessness experienced during the abuse; (e) externalisation of feelings due to social prescriptions that males can act on, but not express, their feelings (Mendel, 1995).

JUDICIAL REVIEW PROCEEDINGS AND PSYCHOLOGICAL ASSESSMENT

As mentioned above, there have been an increasing number of cases being heard by the High Court which seek to prohibit a criminal trial involving a delayed complaint of child sexual abuse. As part of the Judicial Review Proceedings, the court will often request that a psychological assessment be carried out to assist the court in determining the reasons for the delay in reporting. The request for assessment is to ascertain whether the abuse complained of has had any effects, and if so, what effects, including long term and short term effects, on the victim and in particular whether any and if so, which effects may have inhibited him/her from complaining of the said abuse until he/she did so.

The trauma literature suggests, according to Briere (1997), that the amount of posttraumatic symptomatology an individual experiences is a function of at least four broad variables:

1. characteristics of the stressor: in this case, the nature of the abuse;
2. variables specific to the victim: The impact of abuse can vary according to the psychological makeup of the individual child, his or her personal experiences prior to the abuse and resultant coping strategies. However, it is also noteworthy that a number of child molesters report that their assessment of the child's degree of loneliness and distress is a factor in targeting children for sexual abuse and the finding that vulnerable children may be more often targeted by sex offenders is supported by some research on victims (Salter, 1995). According to

Salter, children are in every case hungry for love, but offenders sometimes choose children who are starving for it;

3. subjective response to the stressor: how the child reacted to the abuse; and

4. the response of others to the victim: the social supports available to the child e.g. someone to tell.

In order to assess the impact of a particular event, it is therefore necessary to see the victim and question them in detail about their personal history and current life functioning. This is often experienced as intrusive, triggering anxieties and fears which relate directly to the childhood abuse experience. The author, through her private practice, has been involved in this assessment process and has selected a sample of ten individuals seen over a ten-month period in 1998/1999. The individuals were contacted some time after their assessment and all gave written permission for their material to be used for this paper. Of the sample of ten individuals, seven were men and three were women; all but one of the men were allegedly abused in residential institutions, the exception being a man who was allegedly abused by his employer; all three women were allegedly abused in a non-residential educational institution. Out of the ten, three initiated the report themselves; the remaining seven were approached and asked to make statements to the Gardai as part of ongoing investigations. Most of the latter expressed reluctance initially to make a formal complaint; one individual said he would never have made a formal complaint if he had not received reassurance that he could withdraw at any time. Others referred to their realising that they had a responsibility to other children. Delays in reporting ranged from 20 years to 50 years. The alleged abusers were all male.

The impetus for this paper arose out of the author's concerns arising from these assessments. Firstly, the author was struck by the high level of presenting symptomatology (see Figure 1 below). For the most part, this symptomatology was consistent with the onset of severe distress directly resulting from the legal proceedings. Whilst this is not unusual, these legal proceedings were significantly protracted, in some cases going on for several years. It was clear from the interviews that many individuals had experienced considerable disruption in their lives, in some cases severe marital difficulties since the time of the report. From a psychological point of view, their functioning had deteriorated significantly, they were extremely upset by the resurgence of memories relating to the sexual abuse and this situation was being maintained with little opportunity for resolution by protracted legal investigations and hearings. In addition to the stress experienced as a result of the legal process, all of the interviewees commented spontaneously on how stressful it was for them to participate in the assessment process and discuss experiences which they were actively trying to put behind them. Many noted that if they had known what was to be involved they would never have made the report. Some individuals expressed resentment in having to come for the appointment and all were confused as to the purpose of the assessment. The author has considerable experience of adults seeking counselling for experiences of childhood sexual abuse and in particular of adults' reluctance to report their experiences to the legal authorities. The question of encouraging people to make such reports is a challenge to all healthcare professionals but must also involve our colleagues in the legal professions. The concern therefore arising from these assessments was that this legal procedure would act as an inhibitor to future potential complainants.

In relation to symptomatology presented, eight of the sample met all six criteria for diagnosis of PTSD (DSM IV, 1994) as measured by the Posttraumatic Diagnostic Scale (Foa, 1995), the remaining two meeting all criteria except criterion A, which defines a traumatic event as involving actual or fear of physical injury. Figure 1 depicts the number of scales on the PDS, the Traumatic Symptom Inventory (Briere, 1994) and the Brief Symptom Inventory (Derogatis, 1993) which individuals endorsed at a clinical level of significance.

REASONS FOR DELAYS IN REPORTING

Individuals were asked an open-ended question as to why they did not make a formal complaint earlier than they did. The reasons given are outlined as follows:

Fear that they would not be believed

In all, seven said they did not think they would have been believed and three referred to believing that the Gardai would not believe such a story. One woman described how the alleged perpetrator was seen as a 'gentleman' and 'a saint' in the eyes of her parents. She imagined her mother might have said something like "a good decent man like. . . . don't be telling lies".

Fear of consequences of reporting

Two men said they would be called 'queer'; another two men feared they would be punished e.g. beaten, "I would be put away for saying such a

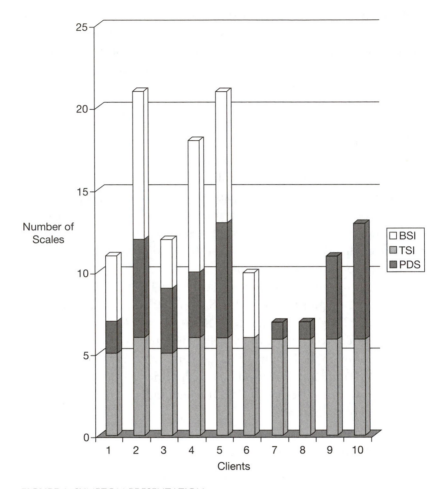

FIGURE 1: SYMPTOM PRESENTATION

thing"; one man said he did not want people to know because of what they would think of him; two women believed that their mother would have felt totally disgraced by a public disclosure. In the latter case, parents had known of the alleged abuse ("it would have destroyed her"). One woman spoke of her fear of retaliation in the local community; another expressed concern for how the court case would impact on her family. Finally, one woman thought that she would need money to pay Solicitor's fees in order to pursue the matter legally and she could not afford this. She also feared that she could be sued for saying something of this nature.

Shame

Most individuals spoke of their embarrassment talking about the alleged abuse, feeling ashamed and disgusted about what happened. Several of the sample had never told anyone prior to making the formal report and had as yet not told significant people in their lives such as close family, employers and friends. One man described how he has even encouraged an individual to make a statement without divulging that he himself has already made a statement.

Abuse as a common experience in institutions

Four individuals noted that it was common knowledge in the institution in which they lived that children were being sexually abused.

Fear of alleged perpetrator

Three individuals referred to their fear of the alleged perpetrator.

Having no one to tell

In particular for those individuals who had allegedly been abused in institutions, the only authority figures available were the staff of the institution who were perceived as allies of the alleged perpetrator. These children did not have access to other professionals outside the institution and many did not have regular contact with their families. Two other individuals believed that to disclose at home would have brought more trouble on them.

Wish to forget about it

This was particularly relevant for people as they reached adulthood. For all of the individuals in this sample, their way of coping with their experiences was to avoid any behaviour which would have triggered memories of the abuse and the concomitant feelings associated with such. "I avoided thinking about it, talking about it, visiting places which would remind me of it, reading abut childhood abuse in newspapers, watching news items on television." Three individuals who had lived abroad for a period of time noted that this had helped them to avoid thinking about their childhood experiences and hearing about child sexual abuse in Ireland.

Lack of appreciation of the impact of the alleged abuse

All of the sample lacked an understanding until more recent years that their experiences were firstly abusive and secondly that they may have had some impact on their development. There was little recognition among professionals, least of all children, of what constituted a "sexual assault". These adults would, as children, have had neither the language to describe nor the understanding to conceptualise the behaviour as sexually abusive.

Many individuals also talked about why they had eventually come to the decision to make a formal complaint. The reason most commonly given was the realisation that the alleged abuser may present a risk to others in those cases where this individual was now married with children of their own, or in positions where they had regular unsupervised access to children through their work. As noted above, only three of the sample had initiated the report. Of those seven who made statements on request, all stated that they did not envisage that they would ever have initiated a report themselves. However, two men talked about their realisation that they were not going to be able to leave this part of their lives behind them unless they co-operated with the investigation. One expressed hope for the future in being able to turn his life around. Another woman talked about the growing compulsion to right the wrong perceived to have been done to her. One woman described her reaction to being approached by the Gardai as one of relief, that at last some action was being taken against the alleged perpetrator.

CONCLUSION

Although the collation of material from the assessment of these ten individuals is perhaps helpful in adding to the literature on why adults have difficulty reporting childhood sexual abuse, the striking feature of this material is that it tells us nothing new. The additional difficulties experienced by those who described being abused in residential institutions are consistent with those written about by Peake and Michaels (1996) in relation to children's reasons for not disclosing abuse in institutions. It therefore begs the question of the necessity of compelling adults to undergo the process of evaluation as part of legal proceedings when these evaluations have the potential to be of themselves traumatic. The courts insist on requesting individual assessment reports and decry the use of general reports from expert witnesses which might prove just as helpful in assisting the fact finders of the legal system, prevent further traumatisation of complainants and if not encourage adults to come forward and perform their civic duty to report crimes at least not deter them further.

REFERENCES

Adler, Z. (1987). *Rape on Trial*, London: Routledge and Kegan Paul.

American Psychiatric Association (1994). *Diagnostic Statistical manual for mental disorders (4th edition)*, Washington DC: American Psychiatric Press.

Blau, I. & Hallahan, E. (1995). Adult Disclosure of C.S.A. prior to and during Counselling – a protective measure for children at risk. Presentation at 11th International Congress on Child Abuse and Neglect, Dublin.

Blau, I. & McElvaney, R. (1999). Mandated Reporting in an adult counselling service. Presentation at 9th Conference of European Association of Psychology and Law, Dublin.

Briere, J. (1995). *Trauma Symtom Inventory*, Odessa: Psychological Assessment Resources.

Briere, J. (1997). *Psychological Assessment of Adult Posttraumatic States*, Washington DC: American Psychological Association.

Denham, J. (1997). B v DPP. (Unreported Judgement).

Derogatis, L.R. (1993). *Brief Symptom Inventory*, Minneapolis: National Computer Systems.

Dublin Rape Crisis Centre (1998). *The Legal Process and Victims of Rape*, Dublin: The Dublin Rape Crisis Centre.

Edwards, S. (1996). *Sex and Gender in the Legal Process*, London: Blackstone.

Elliott, D.M. & Briere, J. N. (1994). Forensic sexual abuse evaluation of older children: Disclosures and symptomatology, *Behavioural Sciences and the Law*, **12**, 261–277.

Esselman, Tomz, J. & McGillis, D. (1997). *Serving Crime Victims and Witnesses*, Washington: U.S. Department of Justice.

Finkelhor, D. (1984). *Child sexual abuse: New Theory and research*, New York: Free Press.

Finlay, C.J. (1986). State (O'Connell) v Fawsitt, IR 362.

Finlay, C.J. (1994) DPP v Byrne.

Foa, E. (1995). *The Posttraumatic Diagnostic Scale*, Washington DC: American Psychiatric Press.

Furniss, T. (1991) *The Multiprofessional Handbook of Child Sexual Abuse*, London: Routledge.

Gannon, J. (1976). State (Healy) v Donoghue, IR 325.

Government of Ireland (1937), *The Irish Constitution*, Dublin: Stationery Office.

Government of Ireland (1998). *Report of the Independent Inquiry into Matters Relations to Child Sexual Abuse in Swimming*, Dublin: Stationery Office.

Greenberg, M.S. & Ruback, R.B. (1992). *After the crime: Victim decision-making*, New York: Plenum Press.

Holmstrom, L. & Burgess, A. (1978). *The victim of rape: Institutional reactions*, New York: Wiley & Sons.

Katz, S. & Mazur, M.A. (1979). *Understanding the rape victim: a synthesis of research findings*, New York: Wiley & Sons.

Keane, F. (1998). C v DPP.

Levine, M. & Doueck, H. (1995). *The Impact of Mandated Reporting on the Therapeutic Process*, Thousand Oaks, CA: Sage.

McColgan, A. (1996). *The case for taking the date out of rape*. London: Pandora

Mendel, M. (1995). *The male survivor: The impact of sexual abuse*. Thousand Oaks, CA: Sage.

Morris, J. (1998). JOC v DPP (unreported).

Murphy, P. (1998). Maximising Community Safety – The Treatment and Management of Imprisoned Sex Offenders, Paper presented at Irish Penal Reform Trust Conference, Dublin.

Peake, A. & Michaels, M. (1996). *Working with Sexually Abused Children*. Oxford Brookes University.

Ruback, R.B. (1993). Comment on Backhman: the victim-offender relationship does affect victims'decisions to report sexual assaults. *Criminal Justice and Behaviour*, **20**, 271–279.

Russell, D. E. H. (1983). The incidence and prevalence of intrafmilial and extrafamilial sexual abuse of female children. *Child Abuse & Neglect*, 7, 133–146.

Russell, D. (1984) *Sexual exploitation: rape, child abuse and workplace harrassment*. California: Sage.

Salter, A. (1995) *Transforming Trauma*. California: Sage.

Skelton, C.A. & Buckhart, B.R. (1980) Sexual assault: determinants of victim disclosure. *Criminal Justice and Behaviour*, 7, 229–236.

Temkin, J. (1987). *Rape and the Legal Process*. London: Sweet and Maxwell.

Torrey, M. (1991). When will we be believed? Rape myths and the idea of a fair trial in rape prosecutions. *Davis Law Review*, 24, 1013.

U.S. Dept. of Justice, Bureau of Justice Statistics (1994), *Criminal victimization in the United States*, Washington DC: U.S. Dept of Justice, Bureau of Justice Statistics.

Winkel, F.W. & Vrij, A. (1993). Rape reporting to the police: exploring the social psychological impact of, *International Review of Victimology*, 2, 277–294.

Chapter 10

DEVELOPING A DESCRIPTIVE MODEL OF THE OFFENCE CHAINS OF NEW ZEALAND RAPISTS: TAXONOMIC IMPLICATIONS

Devon L. L. Polaschek, Tony Ward, Stephen M. Hudson and Richard J. Siegert

Why do men rape? The question reliably sparks debate among researchers and lay people, and is one of the most fundamental issues in understanding rape. A challenge in theorising about rape is heterogeneity, both in characteristics of offenders and in the features of the offence behaviour itself. There is a long history of examining the motives and goals of rapists, and this body of work suggests a number of variables that may be useful in understanding the heterogeneity of rape offending (Polaschek, Ward, & Hudson, 1997).

Knight, Rosenberg and Schneider's (1985) review of rapist typologies described four major components: physical aggression, antisociality, paraphilia and sadism. First, researchers and clinicians have examined the amount of aggression or violence in the offence, and drawn inferences from the level of aggression to its function, as well as to the intentions of the aggressor. Most often, research makes a distinction between instrumental and expressive violence. Instrumental violence is violence in the service of other goals; the rapist uses force sufficient to complete the intended sexual behaviour. Put another way, instrumental violence is aggression as a means to an end. By contrast, expressive violence is aggression in which the main intent is to hurt the victim, and to vent anger rather than to directly alter victim behaviour. However, intentionality may not be related directly either to the level of physical violence or the victim's injuries (Pollard, 1994; Rosenberg, Knight, Prentky, & Lee, 1988). Moreover, violent behaviour commonly involves simultaneous expressive and instrumental intents (Berkowitz, 1993; Indemaur, 1995). In short, this distinction may have more intuitive appeal than practical value.

When relatively low levels of aggression are evident, the second and third major typological components distinguish between offences that appear to result from sexual preoccupations (i.e., paraphilic motives) and those committed in association with antisocial personality features such as impulsivity and low emotional reactivity. When high levels of aggression are a feature, the fourth and final component establishes whether sadism was present or absent. In sadistic assaults the offender inflicts physical harm on the victim to enhance his sexual gratification. Otherwise, he uses violence to hurt the victim for reasons such as revenge, that are not associated with the offender's sexuality per se (Prentky & Knight, 1991; Prentky, Cohen, & Seghorn, 1985).

Many typologies of rape have been suggested over the years, but few have any empirical basis. One of the most widely known is the work of Groth and colleagues (Groth & Birnbaum, 1979; Groth, Burgess, and Holmstrom, 1977). Derived from clinical strategies, this psycho-dynamically oriented classification system describes four different subtypes of rape, based on two major motives: power and anger.

In Groth's view, the main goal of power rape is sexual conquest: using force to make the victim submit reinforces the offender's self esteem. In the first subtype, the *power-assertive* rape, the offender believes it is his right to use rape to express his virility and dominance over women and to keep them "in their place". In the second subtype, the *power-reassurance* rape, the rapist wants to get a woman into a position in which he has her under control, in order to prevent possible rejection and the generation of feelings of personal inadequacy (Groth et al., 1977).

Anger rapes, by contrast, occur when offenders use sexual assault as a vehicle for rage, contempt and hatred for their victim. These offenders use excessive levels of violence, cause serious physical injury to victims, and may force them to engage in humiliating and degrading acts. Often the anger is viewed as arising from the displacement of conflict with significant other women in the perpetrator's life. The offender is said to have negative attitudes to sex and sexual dysfunction is common. The third subtype, *anger-retaliation* rapes, are motivated by revenge and the aim is to hurt and degrade the victim. Lastly, in *anger-excitation* rapes, the perpetrator is sexually aroused by the victim's suffering. In later versions, Groth and colleagues refer to anger-excitation rapes as *sadistic* (Groth & Birnbaum, 1980).

Since its initial development, empirical research on this typology has been sparse. Groth et al. (1977) reported base rates for each rape type, in an examination of 225 offences from a combined sample of offenders and unrelated victims. Overall they found that twice as many offences were classified as power rapes than as anger rapes (65% vs. 35%). Of the power rapes, 52% of the victims' experiences and 38% of offenders' offences were categorised as power-assertive rapes. Of the anger rapes, 40% of the offender sample and 15% of the victims' descriptions were classified as anger-retaliation respectively. Anger-excitation rapes were uncommon, making up 6% of the offenders' and 4% of the victims' samples. Groth and colleagues didn't speculate on the apparent marked differences in frequency of some subtypes across the two samples.

Knight and Prentky (1990; Prentky & Knight, 1991) have developed empirically driven classificatory taxonomies. As with Groth, they are associated with the Massachusetts Treatment Center for serious sexual offenders. The most recent version of their taxonomy, the MTC:R3, contains nine subtypes that are initially organised around four mutually exclusive primary motives for rape. These motives are called *opportunistic*, *pervasive anger*, *sexual* and *vindictive*.

An *opportunistic* rape is motivated by impulsive exploitation of the victim for the purpose of immediate sexual gratification, because the offender finds himself in an environment that affords easy access to sex. *Pervasively angry* rapes occur when an offender with chronic, global, excessive anger loses control of this anger and vents it injuriously on a woman. *Sexual* rapes are driven by protracted sexual fantasies (sadistic or non-sadistic) in an offender who experiences his sexual urges as difficult to control. Lastly, *vindictive* rapes are physically injurious offences carried out by men whose anger and desire to humiliate are exclusively focused on women.

A second-tier social competence variable asymmetrically divides the MTC:R3's four primary motives into 9 subtypes. They are (1) opportunistic–high social competence; (2) opportunistic–low social competence; (3) pervasively angry; (4) sexually sadistic–overt, (5) sexually sadistic–muted; (6) sexually non-sadistic–high social competence; (7) sexually non-sadistic–low social competence; (8) vindictive–moderate social competence; and (9) vindictive–low social competence.

One of the interesting research questions with both Groth's system and the MTC:R3 is the extent to which they may generalise across cultures. There are a number of reasons why we might expect these classification systems not to generalise well. For example, they were developed on a distinctive sample of highly recidivist or highly violent rapists from a large population base, selected for the severity of offence behaviour or underlying pathology. Indeed, early indications regarding generalisability are not entirely encouraging. For example, one assessment using the MTC:R3 with a sample of 80 incarcerated rapists which included some "first offenders" found 25% of the subjects to be unclassifiable. Of the

75% that were classifiable, only one offender was assigned to the "pervasively angry" category (Barbaree, Seto, Serin, Amos, & Preston, 1994).

The present study examines the applicability of Groth's and of Knight and Prentky's classification systems to another sample. It is part of a programme of research in which we have sought to develop descriptive models of offending constructed primarily from information from offenders about how they set about committing their offences. This offence process research provides a novel way of examining the implications of offender heterogeneity for theorising and treatment design. Because offence chain models are based on the temporal sequence of cognitive, affective, volitional and behavioural offence elements, they offer a unique opportunity to examine taxonomic issues in a temporal framework.

The aim of the present study was to develop a preliminary descriptive model of the offending of men who sexually assault adults. The findings are examined with particular emphasis on their implications for offender and offence classification.

METHOD

Participants

Participants were 24 European New Zealand men currently serving a prison sentence for sexual violation or attempted sexual violation of a person over the age of 16 years. They were from five prisons throughout New Zealand. Non-Europeans (New Zealand Maori and men from the other Pacific nations) were intentionally excluded from participation in this first phase of model development, in order to limit the introduction of biases attributable to differences in culture between coders and participants. Of the 32 participants who were approached, 8 declined, yielding a participation rate of 75%.

The average age of participants at the time of the index sexual violation was 31.8 years ($SD = 7.6$, range 21–44 years). Mean sentence length was 7 years ($SD = 2.3$, range 3–10 years). Two participants were on indefinite sentences. Mean age at first conviction was 23.0 years ($SD = 8.5$, range 15–45). Five had no previous convictions. The remaining 19 participants on average had 13.3 previous convictions of which most were property, driving and minor drug offences. Ten had previous convictions for violence and 5 for sexual offending.

There were 31 index (i.e., current sentence) sexual offences involving 27 victims, of whom two were male. Seven offences were against current or estranged wives or de facto partners. Nine victims were strangers, and eight were casual acquaintances. Four offences were committed by fathers and 3 by close friends. Most participants admitted their offending but 11 were in denial; they asserted that they had been involved in consensual sexual activity with the victim. Five men had received psychological treatment related to their offending since commencing their sentence.

Procedure

Demographic and preliminary offence-related information was obtained from participants' institutional files. Following perusal of the file information, participants were interviewed about the target offence and events leading up to it. Interviews were audiotaped for later reference if necessary. However, the main data presented here were derived from an oral narrative of the offence constructed by the offender with prompting from the researcher, and typed into a portable computer by the researcher during the interview. This narrative is referred to as the *offence chain*. Most participants readily described the events that unfolded, but required prompting to included details of their thinking, affective responses and the volitional components of the resulting offence chain. The section of the interview in which data for the offence chain were gathered generally took from 1 to 3 hours to complete.

All data were collected by the first author, who was experienced and trained in this type of interviewing with offenders.

RESULTS

Data analysis procedure

Once the offence chains were developed, they were analysed using Strauss and Corbin's (1990) grounded theory procedures. In the first stage, the narratives were broken down by the first author into meaning units: small blocks of text generally containing single phrases. After this first phase of data analysis, all four authors were involved in different aspects of the data analysis, to maximise the utility and generalisability of the model.

In the second phase of analysis, the meaning units were coded into provisional categories on the basis of their semantic similarity with other units. Descriptive names were developed for each category to best capture the common semantic content of the category at the lowest possible level of abstraction. For example, the meaning unit /she was an attractive girl/ was assigned to the provisional category *attractiveness*. Each meaning unit was assigned to one or more categories (multiple coding; Straus &

Corbin, 1990) and a new category was created if the concept did not fit any existing category. The first 6 offence chains were coded in this way. Once this coding was completed, provisional categories were either combined or subsumed under other, more abstract categories. For example, the provisional category *attractiveness* subsequently became a subcategory of the more abstract category *initial appraisal of the victim*.

Next, further offence chain meaning units from new interviews were coded and used to test the adequacy of these provisional categories. Categories were expanded or collapsed to a more abstract level to accommodate more data, and where necessary new categories were developed to allow new data to be incorporated.

When 10 offence chains had been coded, the derived categories were organised into a preliminary temporal sequence. The process of checking back through the offence chains as we developed the model resulted in further collapsing and refinement of categories. Finally, the remaining 14 offence chains were coded, categorised and used to check the accuracy of the model. Yet more refinement and abstraction, as well as the addition of some new categories led to the final model. A diagrammatic representation was constructed, containing 21 categories and 43 subcategories (see Figure 1).

The preliminary model

For clarity of presentation the model is divided into six phases containing between three and five main categories each. The six phases were: I *Background*, II *Goal formation*, III *Approach*, IV *Preparation*, V *Offence*, and VI *Post-offence*. The full preliminary model (the Rape Model, or RM) is presented in Figure 1. Below we describe the features of the model, phase by phase. Although two of the victims were male, in order to protect their identity, all references to victims use female pronouns.

Phase I: Background factors covers the offender's lifestyle and circumstances in the days, weeks or months prior to offending (see the top of Figure 1). It includes employment, relationships with others, leisure time, finances and alcohol and drug use, as well as the impact of any historical difficulties on day to day living. The two subcategories, *generally positive* and *generally negative*, reflect the overall affective tone of this background. The offender's *style of management* or *coping style* was either problem-based (problems that arose were addressed directly with the offender often regaining positive affect as a result), or *emotion-based* (the offender attempted only to ameliorate the resulting negative affect rather than directly focusing on solving the problem). Emotion-based coping often resulted in temporary positive affect, but over longer time periods, stress and negative affect spiralled because of the accumulation of unsolved problems. *Proximal mood* refers to events of the last few hours. There were three subcategories, *positive*, *depressed* or *angry*.

Phase II: Goal formation begins with the process of establishing the dominant goals that the offence ultimately is intended to achieve. There were two dominant goals, *seeking sexual gratification* and *redressing harm to self*. Those seeking sexual gratification were doing so either to enhance an existing positive mood, or to escape an existing negative mood. Those redressing harm perceived to have been inflicted on them by others sought either to harm someone else directly, or to resolve the problem generating the harm by confronting the person perceived as its source. Once goals were established, offenders began planning. Their explicit plans had three foci: *sexual access*, *sexual assault*, or *non-sexual redress of harm*. Some offenders appeared to do no planning at all, moving straight from deciding on their goal to enacting it.

Phase III: Approach begins with an *encounter with the victim*; the initial approach behaviour that leads to the *communication of intent* to the victim. For some, communication of intent was *indirect*; offenders "chatted up" a victim, grooming her to undermine the likelihood of engendering resistance. With *direct* communication, the offender informed the victim directly of what his goal was, either verbally, or by using direct physical force, such as abducting her and threatening her with violence. *Victims' responses* to this communication were reported by offenders to be either *compliant* or *resistant*. Victims' behaviour was reported as more actively resistant in the approach phase than during the assault itself. However, compliant behaviour was also reported, and offenders often interpreted apparent compliance as indicating implicit consent, despite the coercive context.

Offenders' *evaluation of progress towards goal* was generally based on their interpretation of the victim's response. They made *positive* evaluations when the victim was either perceived to be consenting to sex, or when they thought they had her under control. In *negative* evaluations, the victim was perceived to be thwarting the offender, or disrupting his intentions.

Following evaluation, about one-third of the sample *established secondary goals*. These goals reflected a change in direction. Rapists either added an extra goal to their original one (e.g., getting *sexual gratification* in addition to harming her), or changed the original for a new one (e.g., *victim harm*: deciding to punish the victim instead of *interpersonal*

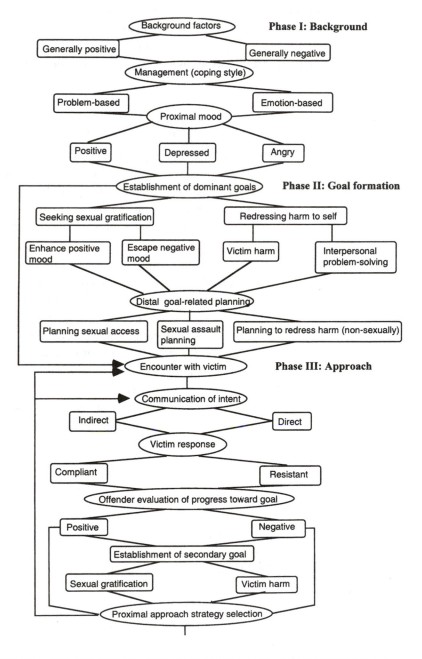

FIGURE 1: THE PRELIMINARY RAPE MODEL SHOWING MAJOR CATEGORIES AND SUBCATEGORIES

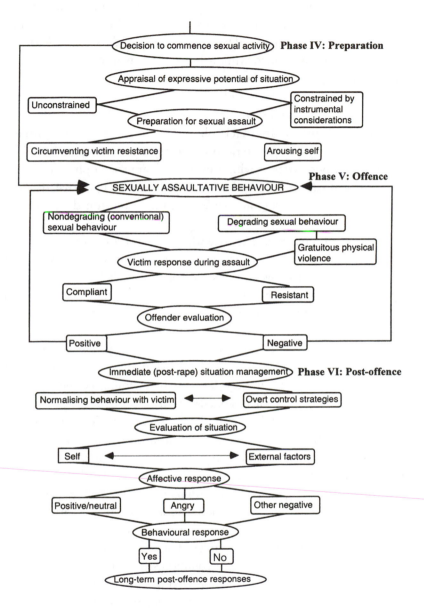

FIGURE 1: CONTINUED

problem-solving: resolving interpersonal conflict). Those who had just made negative evaluations were most likely to form secondary goals. Secondary *sexual gratification* goals were formed by men whose initial dominant goal was non-sexual harm redress. Secondary *victim harm* goals were formed both by men who at first simply wanted sex, and by men whose initial approach to the victim was to solve problems with her. These men were often angry after evaluating their progress, because the victim did not co-operate with their plans.

The length of the approach phase varied greatly. Some offenders completed more than one iteration of it; repetition is represented by the recursive arrows. After moving through the approach phase once, most men, especially those who evaluated their progress as positive, decided to commence sexual activity and so went straight on into the preparation phase.

Phase IV: Preparation begins with the *decision to commence sexual activity*. Having made this decision, a few offenders immediately began their sexual assault. However, most first *appraised the expressive potential of the situation*. This appraisal referred to whether they judged that they could express themselves without concern for environmental or practical *constraints* or whether instead, they judged their behaviour to be *constrained instrumentally*. Constraints came mainly from concern about keeping the victim under control, or the risk of detection by others. Men who were concerned about these factors often committed their rapes very quickly, or interrupted their sexual activity periodically in order to re-exert their control over the victim through renewed violence or threats.

Having appraised the expressive potential of the situation, offenders often engaged in some *sexual preparation*. Here they engaged in activities intended to enhance their own level of arousal, or they carried out behaviour resembling conventional foreplay, apparently to either maintain in their own mind the illusion of victim consent, or in an effort to sexually arouse the victim and so undermine her resistance.

During *Phase V: Offence* a range of sexual behaviour occurred (see second part of Figure 1). The most common sexual behaviour was conventional "missionary position" penile-vaginal intercourse: *nondegrading (conventional) sexual behaviour. Degrading sexual behaviour* was less common; it included anal intercourse, penetration of the victim's vagina with objects, and forcing the victim to perform fellatio. Whether something was classified as degrading or nondegrading depended entirely on what the offender thought or intended, so that hypothetically the same actual behaviour could have occurred in association with either intent.

However, in this sample, the behaviour occurring in each category was relatively distinct. Offenders viewed behaviour other than conventional intercourse as degrading. Conventional intercourse was generally perceived as nondegrading.

Gratuitous physical violence (see right hand side) occurred only in association with degrading sexual behaviour in this sample, and was uncommon during the sexual assault itself. Most violence during the sexual assault was limited to that needed to control or overpower the victim.

The *victim's response* during the rape was again reported as *resistant* or *compliant*. It was followed by an *offender evaluation* that again was either *positive* or *negative*. Evaluations during the offence phase focused on whether offenders felt satisfied about the harm they had caused, or had enjoyed the sexual experience. Offenders with a focus on their own sexual gratification were usually positive unless the victim's behaviour had been sufficiently resistant to interfere with achieving gratification. Some offenders were disappointed because having sex with the victim did not live up to preconceived fantasy. Others simply felt relief at expressing themselves, or already had a sense of dread about the harm they were causing.

Phase VI: Post offence begins immediately following the conclusion of the sexual assault when offenders take stock of the consequences (see the bottom of Figure 1). The phase begins with *immediate (post-rape) situation management*; the offender becomes concerned again with managing the victim and the physical environment. Some offenders engaged in *normalising behaviour*, the function of which seemed to be aimed at maintaining their own or the victim's perception that the interaction has been a consenting one. Offenders talked to victims about their lives, offered them cigarettes or made plans to see them again. *Overt control strategies* were intended to control the immediate risk of apprehension (e.g., tying her up, cutting phone lines, escaping).

In the next part of this phase the offender *evaluates the situation*. This is a much broader evaluation than that at the end of the previous phase. It includes a wider range of factors and a longer time frame, extending both back over the events surrounding the offence(s), and into the future. Evaluation of *external factors* included victim impact and ongoing risk of detection. *Self evaluation* focused on whether dominant goals were achieved and what the short and long term implications were. At this point some offenders first experienced guilt, shock or fear. Others became angry. Some felt satisfied, while others realised for the first time that they had committed a serious crime. In response to these evaluations and affective responses, some offenders selected and implemented a *behavioural response*. This behaviour could be an adaptive response to their evaluation, such as attempting to conceal the crime, or going into hiding. However for many, including most of those who had persuaded themselves that their behaviour was not criminal, this response simply amounted to going home or going to sleep. Most of the offenders in this sample made no serious attempt to evade arrest, even when they acknowledged the criminality of what they had done – behaviour that no doubt accounts in part for why they were incarcerated. Lastly, *long-term post-offence responses* included seeking help in recognition that the offender has a problem, continuing an existing criminal lifestyle, or developing ideas about better strategies for avoiding future apprehension.

DISCUSSION

The primary goal of this research was to develop a preliminary model that described adult sexual assault from an offender perspective. A strength of the RM is the way in which it can accommodate different offenders and offence styles. In general, endeavours to classify such complex human behaviours have been thwarted by their continuously variable nature. Recent research using offence chain models has suggested that they have the potential to distinguish between offenders on the basis of the pathways their offences follow through the model; thus offence pathways may be considered taxa (Hudson, Ward, & McCormack, 1999).

In its preliminary form, it is premature to consider quantifying pathways in the RM. However, even at this early stage there are implications for traditional classificatory systems and we consider these next. Comparing the RM with existing typologies is important because it gives indications of the extent to which the US research reviewed earlier can be adopted in New Zealand, a country substantially influenced by the US, but with less than 2 percent of the US population.

The RM outlines the temporal interaction between cognitive, affective and behavioural features of the offence process. As well, it incorporates motivational variables in the form of the goal setting components. One of its unique features is that it allows for the modification of goals during the course of the offence chain. The RM data analysis suggests that offenders' explicit goals do not necessarily remain static throughout the chain; offenders may change or add goals later on in response to the unfolding interaction with the victim. Some offences occur in the service of enduring goals, or goals set at some temporal distance from the offence, while others are committed almost immediately after the goal is established. The RM allows goals to be set as a function of the interaction with the victim. It makes suggestions about how goals arise from background factors; some goals flow congruently out of the proximal background while others are attempts to change or escape it.

None of the most well known classification systems have based their findings explicitly on the way offences unfold. Instead they have relied on a handful of offence features, and tied these together, often through a common motivational theme. The implications of the RM findings for each of the two typological systems reviewed earlier will be discussed in turn.

Groth's typology

Groth is explicitly clear that rape is not motivated by sexual desire, but is a pseudosexual act; a symptom of psychological dysfunction (Groth & Birnbaum, 1980). However, Groth and Birnbaum (1979) also note that "sexuality is not the only – nor the primary – motive underlying rape" (p.60).

The RM goal of seeking sexual gratification to enhance positive mood seems to have no parallel in Groth's work. These offences lacked overt evidence of a threat to self esteem in the background of the relevant perpetrators. On the contrary it appeared that the rape occurred in the context of routine activity, without any recognisable precipitating event. There was little or no evidence of anxious affect proceeding the offence, and rather than having lost control of their lives, these offenders reported some contentment or complacency with how life was going. Attempts to negotiate a consenting encounter were reported. This is inconsistent with conquest as described by Groth et al. (1977).

The victim's experience was not mentioned by some of these men at any point during the sexual parts of the chain. Its apparent irrelevance suggests that rather than being focused on conquest, they were pre-occupied with the sex itself, and victim response was not a significant element of that experience. Thus this distal goal in the RM provides evidence that disputes Groth's central contention that rape is primarily a pseudosexual act, concerned more with status, hostility, control and dominance (Groth & Birnbaum, 1979). Rather, in the RM there is behaviour that is suggestive of a focus on sexual pleasure and satisfaction, with or without the victim's consent.

The second distal subgoal of *escaping negative mood through sexual gratification* seems more related to Groth's concept of a power or conquest-based motivation. These offenders initially sought consenting sex, but used much more overtly aggressive approach behaviour. They expressed surprise and disappointment when this behaviour didn't result in the victim's consent and indeed, full co-operation with their sexual plans. This process is suggestive of power motivation generated by compensatory processes.

Groth notes that power rapists tend to be anxious before the assault, and feel that their life is out of control, and this is somewhat consistent with those offenders who sought sexual gratification to escape aversive affective states. However, Groth's power rapist "typically reveals no effort to negotiate a consenting encounter" (Groth & Birnbaum, 1980, p. 23). This observation is inconsistent with an analysis of the relevant offences in the RM sample. Offenders reported that they were initially seeking consenting sex and attempting to negotiate sexual access to an available woman. Groth contends that in power rapes, the offender asserts power through controlling a sexual encounter with a woman in order to restore a sense of inadequacy. The offence is triggered by threatening behaviour by others in some other part of the individual's life.

A more parsimonious explanation for the relevant offences in the RM sample is that these offenders sought a pleasurable experience to provide at least temporary relief from negative affect. In this respect their behaviour seems more of an avoidant or palliative coping strategy (see Zamble & Porporino, 1988). Half of the men whose offences were identified as having this goal reported a positive sexual experience immediately afterwards. These reports are at odds with Groth's claims that the offence is not sexually pleasurable.

Evidence consistent with Groth's anger motive was found in the RM amongst those with the harm redress goals. The RM does not conceptualise anger expression as a goal, because anger seemed better represented as an affective correlate that waxed and waned once the main goal was established, reaching a peak usually around the commencement of the sexual assault phase. Groth suggests that with anger-motivated rape, "sexuality has become a means of expressing and discharging feelings of pent-up rage" (Groth & Birnbaum, 1980, p. 21). The first question raised by the RM is "whose sexuality?" Men who committed harm-motivated rapes sometimes explicitly chose rape for its ability to hurt the victim, not for its sexual value to the men themselves. Sexually assaulting another human being is often accurately considered by perpetrators to be one of the most degrading and humiliating acts one adult can do to another. The offender may use objects rather than his own body parts to violate the victim and he may experience no sexual arousal. Does this mean his own sexuality is involved, or is he trying to damage the victim's sense of sexual identity and well-being?

We found little evidence that anger was displaced or particularly "pent-up", as is suggested by Groth. Most victims were the same individuals with whom the offender was in conflict, and the conflict had commenced recently. Immediately prior to forming the intent to commit a sexual assault, a number of offenders were already expressing their anger toward the other party to the conflict, sometimes violently. So it is questionable that sexuality per se has become the means of discharging a build-up of rage. The points of concordance with Groth are that the main goal is to hurt, punish, and degrade, that sexual assault becomes the chosen means of achieving this, and that most of these offences were relatively impulsive and unplanned.

There was one offence in the sample with features consistent with sadism; these features were suggestive of an early stage in the hypothetical development of this sexual preference. Although this offender was aroused by fantasies of raping and by victim distress and fear, he was grateful that the victim wasn't resistant, used minimal violence and made no attempt to commit any unconventional sexual acts or to deliberately injure the victim during the offences. Had the offender continued on offending undetected, escalation in a manner consistent with Groth's observations about sadism might have occurred. However, it has also been noted by others that the ways in which Groth defines sadism (e.g., Groth & Birnbaum, 1979) contradict themselves because he has included both the eroticisation of aggression and expressively aggressive motives (e.g., revenge, punishment) in his definition (Baeza & Turvey, 1999).

Interestingly, Groth suggests threat to self esteem is a feature of power, rather than anger rapes. However, it could be argued that rape by definition must always be about power, since it involves an assault committed against another individual without their consent or by force. Threats to self esteem were most evident in the RM in conjunction with angry affect, and this is consistent with a growing experimental literature, that suggests that ego threats are particularly associated with the generation of angry affect and increased aggressive propensity (Bushman & Baumeister, 1998; Rhodewalt & Morf, 1998). However, as Baumeister, Bushman and Campbell (2000) have noted, the pernicious idea that beneath the surface of an aggressive or violent individual lies hidden low self esteem is itself under substantial threat, because no one has managed to demonstrate it empirically, and conceptually there is substantial evidence that overt low self esteem does not predict the use of aggression towards others.

In summary, the two major sources of differences between Groth's typology and those implicit in the RM come from: (1) the reliance on psychodynamic theory, and on constructs that are not readily observable either by the offender, the victim or the interviewer; and (2) the likely use in Groth's research of a more severely dysfunctional and experienced sample or subsample.

The MTC:R3

Knight and Prentky's (1990) MTC:R3 provides detailed criteria for its use as a classificatory tool. Comparison of the RM with the MTC:R3 is necessarily limited here because we have not yet undertaken formal classification with the MTC:R3 of the cases used to construct the RM.

As we noted, at the broadest level of classification, Knight and Prentky's model divides offences around four motivations; opportunistic, pervasively angry, sexual and vindictive. Below we compare the RM with each of these motivations.

Opportunistic types

Knight and Prentky note that the sexual assault of opportunistically motivated offenders is an impulsive, unplanned predatory behaviour by an offender seeking immediate sexual gratification, using whatever force is necessary, and indifferent to the victim. For the purpose of comparison with the RM, opportunistic motivation may be viewed as relating to a sexual goal, albeit developed in close temporal proximity to offence commission. Within the MTC:R3 itself, opportunism is distinguished from sexually motivated subtypes by the duration between goal formation and achievement (i.e., between deciding to rape, and carrying out the offensive act) and by the main triggers for goal formation. With opportunistic offenders it is suggested that motivation largely develops from environmental factors, particularly the presence of a potential victim in a situation where others are unlikely to prevent the offence from taking place. By contrast, the MTC:R3's sexually motivated offenders demonstrate more enduring sexual motives characterised by extensive fantasising, in the absence of a suitable victim.

There are some significant similarities between RM offences with the goal of *seeking sexual gratification to enhance positive mood* and the opportunistic subtypes. Like Knight and Prentky's opportunist rapes, these offences tend to show minimal planning, a focus on meeting one's own sexual needs rather than on the interpersonal features of a sexual encounter, little violence and indifference to victims and consent.

Many of the rapes by men with positive affect-sexual gratification goals took place after social events in contexts where casual sexual encounters are common. For example, the planning necessary to access a victim after a party, and carry out a low violence sexual act may be minimal. Often in these situations, the victim's ability to even consider consent issues, let alone effectively resist is rendered very low because she is either extremely intoxicated or even asleep at the beginning of the assault. Many offenders would have had opportunity to practise sexual encounters of this kind many times, and so are likely to have some kind of behavioural script for how such events unfold. Knight and Prentky also note that opportunistically motivated offences show little evidence of planning. In a sense this is the "planned opportunism" that Pithers (1993) has referred to, where an offender has a plan, should an opportunity eventuate, but doesn't push to create one.

The RM implies that some MTC:R3 opportunists genuinely may struggle to distinguish their behaviour from non-criminal forms of sex. This difficulty arises partly from their insensitivity to coercion and consent issues and their tendency to set up offences in ways that make the distinction between consent and non-consent a contentious one because they have minimised the likelihood of the victim clearly verbally expressing non-consent (e.g., by assaulting her when she is very drunk or asleep). The RM also implies that the most common affective context for opportunistic offending is a mildly positive or neutral one. Knight and Prentky do not discuss the affective features of opportunistic motivation.

One of the problems with using the MTC:R3 is that classification is made on a mixture of bases, including both offence features and offender history features, extending back into childhood. Yet it is not made explicit how these distal historical features link with the posited motivations. A comprehensive theory of criminal action is needed to expose such links so that they could be used with other samples. Comparing the RM with the MTC:R3 provides examples of why this lack of explicitness might be problematic. A number of men whose distal offence goal was to *escape negative mood through sexual gratification* shared the same MTC:R3 Opportunistic Type childhood and adult characteristics as those seeking sex to enhance positive mood. Yet their motivation to offend often occurred in the context of a prolonged build-up of risk factors, and thus could not be viewed as being elicited merely by a situation with rape potential. That Knight and Prentky's system has been developed using both offender and offence characteristics is understandable, maybe even desirable. However, it may also be its greatest limitation, rendering it sample-bound, and even culture-bound. By the time rapists are admitted into a facility such as the one from which Knight and Prentky drew their sample, they are likely to be experienced offenders, and their experience may have an undetectable yet significant impact on the links between offence characteristics and the essentially static offender history variables.

Pervasively angry type
Knight and Prentky (1990) describe the pervasively angry motivation as if it was an offender trait, characterised by undifferentiated anger, and expressed towards both women and men. There was no one in the RM sample for whom we obtained a history consistent with these criteria. Previous research with a sample similar to ours, by Barbaree et al. (1994), classified only one man to this subtype in a sample of 60. The present research confirms that, consistent with their findings, pervasive anger is a rare motivation.

Sexual types
The placement of sexual motivation types in the MTC:R3 suggests that they are not closely related to the opportunistic subtype. There are two main subtypes of sexual motivation, sadistic and non-sadistic. As we noted earlier, definitions of sadism remain confusing, but its frequency in the RM sample was too low to make comparisons.

Non-sadistic sexual motivation is said by Knight and Prentky to be characterised by protracted fantasies and preoccupations, of a non-sadistic nature. Men committing their offences for the main purpose of seeking sexual gratification to escape negative mood appear related to the MTC:R3 sexually motivated rapists, although these RM offenders seldom disclosed extensive sexual fantasising as an offence precursor. If the two are related, then the RM provides an affective context for sexual motivation. Curiously, Knight and Prentky (1990) make no comment about affective context, although their earlier work (Knight & Prentky, 1987; Knight, Rosenberg, & Schneider, 1985) and that of others (Groth & Birnbaum, 1980), has suggested that protracted sexual fantasies function as a management strategy for negative affective experiences and lifestyle imbalance, serving a compensatory function.

Vindictive types
Knight and Prentky (1990) do not directly discuss the relationship between the second type of anger-related motivation in the MTC:R3,

vindictiveness towards women, and pervasively angry motivation. However, vindictiveness appears to be distinguished from pervasively angry motivation by intent, not just to punish, but to degrade and humiliate (see MTC:R3 criteria, u.d.). Vindictives are said to have lower levels of lifestyle impulsivity, and little evidence of violence towards males.

The most related RM goal would be that of *redressing harm to self*, especially through *victim harm*. This goal was associated with predominantly angry affect during the offence. Anger also was common during the approach phase. Once again, the RM may be able to provide a context for the generation of the affect, and the development of vindictive motivation that complements the MTC:R3 research.

In the RM sample, specific triggers were identifiable for men who were redressing harm to themselves. The most common was some kind of interpersonal conflict with a woman. Knight and Prentky (and Groth before them) suggested that this conflict ignited some reservoir of rage located within the offender. By contrast in the majority of RM cases the conflict drove some effort to reduce the anger by resolving the issues, at least from the offender's point of view. The RM data imply that Knight and Prentky's description not only shows its psychodynamic roots, but also probably describes a greater degree of pathology than was found in the RM's angry offenders. Angry motivation for RM offenders was generally tied to particular situations and women rather than being free-floating as Knight and Prentky suggest. These interpersonal situations usually involved conflict between the offender and the victim. It is possible that further development of this perturbing style of dealing with interpersonal problems may, in time, grow unchecked into generalised hatred of women and result in the commission of vindictive rapes, triggered solely by internal cues and perpetrated against uninvolved women. That the two samples may contain offenders at these different developmental stages may explain why the MTC:R3 no longer suggests an environmental context for anger rapes, although earlier related work did (Prentky, et al., 1985).

Conclusions about the MTC:R3

Overall, one of the major limitations of the MTC:R3 for understanding the offence process is that it gives no indication of the stability or otherwise of the motivations posited, with the exception of the Opportunistic subtype where the duration between goal formation and action is suggested to be brief. However, if an offender is pervasively angry or pervasively sexually preoccupied, then what causes an offence to occur at a particular point? It is of at least theoretical interest to establish whether triggers develop from external (i.e., interpersonal conflict) to internal and cognitive (i.e., misperception of intent of a woman's behaviour) with offender development and offence experience.

Knight and Prentky are vague about how the four primary motivations were derived. They write "although this system was generated from a bottom-up structuring of similar types, a hierarchical organisation of types in terms of motivational components naturally emerged" (1990, p. 46). It is also not clear what sources of data were most informative in this respect. This knowledge is important for comparative purposes since the RM was derived mainly from offender information; information from the victim or other sources was of variable quality and provided little in the way of information about goals. By contrast, the data from the MTC were likely to be much richer, given that the offenders were in a treatment facility for lengthy periods. Nevertheless the comparisons made with the RM suggest that the MTC:R3 is likely to require some adaptation for ready use with less restrictively selected samples.

Clearly the RM has more potential for examining taxonomic issues than we have been able to demonstrate here. Even at this point it is proving to be a useful tool for examining the degree of fit between existing US research and other offender samples. We have demonstrated here that some aspects of Groth's and of Knight and Prentky's taxonomies appear to correspond closely to features of this New Zealand sample, but that other features appear absent or do not relate to each other in the expected manner. Whether these differences are limited to the small sample discussed here, or represent genuine cultural differences in criminal behaviour is a question for future research.

We have already begun work on deriving reliable pathways through the model, that account for all of the sample. Our future plans include extending the sample size and diversity, inclusion of new offence chains gathered and analysed by other researchers, and including Maori and Pacific offenders. This future research will help streamline the RM and will provide more information about its adequacy. The larger sample will also be used to examine whether the offenders on each pathway differ in their personal or offence characteristics. Preliminary quantitative analysis suggests that they do.

The value of descriptive models like the one presented here is that they are tightly connected to the data on which they are built. Descriptive models of how offenders go about offending have considerable taxonomic potential and they provide a way of checking that higher level theory development really is grounded in what offenders do, rather than what we think they do.

ACKNOWLEDGEMENTS

This research was supported by funding grants to the first author, from the NZ Department of Corrections and the Victoria University of Wellington Internal Grants Committee. We would like to thank Dr Maryanne Garry for her helpful comments on earlier versions of this chapter.

REFERENCES

Baeza, J. J., & Turvey, B. E. (1999). *Sadistic behavior: A literature review*. [On-line]. Available: http://www.corpus-delicti.com/sadistic_behavior.html

Barbaree, H. E., Seto, M. C., Serin, R. C., Amos, N. L., & Preston, D. L. (1994). Comparisons between sexual and nonsexual rapist subtypes: Sexual arousal to rape, offense precursors, and offence characteristics. *Criminal Justice and Behavior, 21*, 95–114.

Baumeister, R. F., Bushman, B. J., & Campbell, W. K. (2000). Self-esteem, narcissism, and aggression: Does violence result from low self-esteem or from threatened egotism? *Current Directions in Psychological Science, 9*, 23–29.

Berkowitz, L. (1993). *Aggression: Its causes, consequences and control*. New York: McGraw-Hill.

Bushman, B. J., & Baumeister, R. F. (1998). Threatened egotism, narcissism, self-esteem, and direct and displaced aggression: Does self-love or self-hate lead to violence? *Journal of Personality and Social Psychology, 75*, 219–229.

Groth, A. N., & Birnbaum, H. J. (1979). *Men who rape: The psychology of the offender*. New York: Plenum.

Groth, A. N., & Birnbaum, H. J. (1980). The rapist: Motivations for sexual violence. In S. L. McCombie (Ed.), *The rape crisis intervention handbook: A guide for victim care* (pp. 17–26). New York: Plenum.

Groth, A. N., Burgess, A. W., & Holmstrom, L. L. (1977). Rape: Power, anger, and sexuality. *American Journal of Psychiatry, 134*, 1239–1243.

Hudson, S. M., Ward, T., & McCormack, J. C. (1999). Offense pathways in sexual offenders. *Journal of Interpersonal Violence, 14*, 779–798.

Indemaur, D. (1995). *Violent property crime*. Leichhardt, NSW, Australia: Federation Press.

Knight, R. A., & Prentky, R. A. (1987). The developmental antecedents and adult adaptations of rapist subtypes. *Criminal Justice and Behavior, 14*, 403–426.

Knight, R. A., & Prentky, R. A. (1990). Classifying sexual offenders: The development and corroboration of taxonomic models. In W. L. Marshall, D. R. Laws, & H. E. Barbaree (Eds.), *Handbook of sexual assault: Issues, theories, and treatment of the offender* (pp. 23–52). New York: Plenum.

Knight, R. A., Rosenberg, R., & Schneider, B. A. (1985). Classification of sexual offenders: Perspectives, methods, and validation. A. W. Burgess (Ed.)., *Rape and sexual assault: A research handbook* (pp. 222–293). New York: Garland.

Malamuth, N. M., Heavey, C. L., & Linz, D. (1996). The confluence model of sexual aggression: Combining hostile masculinity and impersonal sex. *Journal of Offender Rehabilitation, 23*, 13–37.

Marlatt, G. A., & Gordon, J. R. (Eds.). (1985). *Relapse prevention: Maintenance strategies in the treatment of addictive behaviors.* New York: Guilford.

MTC:R3 criteria (Version 1; u.d.). Unpublished manuscript.

Pithers, W. D. (1993). Treatment of rapists: Reinterpretation of early outcome data and exploratory constructs to enhance therapeutic efficacy. In G. C. N. Hall, R. Hirschman, J. R. Graham, & M. S. Zaragoza (Eds.), *Sexual aggression: Issues in etiology, assessment, and treatment* (pp. 167–196). Washington D. C.: Taylor & Francis.

Pithers, W. D., Marques, J. K., Gibat, C. C., & Marlatt, G. A. (1983). Relapse prevention with sexual aggressives: A self-control model of treatment and maintenance of change. In J. G. Greer & I. R. Stuart (Eds.), *The sexual aggressor: Current perspectives on treatment* (pp. 214–234). New York: Van Nostrand Reinhold.

Polaschek, D. L. L., Ward, T., & Hudson, S. M. (1997). Rape and rapists: Theory and treatment. *Clinical Psychology Review, 17,* 117–144.

Pollard, P. (1994). Sexual violence against women: Characteristics of typical perpetrators. In J. Archer (Ed.), *Male violence* (pp. 170–194). London: Routledge.

Prentky, R., Cohen, M., & Seghorn, T. (1985). Development of a rational taxonomy for the classification of rapists: The Massachusetts treatment center system. *Bulletin of the American Academy of Psychiatry and Law, 13,* 39–70.

Prentky, R. A., & Knight, R. A. (1991). Identifying critical dimensions for discriminating among rapists. *Journal of Consulting and Clinical Psychology, 59,* 643–661.

Rosenberg, R., Knight, R. A., Prentky, R. A., & Lee, A. (1988). Validating the components of a taxonomic system for rapists: A path analysis approach. *Bulletin of the American Academy of Psychiatry and the Law, 16,* 169–185.

Rhodewalt, F., & Morf, C. C. (1998). On self-aggrandizement and anger: A temporal analysis of narcissism and affective reactions to success and failure. *Journal of Personality and Social Psychology, 73,* 672–685.

Strauss, A., & Corbin, J. (1990). *Basics of qualitative research: Grounded theory procedures and techniques.* Newbury Park, CA: Sage.

Ward, T., & Hudson, S. M. (1998). A model of the relapse process in sexual offenders. *Journal of Interpersonal Violence, 13,* 700–725.

Zamble, E. & Porporino, F. J. (1988). *Coping, behavior, and adaptation in prison inmates.* New York: Springer-Verlag.

Chapter 11

SITUATIONAL FACTORS IN SEXUAL OFFENDING

John Murray

Sexual assaults are criminal events the literature generally examines from psychological or socio-cultural perspectives. While these perspectives describe crucially importance aspects of sexual assaults, such as treatment, causes and origins, they nevertheless provide a lop-sided view of the behaviour. The literature, most probably reflecting the convicted status of their forensic subjects, implies the sexual aggressor proceeds inexorably towards offending and cannot be deflected. However, sexual assaults do not occur in a vacuum. For example, they occur most frequently on weekends, during the hours of darkness and more likely involve the victimisation of younger women (Meilman & Haygood-Jackson, 1996). This suggests that factors other than psychological or socio-cultural phenomena are crucial offence components. An understanding of situational factors, apart from providing information on a neglected research area can form the basis for constructing community preventive programs and inform therapy, particularly relapse prevention.

This chapter argues that sexual offending involves a complex psychological/socio-cultural/situation interaction, but the first two elements are over-represented in interpreting the offence. While the individual may be readied for sexual offending by psychological and socio-cultural factors, the situation exerts a considerable influence over the act. An example from suicide prevention illustrates this interaction. Clarke (1999) reported that suicide, a perceived deviant act committed by desperate people, was reduced by 30 percent when in the 1960's the English switched from lethal to non-lethal household gas. By removing easy access to facilitators the suicide rate was reduced. Similarly, Lasley (1998) reported that blocking automobile access to high-risk sites significantly reduced gang homicide and drive-by shootings. In both these cases, the "root-cause" of the problem was not eliminated, e.g. depression, anti-social personality, poverty, but opportunities were reduced. These two cases suggest that situations, far from being neutral platforms on which the drama is acted, also control and influence behaviour in a manner not explicitly recognised in the literature, especially the sexual offence literature. This is not to suggest that sexual offences are simply functions of situational imperatives, as there will always be calculated and planned attacks motivated by psychopathology, but an understanding of situation opens new vistas for investigations and prevention.

Situational crime prevention has achieved considerable success in reducing a variety of crimes (Clarke, 1995), however, this begs the question of whether the underlying principles are applicable to sexual offending. If sexual offending is viewed within the context of a crime similar to other crimes, and not imbued with special qualities of separateness because of its sexual and gendered aspects, situational crime prevention may have considerable preventative and explanatory utility. Currently there is a dearth of information on the situational aspects of sexual assaults and this research is an attempt to address this position. Another advantage of investigating sexual offences from a situational perspective is the emphasis on the crime rather than the offender (Weisburd, 1997). Finally, a situational analysis offers the hope of practical preventative solutions to sexual assault at the community level, something current approaches do not address systematically.

This chapter briefly reviews socio-cultural and psychotherapeutic theories of sexual offending as well as discussing their limitations. Situational crime prevention theory is then examined, including its ability to offer antidotes to sexual offending.

THEORIES OF SEXUAL OFFENDING

There is an extensive literature describing the genesis of sexual assault with socio-cultural and/or psychological explanations predominating as the main theoretical underpinnings. These theories generally ascribe external and/or internal motivations to the offender and do not accord situational factors much causative utility. This chapter now briefly examines the two main theories of sexual offending.

Socio-Cultural Explanations
Socio-cultural explanations locate the causes of rape and sexual assault within the fabric of western culture and society (Jenkins, 1997). Brownmiller's (1975) thesis that rape is "nothing more or less than a conscious process of intimidation by which all men keep all women in a state of fear" remains the classic definition of this position. Sexual assault is not seen as a sexual act per se, but as deviant behaviour serving

non-sexual needs, such as domination, and cannot be seen as isolated from the patriarchal fabric of society in which it occurs (Hazelwood & Burgess, 1995). Brownmiller (1975) also argued that rape serves a political function by preserving a patriarchal system that benefits all men, including those who do not rape. This model soon became the dominant ideology explaining sexual assault although it has been called into question with some contemporary research (Levi, 1994; Smith & Bennett, 1983).

Nevertheless, there is considerable evidence supporting the socio-cultural origins of sexual assault. With one in four male North American undergraduates holding beliefs that rape is provoked by the victim, that any woman can prevent rape and women frequently cried rape falsely, provides some indication to the extent with which rape myths permeate society (Holcomb et al., 1991). While sexual assault is commonly perceived as the behaviour of sick or criminal men, rape supportive attitudes are widely held in the general community. Malamuth's (1981) study reported 35% of "normal" men in his sample expressed some likelihood of raping. Similarly, Koss et al. (1987) found 25% of 2,972 men sampled admitted involvement in some form of sexual aggression and 7.7% of men reported perpetrating an act that met the legal definition of rape or attempted rape. Spangaro (1992) also reports that approximately half of all Australian women experience some serious sexual violence. Findings such as these suggest that western society promotes a hegemonic masculinity and a callous disregard for the position of women, objectification of women and support for men who sexually abuse women (Schwartz, 1997).

However, Levi (1994) argues that the socio-cultural explanations of rape grossly over-predict its occurrence and men's attitude to women fails to account for the fact that few rapists offend as frequently as their individual and gendered value systems would suggest. In addition, most of the studies on sexual offenders relate to incarcerated or hospital populations, which limits their generalisability.

Psychological Explanations
The other major explanatory theory describing sexual assault is psychological. Psychology provides numerous models of sexual offending causality but they overwhelmingly, but not exclusively, attribute behaviour internally to dispositional factors (Vaughan & Hogg, 1998). Some psychological explanations stem from various childhood psychosocial schemata involving a dysfunctional childhood characterised by poor parental role modelling, severe and inconsistent discipline, with the fathers

often aggressive, drunken and in trouble with the law (Maginnis, 1998; Marshall & Barabee, 1989). Other psychological studies have attempted to delineate personality profiles of sexual aggressors, but no unitary profiles can be determined for spouse abusers, child sexual offenders or other types of abusers (Jenkins, 1997). Malamuth et al. (1993) reached a similar conclusion that personality deficits failed to show correlation with sexual assault. Other approaches describing the origins of sexual assault, especially rape, include attempts to classify rapists according to their behavioural patterns that categorise motives into displaced aggression, compensatory, sexual-aggressive and impulsive (Cohen, Seghorn & Calmas, 1969). The unifying theme of psychological approaches is acceptance of dispositional or internal causes of sexual offences especially in its treatment and clinical manifestations.

While most psychological explanations of sexual offences discount situations, this is not universally true. Relapse prevention, the most widely used treatment with sexual offenders, while positing no cure, emphasises self-regulatory behaviour and avoidance of high-risk situations. High-risk situations as utilised in relapse prevention do not accord situations themselves causative power. For example, a rapist walking aimlessly through darkened streets is considered to be in a high-risk situation, but the power of the situation to influence his behaviour is rarely considered. In a similar vein, Marshall & Barbaree (1989) discuss situational theories of sexual violence in terms of momentary misinterpretations of behaviour, the use of alcohol or intoxicants, overwhelming sexual arousal or insanity, but assert that by themselves these will not serve as explanatory theories. The discussion of situations in the sexual assault literature seems to occur more in terms of a background to the offence rather than having causative utility.

Limitations of Psychological and Socio-Cultural Approaches
Whatever the merits of socio-cultural and psychological models in describing the causes of sexual offending, their efficacy as preventative or curative methodologies is open to question. Easteal (1993) saw rape prevention in terms of changing social attitudes, law reform, significant modification of gender roles and gendered stratification and de-emphasising violence. Since we do not live in a utopian society, Easteal (1993) suggested precautionary, but crude situational measures, such as learning self-defence, knowing sexual rights, being cautious on dates, using dead-locks and parking cars in well-lit areas. However, it is difficult to imagine any additional precautionary measures women can undertake. For example, Prentky (1995) argues that there is a fear which forces potential

victims to schedule their daily activity around issues of safety and this fear has become the norm.

Another deficit in the current approaches to sexual offending is their inability to realistically address sexual offending prevalence. Recourse to statistics will help clarify this. Since the majority of sexual offenders are not prosecuted, let alone jailed or supervised, it is difficult to imagine that therapeutic interventions, even if successful, can impact significantly on sexual offending (Violence Against Women, 1994). Indeed, only 20% of rapes may be reported to the police (Teets, 1997).

In addition, the efficacy of treatment is still unknown. Herman (1990) posits that treatment for sexual offenders must be considered entirely experimental and claims of therapeutic success should be offered with great caution and received with healthy scepticism. Marshall et al. (1998) offer a similar observation reporting that it remains to be demonstrated that treating sex offenders reduces recidivism although there is good grounds for optimism.

It is obvious that other approaches to dealing with sexual offending are required. The socio-cultural and psychological explanations individually and combined still cannot fully account for the incidences of sexual assault. While these explanations have some efficacy in describing the genesis of sexual assault, other factors must be propitious if an offence is to occur. Rape, for example, is not a random event (Bohmer & Parrot, 1993; Hazelwood & Burgess, 1995; Schwartz & DeKeseredy, 1997; Stevens, 1994) and circumstances must be advantageous for the offender before he proceeds with the offence (Gabor, 1994; Vogelman, 1990). Rapes occur in relatively secure environments for the rapist where he is unlikely to be disturbed and the victim is alone (Ploughman & Stensrud, 1986; Vogelman, 1990). Rapes also occur more frequently indoors (Greenfeld, 1997; Quinsey & Upfold, 1985); on weekends (John, 1978; Simon, 1997); in the evening with younger rather than older women as the primary targets (Greenfeld, 1997). The non-random occurrences of sexual assaults suggests that considerations other than social or psychological factors are operating (Ploughman & Stensrud, 1986). Taken together, it seems cultural and psychological factors often prepare the perpetrator for sexual assault, but situational elements generally determine if, when, and where the offence will occur. However, sexual assaults can also be largely situational in causation, for example, when soldiers rape for unit "solidarity" purposes.

Gonsiorek, Bera, and LeTourneau (1994) proposed a model that combined psychological, socio-cultural and situational factors within a coherent explanation. Socio-cultural and psychological factors pre-disposed the individual for sexual aggression but situational factors had to be advantageous for the offence to occur. However, their concept of "situational opportunity" as an initiator was conceived in a narrow victim-availability model. Situational opportunity or situation–persons interactions were not developed in their model.

While both Relapse Prevention and Gonsiorek & Bera's (1994) model recognise situational factors in sexual offending, another major theoretical school has applied situational factors to non-sexual crimes, and with some success.

SITUATIONAL CRIME PREVENTION

Although situational explanations of sexual assault could be included under the psychological explanations they will be discussed separately given the growing criminological literature related to situational crime prevention. Situational crime prevention is an opportunity reduction strategy based on the assumption that criminals rationally select targets and that chance of victimisation can be reduced by increasing the effort, increasing the risk, reducing the rewards and setting rules (Clarke, 1995). It is more concerned with the immediate and non-dispositional causes of crime, to reduce opportunities for its occurrence and increasing the associated risks (Downes, 1997). It is underpinned by a number of criminological theories, two of the more important being rational choice and routine activity theory.

The rational choice component perceives offenders as active, albeit "imperfect" decision makers (Rosenbaum, Lurigio, & Davis, 1998) who make decisions on a cost/benefit analysis and so exploit criminal oppor-tunities for their benefit. Their decision does not have to be "carefully preconceived and planned or require hierarchical, sequential decision making" (Cromwell, Olson, & Avary, 1991). The criminal seeks to benefit from crime, without taking undue risks, and exploits opportunity as it occurs. The offender does not necessarily have a strong motivation to offend but if circumstances are propitious, the offence may occur. Conversely, in the absence of favourable situational conditions the offence may not occur.

Also supporting the situational crime prevention approach is routine activity theory, which argues that an offence occurs when a motivated offender, suitable victim and an absence of guardians coincide in time and space. Cohen and Felson (1979), in developing this criminological theory,

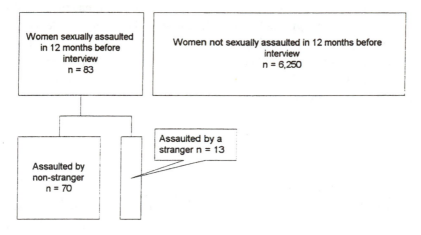

FIGURE 1: SCHEMA OF INVESTIGATIVE PROCESS

argued that variations in burglary rates were associated with changes in the working habits of suburban residents; their houses were empty during the day because both partners worked and there was more "stealable" property available like televisions. As people go about their normal business, they may expose themselves to higher risks of victimisation.

Difficulties in Applying Situational Factors to Sexual Assaults
Situational crime prevention is directed at highly specific forms of crime (Clarke, 1992) and underpinned by the crucial role of the person–situation interaction (Wortley, 1997). Application of situational crime prevention interventions has reduced crime in a variety of circumstances and offence types (Clarke, 1992, 1997), ranging from graffiti reduction (Wilson, Lincoln, & McGilvray, 1995) to robbery (Indermaur, 1995). However, situational crime prevention has been under-researched for its applicability in sexual offending, perhaps reflecting difficulties in applying this approach and because of the dominance of deviance models.

One of these difficulties is that situational crime prevention seems to work best when applied to tangible target sites like banks, telephone boxes and fighting outside pubs where the full range of situational crime prevention techniques can be introduced. However, sexual assault is qualitatively different to the usual situational crime prevention targeted offences. Sexual offences, although occurring more frequently in certain times and places, still occur over large time and space spans. Thus usual interventions effective in restricted sites are difficult to introduce. Although applying situational crime prevention to sexual offending is methodologically challenging it should not be avoided: it has the promise of identifying new approaches to reducing sexual assault prevalence.

It is important to emphasise that sexual assaults are carried out volitionally with responsibility being totally borne by the perpetrator.

Specifically, this chapter examines the role of situational factors in discriminating between victims and non-victims on the Women's Safety: Australia (1996) survey.

METHOD

Women's Safety Survey

The Australian Bureau of Statistics conducted a women's safety survey (Women's Safety: Australia, 1996) from February to April 1996, to provide information on women's safety at home and in the community, with a particular emphasis on emotional, physical and sexual violence. Data was collected from 6,333 female respondents over the age of 18 years. Participation in the survey was voluntary but 22% of women refused to participate. Due to constraints on the length of the interview information was only collected on the last incident of physical and sexual victimisation.

Two questionnaires were developed for household and personal use. The former collected basic demographic data from any responsible adult in the household, e.g. age, sex, relationships. If there was any woman in scope she was advised of the general nature of the survey and invited to participate. The questionnaire was designed so that less personal and intrusive questions were asked first. Subjects were advised when the interview focus was to change to sexual and physical assaults, and given the opportunity to withdraw. Participants were also given the option of a telephone interview but most of the interviews were conducted face-to-face. All interviews were conducted in private to ensure the safety of the respondents. Only women interviewers were used and they were given additional special training to enable them to deal with issues associated with violence against women.

Strategy of Analysis

Two analyses of the data were undertaken. The first analysis investigated male initiated sexual assaults by comparing women who had been sexually assaulted in the 12 months before the interview with the remainder of the survey across situationally relevant independent variables (detailed shortly). The second analysis focused on the women sexually assaulted by a male in the 12 months before the interview based on the perpetrator's familiarity to them i.e., stranger or non-stranger status across similar independent variables in the first analysis (Figure 1). Restricting the analysis to recent victims is more likely to capture the dynamic nature of the independent variables.

Variables Used in Analysis

The variables included in this analysis were chosen based on their situational crime prevention potentiality and utility. They comply with the operational definition of situations provided above. This chapter now briefly examines the independent and dependent variables used in the analysis and the rational for their inclusion.

Marital status: A woman's marital status may reduce the possibility of sexual assault (Newton-Taylor, DeWit, & Gliksman, 1998). A woman in a relationship is less likely to be out of an evening or in dangerous situations by herself. Unmarried women are more likely to be involved in the dating scene and thereby exposing themselves to high-risk situations.

Educational Qualifications: Educational qualifications are generally associated with high socio economic status and can be expected to reflect lifestyle factors such as living in lower crime rate environments which could effect victimisation rates. Younger women are more likely to have higher levels of education than the older generation and have a greater understanding of what constitutes sexual assault (Riopelle, Bourque, Robbins, Shoaf, & Kraus, 2000).

Childhood sexual abuse: Childhood sexual abuse is a risk factor because of the traumatising effect it exerts over its victims and dys-functional sequelae (Mammen & Olsen, 1996). The literature has reported greater probability of adult re-victimisation of childhood sexual abuse victims (Beitchman et al., 1991; Couarelos & Allen, 1998; Himelein et al., 1994). Fergusson et al. (1997) interpret the dysfunctional sequelae of childhood sexual abuse in terms of dysfunctional family dynamics and social disadvantage, all of which were related to sexual vulnerability in adolescence. They also suggested childhood sexual abuse was associated with early sexual activity, which exposed the woman to heightened risks of other adverse outcomes in adolescence (Rickert & Wiemann, 1998).

Prior Physical Attack History: This variable may provide some indication of a woman's general vulnerability. Sexual physical assaults may be related to similar social, family and other variables (Huddleston, 1991).

Victim Age: The literature has demonstrated a strong relationship between age and sexual assault victimisation (Russell, 1984; Salter, 1992) and perpetrator (Salter, 1992). Specifically, most victims of sexual assault were young (Koss et al., 1987) with the vast majority of rape victims between the age of 11 and 30 (Russell, 1984). Katz & Mazur (1979) also report that risk of sexual assault declines steadily as women get older.

Younger women are at greater risk of sexual assault because of their greater exposure to dangerous situations and potential aggressors through their involvement in the dating scene (Ullman, 1997; Vicary, Klingaman, & Harkness, 1995). They may also have not yet developed sexual assault avoidance skills.

Alcohol Involvement: Alcohol usage by both victim and perpetrator has long been recognised as a risk factor for sexual assault (ElSohly & Salamone, 1999; Emmert & Kohler, 1998). This variable is only used in the Stranger/Non-stranger analysis.

Situations Operationally Defined

Situations in the situational crime prevention literature usually refer to opportunity, proximity or temporal influence associated with the criminal event. However, the use of situational factors may be limited in situational crime prevention interventions as they may be applied in sexual offences. For these reason situations are operationally defined as non-personality or non-dispositional factors thought to be associated with sexual offending. This broader operational definition allows for a more comprehensive investigation of causative elements in sexual offending that are not fastened by ties of opportunity, proximity or time.

If sexual assault can be significantly explained by situational factors it opens up avenues for new preventative approaches: it is easier to manipulate situations than personality. Whilst acknowledging that sexual assault cannot be totally "designed out" by situational interventions, it may prove to have offence reduction efficacy. Fresh insight into the prevention and treatment of sexual offending at both the community and therapeutic levels may be elicited. The first step in applying situational crime prevention to sexual offending necessitates the identification of situational markers. Identification of these markers will provide new avenues for community level and therapeutic interventions such as relapse prevention. It will also provide insights into identifying factors, which could explain differences between sexual assaults perpetrated by strangers and non-strangers.

Independent Variables

The independent variables used in the first analysis were:

- Marital status of the respondent;
- Educational achievement of respondent;
- Childhood sexual abuse history;
- Physical attack since age 15; and
- Age of respondent.

These variables were again used in the second analysis in addition to the variable measuring involvement of alcohol in the offence.

Statistical Analysis

Logistic regression was used in the first analysis given the dependent variable was dichotomous, sexual assault or non-sexual assault and the independent variables were a combination of dichotomous and ordinal (e.g., respondent's age). Logistic regression estimates the probability of an event occurring.

The second analysis applied cross-tabulation and Chi analysis to the victims of sexual assaults occurring in the past 12 months.

RESULTS

The first statistical process consisted of a logistic regression analysis performed through SPSS to assess the probability of being sexually assaulted in the 12 months before the survey interviews across marital status, level of education, history of childhood sexual abuse, history of adult sexual assault and respondent's age. All of the survey's 6,333 cases were included in the analysis consisting of 83 victims and 6,250 non-victims.

The analysis produced a model fit based on the five independent variables (see Table 1). X^2 (128.95, df 5, $p = 0.00$). Every independent variable in this analysis was significant. While producing significant results the logistic regression was unable to correctly classify any of the women sexually assaulted. An overall correct classification of 98.69 % was achieved but the majority of these were the correct classification of the major category, non-assaulted women. Indeed blindly allocating women to this category produced a success rate of 98 %, which is a minuscule improvement over chance. The difference in category sizes most probably accounted for this unimpressive overall classification rate.

Table 1: Parameter Estimates for Multivariate Main Effects Predicting Probability of Sexual Assault 12 Months before Interview

Variable	B	S.E.	Wald	Sig.	exp(B)	CiL	CiH
Marital Status	1.31	0.25	27.82	0.00	3.74	2.27	6.05
Education	0.49	0.22	4.70	0.03	1.63	1.06	2.51
Child Sex Abuse	0.60	0.26	5.28	0.02	1.82	1.09	3.03
Physical Attack	1.36	0.25	29.73	0.00	3.89	2.39	6.36
Age	−0.27	0.06	18.12	0.00	0.76	0.68	0.86

To examine the effect of the independent variables on the sexual assault status of the subjects more clearly, a second set of comparisons using bivariate analysis – cross-tabulations were carried out. These comparisons are included in the body of the results.

Age

Age decreased the probability of sexual assault. Table 1 lists an odds-ratio of 0.76 for the independent variable age. Specifically, each subsequent age grouping has a 0.76 probability of reporting a sexual assault than the preceding age grouping. However, the magnitude of the decreasing probability is not sufficiently described by this single statistic. The sexual assault adult victimisation reporting rate varies from a low of 14.5% to a high of 31% until age 45 before dropping back to single digit reporting rates.

Table 2 details the cross-tabulations of age and sexual assault victimisation. Women in the pre-menopausal age ranges, 18 to 44, report the highest victimisation rates, with women in the 35–44 age group reporting the highest victimisation levels. However, women in the next age group report less than a quarter of victimisations of the 35–44 age group. Women in the post-menopausal ages, 45–60+, account for almost 11% of the sexual assaults.

Table 2: History of Sexual Assault by Age

Age	Not sexually assaulted		Sexually assaulted	
	No.	%	No.	%
18–24	673	10.80	22	26.50
25–29	641	10.30	12	14.50
30–34	809	12.90	14	16.90
35–44	1,441	23.10	26	31.30
45–54	1,068	17.10	6	7.20
55–59	329	5.30	1	1.20
60+	1,289	20.60	2	2.40
Total:	6,250		83	

Childhood Sexual Abuse

A history of childhood sexual abuse is a major risk factor for subsequent sexual offending. Examination of Table 1 reveals that childhood sexual abuse increases the probability of adult sexual assault re-victimisation by a factor of 1.8. Almost a quarter of the women sexually assaulted in the year before being interviewed were childhood sexual abuse victims. More than 11% (710) of respondents were victimised as children (see Table 3).

Table 3: History of Childhood Sexual Abuse by Adult Sexual Assault

Sexually assaulted as a child	Not sexually assaulted		Sexually assaulted	
	No.	%	No.	%
No	5,562	89.00	61	73.50
Yes	688	11.00	22	26.50
Total:	6,250		83	

Physical Attack

The logistic regression analysis calculated a 3.89 greater probability of being sexually assaulted if the woman had been physically assaulted since the age of 15. Almost 70 % of the women sexually assaulted in the year before being interviewed had been physically assaulted. The survey results provide no indication if the physical attack was related to the sexual assault but on the evidence of the logistic regression and cross-tabulation table (Table 1) physical assault is strongly associated with sexual assault.

Table 4: History of Physical Attack by Sexual Assault in 12 Months Before Interview

Physical Attack	Not sexually assaulted		Sexually assaulted	
	No.	%	No.	%
No	4,506	72.10	25	30.10
Yes	1,744	27.90	58	69.90
Total:	6,250		83	

Marital Status

Table 5 indicates that women not in relationships accounted for 71% of sexual assaults in the last year before being interviewed. The logistic regression analysis (Table 1) calculates that a woman not in a relationship has a 3.74 greater probability of being sexually assaulted than a woman in a relationship.

Table 5: Adult Sexual Assault by Being in Relationship

	Not sexually assaulted		Sexually assaulted	
Relationship	No.	%	No.	%
Yes	4,164	66.60	24	28.90
No	2,086	33.40	59	71.10
Total:	6,250		83	

Educational Qualifications

The logistic regression calculated an odds-ratio of 1.63 greater probability of sexual assault for women with a post-highschool education. Table 6 tabulates the results of the bivariate analysis. No easily discernible trends are evident although women with post-highschool education are at greater risk of sexual assault.

Table 6: History of Sexual Assault by Educational Qualifications

	Not sexually assaulted		Sexually assaulted	
Educational Qualification	No.	%	No.	%
High School or less	3,570	57.10	37	44.60
Post-High School	2,680	42.90	46	55.40
Total:	6,250		83	

The second data analysis used cross-tabulations and Chi-square to examine the data. Thirteen women were assaulted by strangers and 70 by non-strangers in the 12 months before being interviewed. The independent variables used in this analysis consisted of marital status, qualifications, childhood sexual abuse, physical attack, age and if alcohol was involved in the offence. None of the comparisons were significant at the p. = 0.05 level, indicating no statistical difference between the groups.

DISCUSSION

The aim of this chapter was to determine if situational factors predicted sexual assaults. More specifically, it aimed to investigate the role of situational factors in predicting sexual assaults in the 12 months before the respondents were interviewed in the Women's Safety Survey (Australian Bureau of Statistics, 1996) and secondly to examine the effects of situational factors on the sexual victimisation of the women identified in the first study. The dependent variable in the first analysis was sexual assault status in the 12 months before the interview. The dependent variable in the second analysis was the stranger/non-stranger status of the male sexual aggressor in the offence occurring in the 12 months before the interview. The independent variables were marital status, education, childhood sexual abuse, adult physical abuse, age and involvement of alcohol. Overall, the results indicated that situational factors were associated with sexual assault victimisation but no significant differences were found between stranger and non-stranger initiated sexual assaults. This latter finding suggests that the factors making a woman vulnerable to sexual assault, make her vulnerable to both stranger and non-stranger depredations. It is noteworthy that all predictor variables in the logistic regression were significant, with marital status and history of adult physical assault recording the strongest effect. While all of the predictor variables used in the logistic regression were statistically significant, the analysis was not able to correctly classify victims of sexual assault with any precision. This was most probably a function of the inequality of the category sizes affecting the analysis.

The first main finding of this analysis was that situational factors vary the probability of women's lifetime sexual assault victimisation. This finding provides support for a central assertion of this chapter that sexual offences are motivated by phenomena other than non-dispositional or socio-cultural factors. Tentative conclusions can be drawn from this data. Sexual assaults are not randomly visited on women. Marital status provides the strongest evidence of this with almost 70 % of women not in partnerships being victimised. This result is probably tapping the women who have left relationships because of violence and younger women who are the primary target of sexual violence (Greenfeld, 1997). Similarly, the high number of women sexually assaulted who have completed post-highschool education probably reflects the preponderance of younger women who are more likely to be higher educated than their mothers. It also probably reflects that young women are more aware of behaviour constituting sexual assault and are willing to define it as such (Ullman, 1997). Childhood sexual abuse is also a predictor of adult victimisation. A woman sexually assaulted as a child has a 1.8 greater probability of being assaulted as an adult. The mediating mechanism for this subsequent abuse is not fully understood but is highly likely to involve women placing themselves in high-risk situations as a result of the traumatising effect of their childhood experience. The traumatising effects of childhood sexual abuse are also more likely to leave the woman with lowered self-esteem and a reduced ability to cope with potentially hazardous situations, especially when her judgment is impaired by alcohol (Beitchman, Zucker, Hood, daCosta, Akman & Cassavia, 1992; Greenfeld, 1997). Prior adult physical attack is a significant predictor of sexual assault by increasing the probability of being sexually assaulted almost four times than for women not physically assaulted. It is possible that the same man is both sexually and physically assaulting the victim and that physical and sexual assaults are part of a cluster of violence with some men being indiscriminate in using violence against women. Age provides some protection from sexual assault for a woman with each age grouping in the survey having a 77 % lower risk of sexual assault than the preceding one. This was especially noticeable after age 45 when the sexual assault rate was reduced to single digits. It seems that if a woman can negotiate the young adult age range of 18 to 24 without being sexually assaulted she faces only a relatively low increase in probability of sexual assaults thereafter although there is an increase in the 35–44 year age group. This suggests that young women devise sexual assault preventative strategies that reduce their risk.

The second analysis was unable to separate stranger and non-stranger initiated sexual assaults through the predictor variables used in the analysis. In other words, victims and non-victims of sexual assault statistically differ across the predictor variables while no statistical difference could be found between stranger and non-stranger initiated assaults. It seems that whatever factors make a woman vulnerable to sexual assault, she is vulnerable to victimisation by males known and unknown to her. It is possible that perpetrators hunt for victims exhibiting certain characteristics or in certain situations, but it does suggest the need for more research to clarify this issue before any firm conclusion can be drawn.

The above findings have implications for the reducing of sexual assaults using situational crime prevention approaches. First, as women who have been sexually abused in childhood are at significantly greater risk of adult re-victimisation, greater resources should be directed towards these victims (Couarelos & Allen, 1998). Such approaches targeting victims of childhood sexual abuse allow for better use of scarce sexual assault prevention resources and has potential to reduce subsequent re-victimisations. On a broader scale, these results provide indications that sexual assaults are more prone to situational factors than previously acknowledged in the literature. Although it has to be acknowledged that these results do not allow far-reaching conclusions to be drawn regarding the efficacy of situational crime prevention in reducing sexual offending, they nevertheless indicate that this approach should be explored.

The results of this study suggest that situational factors have utility in preventing sexual assault. Identification of situational characteristics associated with sexual assault provides strong hints that these offences are capable of reduction through manipulation of environmental, physical and situational factors. It is obvious that further investigations into the role of other situational factors are required to identify factors with sexual assaultive prevention utility. In particular, more details on type of residence, exact location of the assault and how the offender gained entry need closer examination.

Socio-cultural and psychological variables nevertheless impress as important elements in the decision to offend. They seem to function as the building blocks for the sexual offending decision but the behaviour must be expressed in a physical location and the offender, based on situational crime prevention theory, must maximise his probability of avoiding apprehension. These findings provide tantalizing hints that sexual offending is informed by situational factors and further investigation is required. In particular, location factors such as distance from main roads, how entry was gained to the sexual assault site and type of dwelling may reveal a clearer picture of sexual offending than the relatively crude situational variables available for this study.

Conclusions that can be drawn from this study are that sexual assault victimisation can be predicted from victims' characteristics and situational variables. The analysis was strongest in separating non-victims from victims by achieving almost perfectly successful classification but conversely unable to successfully classify victims. This latter result is most probably a function of the group inequality sizes in the analysis. It also seems possible that perpetrators probably hunt for, or are aware of vulnerability factors in their victims. Given that 16 % of Australian women are sexually assaulted, greater effort should be expended in advising women of re-victimisation probability (Australian Bureau of Statistics, 1996).

The findings in analysis one and two were consistent with other studies of situational factors (Grabosky & James, 1995) that factors other than dispositional ones contribute to the decision to offend. While the results could not be construed as clearly identifying specific situational factors that can immediately contribute to a reduction in sexual offending, it does suggest that situational factors are worthy of further investigation.

REFERENCES

Australian Bureau of Statistics. Women's Safety Survey (1996). Canberra, Catalogue No. 4128.0.

Beitchman, J. H., Zucker, K. J., Hood, J. E., daCosta, G. A., & Akman, D. (1991). A Review Of The Short-Term Effects Of Child Sexual Abuse. *Child Abuse and Neglect*, 15(4), 537–56.

Bohmer, C., & Parrot, A. (1993). *Sexual Assault on Campus: The Problem and the Solution*. NY: Lexington.

Burgess, A. G., Burgess, A. W., & Hazelwood, R. R. (1995). Classifying Rape and Sexual Assault. In R. R. Hazelwood, & A. W. Burgess (Editors), *Practical Aspects of Rape Investigation: A Multidisciplinary Approach* (pp. 193–203). Boca Raton, Florida: CRC Press.

Clarke, R. V. (1992). Introduction. in Ronald V. Clarke (Editor), *Situational Crime Prevention: Successful Case Studies*. New York: Harow and Heston.

Clarke, R. V. (1997). Introduction. In Ronald V. Clarke (Editor), *Situational Crime Prevention: Successful Case Studies* (, Chap. Second Edition,). Guilderland, NY: Harow and Heston.

Clarke, R. V. (1995). Situational Crime Prevention. In Michael Tonry, & David P. Farrington (Editors), *Building a Safer Society: Strategic Approaches to Crime Prevention* (Crime and Justice: A Review of Research. Edited by Michael Tonry ed., Vol. 19 pp. 91–150). Chicago: The University of Chicago Press.

Clarke, R. V. (1999). *Situational Crime Prevention – Everybody's Business*. Australian Crime Prevention Council.

Cohen, L., & Felson, M. (1979). Social Change And Crime Rate Trends: A Routine Activity Approach. *American Sociological Review*, 44.

Cohen, M., Seghorn, T., & Calmas, W. (1969). Sociometric Study Of The Sex Offender. *Journal of Abnormal Psychology*, (74), 249–255.

Couarelos, C., & Allen, J. (1998). Predicting Violence Against Women: The 1996 Women's Safety Survey. *Crime and Justice Bulletin, No. 42*(NSW Bureau of Crime Statistics and Information).

Cromwell, P. F., Olson, J. N., & Avary, D. W. (1991). *Breaking and Entering: An Ethnographic Analysis of Burglary*. Newbury Park, California: Sage.

Downes, D. (1997). Macro and Micro Issues in Urban Crime and Delinquency. *http://cl24.uwe.ac.uk/commsafe/eudacc95/downes.htm 6.2.97*.

ElSohly, M. A., & Salamone, S. J. (1999). Prevalence Of Drugs Used In Cases Of Alleged Sexual Assault. *Journal of Analytical Toxicology*, 23(3), 141–6.

Emmert, C., & Kohler, U. (1998). Data About 154 Children And Adolescents Reporting Sexual Assault. *Archives of Gynecology and Obstetrics*, 261(2), 61–70.

Fergusson, D. M., Horwood, L. J., & Lynskey, M. T. (1997). Childhood Sexual Abuse, Adolescent Sexual Behaviors And Sexual Revictimization. *Child Abuse And Neglect*, 21(8), 789–803.

Gabor, T. (1994). *'Everybody Does it!' Crime by the Public*. Toronto: University of Toronto Press.

Gonsiorek, J. C., Bera, W. H., & LeTourneau, D. (1994). *Male Sexual Abuse: A Trilogy Of Intervention Strategies*. Thousand Oaks: Sage Publications.

Grabosky, P., & James, M. (1995). *The Promise of Crime Prevention: Leading crime prevention programs*. Canberra, Australia: Australian Institute of Criminology.

Greenfeld, L. A. (1997). *Sex Offenses and Offenders: An Analysis of Data on Rape and Sexual Assault*. U.S. Department of Justice, Office of Justice Programs, Bureau of Justice Statistics.

Herman, J. L. (1990). Sex Offenders: A Feminist Perspective. In W. L. Marshall, D. R. Laws, & H. E. Barbaree (Editors), *Handbook of Sexual Assault: Issues, Theories and Treatment of the Offender*. New York: Plenum.

Himelein, M. J., Vogel, R. E., & Wachowiak, D. G. (1994). Nonconsensual Sexual Experiences In Precollege Women: Prevalence And Risk Factors. *Journal of Counseling and Development; 1994 Mar–Apr Vol 72(4) 411–415.*

Holcomb, D. R., Holcomb, L. C., Sondag, K. A., & Williams, N. (1991). Attitudes About Date Rape: Gender Differences Among College Students. *College Student Journal; 1991 Dec Vol 25(4) 434–439.*

Huddleston, S. (1991). Prior Victimization Experiences And Subsequent Self-Protective Behavior As Evidenced By Personal Choice Of Physical Activity Courses. *Psychology A Journal of Human Behavior; 1991 Vol 28(3–4) 47–51.*

Indermaur, D. (1995). Reducing the Opportunities for Violence in Robbery and Property Crime: The Perspectives of Offenders and Victims. In *Crime Prevention Conference 1994, Conference Papers Crime Prevention Conference 1994, Conference Papers* (pp. 127–148).

Jenkins, A. (1997). *Invitations to Responsibility: The Therapeutic Engagement of Men Who are Violent and Abusive.* Richmond, South Australia: Dulwich Centre Publications.

John, H. W. (1978). Rape And Alcohol Abuse: Is There A Connection? *Alcohol Health and Research World; 1978 Spr Vol 2(3) 34–37.*

Katz, S., & Mazur, M. (1979). *Understanding The Rape Victim: A Synthesis Of Research Findings.* New York: John Wiley.

Koss, M. P., Gidycz, C. A., & Wisniewski, N. (1987). The Scope of rape: Incidence and prevelance of sexual aggression and victimization in a national sample of higher education students. *Journal of Consulting and Clinical Psychology, 55*(162–170).

Koss, M. P., Goodman, L. A., Browne, A., Fitzgerald, L. F., Keita, G. P., & Russo, N. F. (1994). *No Safe Haven: Male Violence Against Women at Home, at Work, and in the Community.* Washington, DC: American Psychological Association.

Lasley, J. (1998). *"Designing Out" Gang Homicides and Street Assaults.* (Report No. NCJ 165041). U.S. Department of Justice, Office of Justice Programs, National Institute of Justice.

Levi, M. (1994). Violent Crime. M. Maguire, R. Morgan, & R. Reiner (Editors), *The Oxford Handbook of Criminology.* Oxford: Clarendon Press.

Maginnis, R. L. (1998). Policing Sex Offenders. *http://www.capitalresearch.org/frc/insight/is94g2cr.html 1.2.98.*

Malamuth, N. M. (1981). Rape Proclivity Among Males. *Journal of Social Issues; 1981 Vol 37(4) 138–157.*

Malamuth, N. M., Heavey, C. L., & Linz, D. (1993). Predicting Men's anti-Social Behaviour Against Women: The Interactions Model of Sexual Aggression. In G. C. N. Hall, R. Hirschman, J. R. Graham, & M. S. Zavagoza (Editors), *Sexual Aggression: Issues in Etiology, Assessment and Treatment.* New York: Taylor and Francis.

Mammen, G., & Olsen, B. (1996). Adult Survivors Of Childhood Sexual Abuse. Do I Have Them In My Practice? *Australian Family Physician, 25*(4), 518–24.

Marshall, W. L., & Barabee, H. E. (1989). Sexual Violence. In K. Howells, & C. Holin (Editors), *Clinical Approaches to Violence.* New York: Wiley.

Marshall, W. L., Fernandez, Y. M., Hudson, S. M., & Ward, T. (1998). Conclusions. In W. L. Marshall, & Y. M. Fernandez (Editors), *Sourcebook of Treatment Programs for Sexual Offenders.* New York: Plenium Press.

Meilman, P. W., & Haygood-Jackson, D. (1996). Data On Sexual Assault From The First 2 Years Of A Comprehensive Campus Prevention Program. *Journal of the American College Health, 44*(4), 157–65.

Newton-Taylor, B., DeWit, D., & Gliksman, L. (1998). Prevalence And Factors Associated With Physical And Sexual Assault Of Female University Students In Ontario. *Health Care Women International, 19*(2), 155–64.

Ploughman, P., & Stensrud, J. (1986). The Ecology Of Rape Victimization: A Case Study Of Buffalo, New York. *Genet Soc Gen Psychol Monogr, 112*(3), 303–24.

Prentky, R. (1995). A Rational for the Treatment of Sex Offenders: Pro Bono Publico. J. McGuire (Editor), *What Works: Reducing Reoffending: Guidelines from Research and Practice*. Chichester: John Wiley and Sons.

Quinsey, V. L., & Upfold, D. (1985). Rape Completion And Victim Injury As A Function Of Female Resistance Strategy. *Canadian Journal of Behavioural Science; 1985 Jan Vol 17(1) 40–50*.

Rickert, V. I., & Wiemann, C. M. (1998). Date Rape Among Adolescents And Young Adults. *J Pediatric Adolescence Gynecology*, 11(4), 167–75.

Riopelle, D. D., Bourque, L. B., Robbins, M., Shoaf, K. I., & Kraus, J. (2000). Prevalence of Assault and Perception of Risk of Assault in Urban Public Service Employment Settings. *International Journal of Occupational and Environmental Health*, 6(1), 9–17.

Rosenbaum, D. P., Lurigio, A. J., & Davis, R. C. (1998). *The Prevention of Crime: Social and Situational Strategies*. Scarborough, Ontario, Canada: Wadsworth.

Russell, D. E. H. (1984). *Sexual Exploitation: Rape, Child Sexual Abuse, and Workplace Harassment*. Newbury Park: Sage.

Salter, A. C. (1992). Epidemology of Child Sexual Abuse. In W. O'Donohue & J.H. Geer (Editors), *The Sexual Abuse of Children: Theory and Research* (Vol. 1, pp. 108–138). New Jersey.

Schwartz, M. D., & DeKeseredy, W. S. (1997). *Sexual Assault on the College Campus: The Role of Male Peer Support*. Thousand Oaks, California: Sage Publications.

Simon, R. I. (1997). Bad Men Do What Good Men Dream: A Forensic Psychiatrist Illuminates the Darker Side of Human Behavior. *http://www.appi.org/simona.html 14.10.97*.

Smith, M. D., & Bennett, N. (1983). Poverty, Inequality and Theories of Forcible Rape. *Crime and Delinquency*, 31, 295–305.

Spangaro, J. (1993). In Patricia Weiser Easteal (Editor), *Without Consent : Confronting Adult Sexual Violence : Proceedings Of A Conference Held 27–29 October 1992*. Canberra: Australian Institute of Criminology.

Stevens, D. J. (1994). Predatory Rapists And Victim Selection Techniques. *Social Science Journal; 1994 Vol 31(4) 421–433*.

Teets, J. M. (1997). The Incidence And Experience Of Rape Among Chemically Dependent Women. *J Psychoactive Drugs*, 29(4), 331–6.

Ullman, S. E. (1997). Review and Critique of Empirical Studies of Rape Avoidance. *Criminal Justice and Behavior*, 24(2), 180.

Vaughan, G. M., & Hogg, M. A. (1998). *Introduction to Social Psychology*. Sydney: Prentice Hall.

Vicary, J. R., Klingaman, L. R., & Harkness, W. L. (1995). Risk Factors Associated With Date Rape And Sexual Assault Of Adolescent Girls. *Journal of Adolescence; 1995 Jun Vol 18(3) 289–306*.

Vogelman, L. (1990). *The Sexual Face of Violence: Rapists on Rape*. Johannesburg: Raven Press.

Weisburd, D. (1997). *Reorienting Crime Prevention Research And Policy: From The Causes Of Criminality To The Context Of Crime*. (Report No. NCJ 165041). U.S. Department of Justice, Office of Justice Programs, National Institute of Justice.

Wilson, P., Lincoln, R., & McGilvray, S. (1995). Solving the Problem of Graffiti through Crime Prevention Strategies. In *Crime Prevention Conference* Brisbane: Centre for Crime Policy and Public Safety.

Wortley, R. (1997). Reconsidering the Role of Opportunity in Situational Crime Prevention. In G. Newman, R. V. Clarke, & S. G. Shoham (Editors), *Rational Choice and Situational Crime Prevention: Theoretical Foundations*. Dartmouth: Aldershot, England.

C

VIOLENT OFFENDERS AND OFFENCES

Chapter 12

VIOLENT CRIME AND OFFENDING TRAJECTORIES IN THE COURSE OF LIFE: AN EMPIRICAL LIFE-SPAN DEVELOPMENTAL TYPOLOGY OF CRIMINAL CAREERS

Klaus-Peter Dahle

PROGRESS AND DEFICITS IN UNDERSTANDING DELINQUENT CAREERS

Advances in criminological research have broadened our knowledge regarding the origins of antisocial behaviour and the conditions initiating and maintaining delinquent development in the last years. At the same time, the focus of interest has turned from single delinquent acts towards the processes leading to a criminal development. Modern developmental theories, such as the "Life-Course-Theories", currently rank among the most promising theoretical innovations. This trend was given impetus by modern longitudinal research, which has opened up possibilities for investigating developmental processes in progress. There is also an increased number of theories on the nature of these processes. The concept proposed by Buikhuisen (1990) will serve as an example, but other authors like Dumas (1992), Farrington (1996), Loeber (1990), Lösel & Bender (1998), Moffitt (1993) have also expressed similar ideas.

In accordance with general opinion and empirical evidence, Buikhuisen assumes an accumulation of different bio-psycho-social hazards as the main risk factors for an antisocial delinquent development (see Figure 1). His model demonstrates probable influencing structures with special attention to three areas of childhood socialization: family, school as a field for social learning and finally school as an educational institution. According to Buikhuisen, the typical pattern of delinquent development is characterized by failure in all of these fields, and the model draws on a number of criminological theories to explain the particular influences and effects in detail. On the whole, the concept appears to be compatible with modern developmental approaches. Furthermore, modern longitudinal research has provided ample evidence supporting most of the assumed connections.

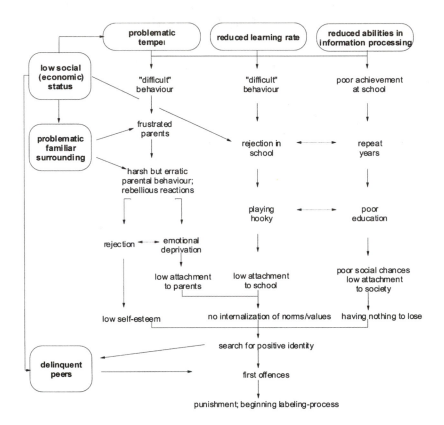

FIGURE 1: CONCEPT OF A TYPICAL ENTRY IN A DELINQUENT DEVELOPMENT
(according to Buikhuisen, 1990; supplemented by Lösel & Bender, 1998)

However, a great deal more is known about early risk factors and typical delinquent development during childhood, adolescence and early adulthood, than about the further processes during the later stages of life. This deficit can probably be attributed mainly to methodological obstacles. Prospective longitudinal studies must be performed on a very long-term basis to follow the line from early childhood to late adulthood. Since such long periods of time usually involve very high shrinkage rates of the sample, such studies would have to start with an appropriately large sample. Furthermore, considering the possibility of late criminal development, originating from circumstances during later periods of life rather than from early childhood factors, the sample should not consist only of early-high-risk groups. All these methodological problems complicate a systematic analysis of delinquent careers in the literal sense of a "life span developmental approach".

THE BERLIN CRIME STUDY

Design and Sample

The Berlin Crime Study attempted to solve the above-mentioned problems by choosing a mixed design with both a retrospective and a prospective component. The study was based on a random sample of about 400 (n=397) adult male offenders who entered the Berlin prison system during the first few months of 1976. Every fourth German-speaking newcomer 21 to 45 years old and with no significant mental impairment was included. The basic examination included extensive interviews (biography, social and sexual history, self-reported delinquency, experience with social and penal institutions, attitudes, etc.), physical and neurological examinations (including electroencephalographic examination), psychological testing (personality, cognitive and intellectual capacity, clinical tests, attitude scales, etc.) and, last but not least, the study of their files. During this basic examination, the story of each subject's life was also recorded. This is the retrospective part of our study[1]. In several steps, we try to understand the subsequent developmental course of the subjects since 1976 by studying their later prison files, analyzing their legal records (up to 1998) and reviewing their health records. Furthermore, we are preparing a personal re-examination of the subjects which is scheduled for the years 2000/2001.

At the time of the basic examination in 1976, the subjects had a mean age of about 30 years (M=29.83; SD=5.35) with a range of 21 to 45 years. The mean age is currently about 53 years, so that the study can now analyze a comparatively long period of life. The distribution of the offences underlying the imprisonment in 1976 corresponded to the typical situation of unselected prison populations: non-violent offences against property clearly dominated (48%), followed by fraud (10%), robbery (9%) and bodily harm (9%). Other crimes like sexual offences (3%), homicide (2%) and others were less frequent.

Recidivism 1976–1998

In assessing the development of the sample since 1976, it must first be considered that 67 of the 397 subjects, i.e. nearly 17%, died since 1976. We have not yet been able to determine the cause of the high mortality rate but are trying to obtain this information from the files of the public health offices. We do know, however, that the causes of death cannot be simply related to the older age groups. There is a connection with age, in that a particular phase of life in the age range of 30 to 45 was associated with a high risk of death. During this period, the subjects had an up to thirty times higher risk of death than the general male population in Germany. However, there were no significant differences before or after this period. Secondly, the risk of death was considerably higher among the subjects addicted to drugs or alcohol, but addiction does not fully explain this phenomenon. We hope to get more information from the public health files.

About 31% of the survivors showed no recidivism after 1976. The others were repeat offenders with a mean of 6.4 new sentences thus far (SD=3.7). However, 24% of them (17% of all survivors) were not arrested again after committing minor offences resulting only in fines or probation. Finally, 170 subjects (52% of the survivors) returned to prison at least once, but most of them even more often (M=4.92; SD=2.85). The total time of imprisonment since release from prison in 1976 was 807 years (M=57 months; SD=41.6). Moreover, 40 subjects (12% of the survivors) were repeat offenders who had committed at least one very serious violent crime after 1976 (defined as robbery, grievous bodily harm, rape or homicide that resulted in a penalty of at least 4 years of imprisonment).

TYPES OF CRIMINAL DEVELOPMENTS IN THE COURSE OF LIFE

One of the main objectives of the Berlin Crime Study is to investigate the distribution of delinquent activity during the course of life and to identify typical patterns and types of criminal careers. For this reason, a cluster analysis[2] of the longitudinal criminological data was performed with the following variables: age at the first and last official offence, and for every 4-year interval since the age of 14[3] as well as the number of offences and the time the subjects spent in prison (or very exceptionally in forensic psychiatric institutions). The analysis disclosed five types of criminal careers.

Figure 2 illustrates the typology on the basis of the average length of time the subjects spent in prison during the different periods of life. This variable appeared to be a characteristic indicator of delinquent activity, since it is affected by both the frequency and gravity of crime. However, please note that there is a bias in the transitions between youth, early adulthood and adulthood because the probability of being sent to prison differs for these age groups. According to the German penal code, a long prison term is unlikely for juveniles. The bar graph shows the average time of imprisonment for the whole sample with a wide plateau-like peak between the ages of twenty and forty.

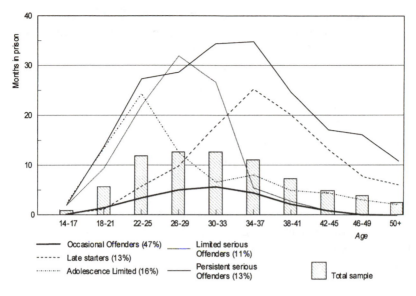

FIGURE 2: TYPES OF CRIMINAL CAREERS IN THE COURSE OF LIFE
(regarding times of imprisonment; from Dahle, 1998)

Late-Starting Careers
Occasional Offenders

From a life-span developmental point of view, the first (and largest) group showed quite a low degree of delinquency in the course of their life. That is why we call them "occasional offenders". They comprised about 47% of the sample, but this is probably an overestimation with regard to the original sample. There is every reason to believe that the majority of the dead subjects belonged to the other groups. The real share of "occasional offenders" is more likely to be about a third in our cross-section of the prison population.

The most important criminological characteristics of the occasional offenders were an extensive specialization in a particular kind of delinquency (monotropic delinquency) and a largely crime-free childhood and youth; the mean age at their first offence was M=24.57 (SD=5.89). In accordance with the late development of delinquency, their burden of early biological, biographical, social and psychological risk factors seemed to be rather low. Also, the course of their early development was not extremely abnormal: poor conduct, early runaway, failure at school or vocational training were clearly below average.

In spite of these similarities, a further examination of the occasional offenders yielded two subgroups, whose differences disappeared, however, in the average-based view of the cluster analyses. That is, half of them offended very rarely in the course of life (often once, but not more than three times). The others offended repeatedly at regular intervals of about three or four years, but only with misdemeanours, such as petty larceny, driving without a licence, other traffic offences or alcohol-related incidents. In contrast to this, the first-mentioned subgroup was very heterogeneous in their offences, which ranged from dereliction of duty and fraud to serious and violent delinquency such as robbery, sexual offences (incestuous child abuse) and, in one case, homicide (murder of spouse).

Regarding possible background factors, an increasing number of critical life events were found for those occasional offenders who committed more serious crimes. These were cases of economic bankruptcy, adultery or other partnership crisis, gambling, debts and similar events. This finding combined with the absence of early risk factors suggests that events occurring in later phases of life may be of decisive importance for this type of delinquent career.

Late-Starting Offenders

Another group (13% of the sample) with a comparatively low burden of early biopsychosocial risk factors and little trouble during childhood development, had a largely crime-free youth[4]. They committed their first offence at a mean age of about 24 years (M=23.79; SD=5.65), but, since they then started quite a remarkable career, we call them "late starters". Up to 1998, they had an average of 17 entries in their legal records (M=17.0; SD=6.27) and spent an average of about 10 years in prison (M=9.86; SD=4.03). Their delinquent activity had a peak in the second half of the fourth decade, but more than 60% were still offending in the last five years. It is remarkable that the late starters as well as the occasional offenders showed a clear preference for specialization (monotropic delinquency). Most of them committed fraud or burglary, though a few were implicated in more violent crimes such as robbery.

Despite the delay in beginning their career, the late starters had no noticeable accumulation of particularly stressful or burdening life events. On the other hand, there was a peculiarity with regard to their criminal attitudes. The psychological scales as well as the interview data of this group gave the strongest impression of an extensively internalized image of being a professional criminal. This may indicate that this type of career may originate from more rational decisions in later phases of life than from adverse developmental circumstances, hazards or life events.

Early-Starting Careers

In contrast to the first types of criminal careers, the remaining three all began with official delinquency and offences committed in early youth. According to their own account, however, over 60% of these offenders already started in childhood. Another common feature of the following three groups is polytropic delinquency. All early starters showed a varied mixture of delinquent and criminal behaviour in the course of their lives, including larceny, robbery, bodily harm, traffic offences and varying antisocial behaviour during childhood. Finally, an enhanced burden with early risk factors was found for all of these early starters. However, there were particular patterns in their biographical backgrounds that seemed decisive for their later development.

Adolescence-Limited Offenders

One of the early-starting groups (16%) had already reached the peak of their criminal activity in their early twenties. After that, the gravity and frequency of their criminal behaviour slowly decreased. Around the age of 30, some of them had succeeded in not re-offending again. However, most of them (about 2/3) showed lasting delinquent behaviour, but its nature had clearly changed while they were in their twenties. Their early offences during youth were committed almost exclusively in the context of peer groups, whereas the later delinquent activities were more individual. They were very often misdemeanours associated with addictive problems. Since their delinquent activities peaked early and showed a plain marked downward trend in the second decade of life, we classified these individuals according to Moffitt's developmental typology (1993) as adolescence-limited offenders[5].

The early risk factors in this group were clearly concentrated in the early familial sphere. The families were characterized by very low social ranks and an accumulation of multiple family problems, like unemployment, drinking parents, early loss of the natural father and repeated changes of the father figure, large families with many children, delinquency, etc. On the other hand, there was no marked increase in either biological risk factors or early conduct problems. According to their own account, their typical development of delinquency was characterized by an early emotional detachment from the family and a simultaneous search for company and compensation among peer groups, that led to the first offences.

To apply these characteristics to Buikhuisen's (1990) concept of the typical process of delinquent development, the focus of developmental problems of our adolescence-limited offenders appears to lie in hazards during family socialization. It is true that almost all of them also had trouble at school, and most of them failed to get a proper education. However, failure occurred comparatively late and seemed to be the consequence of an ongoing delinquency.

The following will give some further insights into their later life. They appeared to have poorer social relationships than all other groups. In spite of their early and intensive contacts with peer groups during adolescence, they reported very few friendships, partnerships or sexual contacts. They thus got the fewest visits of all groups during imprisonment. The psychological tests characterized the adolescence-limited offender group as the most neurotic one with high levels on scales measuring depression, emotional instability and reactive aggressiveness. There was a disproportionately high number of subjects at risk of developing addictive problems, and during imprisonment they gave the impression of being unmotivated (e.g., at work), unreliable and undisciplined with frequent incidents involving alcohol and drugs.

Limited Serious Offenders

Another group (11%) with an early-starting delinquent history continued their career for a longer time. In their twenties, they showed a dramatic increase in the gravity of their criminal behaviour, advancing to serious and violent crime. As in the case of all early-starting offenders, the general nature of the delinquency was a varying mixture of offences. In contrast to the adolescence-limited group, however, this subgroup was not restricted to group delinquency. However, the most remarkable and characteristic criminological aspect was a discontinuation of criminal activities around the age of about thirty. Thus we call them "limited serious offenders". These subjects most often gave up their career abruptly and usually did not re-offend after release from a long imprisonment.

With regard to early biopsychosocial risk factors, the focus of burden in this group seemed to centre on biological factors. The number of (self-reported) complications during pregnancy or birth were clearly enhanced, and there was an increased occurrence of early developmental delay and early conduct disorders. However, their cognitive abilities (intelligence, concentration) appeared to be clearly above average at our basic examination in 1976 and were the best of all groups. In spite of these abilities, however, most of them failed school at a very early age. The percentage of subjects who repeated grades, the number of school dropouts and finally the number of subjects without vocational training were the highest of all groups. On the other hand, the family situation appeared to be relatively normal. There was even some indication of an above-average attachment. For example, the limited serious offenders got the most frequent visits in prison. In particular, their parents came most regularly, even during a long prison term.

Applying these characteristics to Buikhuisen's (1990) concept of an incipient delinquent development, the focus of hazards of the limited serious offenders appears to centre more on school socialization than on family. Given a biological (i.e. temperamental) and neurological pre-disposition, the subjects showed a high level of maladjusted, hot-tempered behaviour, and it seems that school failed to deal with these increased demands.

The most striking psychological feature of the limited serious offenders was a high tendency towards mental crisis, whereas their self-descriptions in the psychological tests conveyed the impression of mental stability. However, more than 36% (the average was about 19%) had attempted suicide. Furthermore this group appeared to be a rather difficult one during imprisonment. They had the most attempted suicides in prison, all cases of "prison tantrum", and most of the aggressive outbursts as well as most cases of escape and attempted escapes.

Persistent Serious Offenders

Finally, one group comprising about 13% of our sample has remained among the most serious offenders during the course of their lives thus far. Up to 1997, only 20% of them had succeeded in dropping out of a criminal career (a dropout being defined as a person who did not re-offend for at least the last five years), and the average length of time the subjects of the persistent group had spent in prisons by 1997 was about 17 years (M=17.03; SD=5.77). They also had the highest recidivism speed. Referring to our index arrest in 1976 for example, 62% were already in prison again 12 months after their release, 91% after 2 years and 100% after 3 years. Finally, almost 40% (39.47%) offended at least once with a very serious violent crime. Based on these criminal characteristics, we called this group "life course persistent serious offenders". It is worth mentioning that the offending trajectories in their course of life appear to be very similar to those found for psychopathic offenders (Hare, McPherson and Forth, 1988). As a rule, the type of crime was quite heterogeneous among all early-starting groups. However, there was one special feature: the persistent offenders typically started with individually committed offences.

As expected, early risk factors were most prominent in the persistent offender group. It was not so much a particular pattern of risks that characterized the subject's early socialization, but the overall accumulation of obstacles was clearly above average in all biopsychosocial areas. It appears that an unspecific accumulation of risks in various fields and the absence of potential protective factors provided the basis for this kind of development. However, there was a particular behavioural pattern in early life. Against the background of increased family problems and experiences of rejection and failure at school, these subjects tended to become equally detached from family and school, but without joining peer groups. During childhood the typical persistent offender was a loner, who played hooky, often ran away and roamed about alone when the first offences were committed.

In accordance with Buikhuisen's developmental concept (1990), these subjects obviously had problems in all areas of socialization. Thus it seems that accounts of their early life fit the model quite well. However, these subjects did not need contact with delinquent peer groups to start offending, as Buikhuisen assumed. It is true that almost all of them also offended within the framework of group activities, but contact with other juvenile delinquents appears to be more a consequence of sanctions imposed in conjunction with an ongoing delinquent development.

The following will give some further insights into the later life of the persistent offenders. A number of special attributes were found when examining personality factors (e.g., a high level of trait aggression), life-style (e.g., enhanced promiscuity or a high regard for status symbols) and attitude patterns (e.g., high distrust of prison staff). These were to be expected. However, a surprising finding relates to their behaviour in prison. Unlike the other two early-starting groups, the persistent offenders seemed quite inconspicuous: they were disciplined and usually rather reliable. Thus predictive expert opinions tended to underestimate the risk of recidivism quite often.

SEVERE VIOLENT CRIME IN THE COURSE OF LIFE

To assess the probability of committing serious violent crime, we formed an extreme group of subjects who had offended in this way at least once in the course of their lives. As already mentioned, we defined robbery, grievous bodily harm, rape and homicide as "serious violent crime", provided that it resulted in a penalty of at least 4 years of imprisonment. Admittedly, the definition is somewhat arbitrary. However, it was chosen to obtain a large enough extreme group for further analysis and led to a selection of about 10% of the sample with the severest crime (k=59 single acts: 61% robbery; 22% rape; homicide and bodily harm with 8.5% each). However, it should be noted that again there is a bias with regard to the earlier periods of life. Under the German penal code, juvenile offenders normally run quite a low risk of being sentenced for 4 years or longer, even in cases of serious violent crime. The selection may thus underestimate harmful crime during adolescence.

It was to be expected that the probability of committing severe violent crime in the defined manner clearly differed among the five types of criminal careers. Almost half (49.2%) of these crimes were committed by the 13% comprising the group of persistent serious offenders (39.5% of this group were involved in this way, half of them repeatedly). Furthermore, another quarter (25.4%) of these acts were committed by the 11% comprising the limited serious offenders (24.2% of this group were involved, again half of them repeatedly). This means that altogether nearly one quarter of the subjects were responsible for three quarters of the severe violent crime. The next group included the adolescence-limited offenders who committed about 12% of the violent acts (10.6% were involved, one of the subjects twice), followed closely by the late starters with 10.2% (only three subjects of this group were involved, but all of them repeatedly). Thus, the rate of serious violent crime in these two groups was approximately equivalent to the mean rate in the whole sample. In contrast, only two incidents (3.4%) – one case of homicide and one case of robbery – could be allocated to the 47% of the sample comprising the group of occasional offenders. Statistical tests confirmed that the differences in the rates of serious violent crime were highly significant between the groups. Fisher's exact test yielded a score of about 38 (37.95; p<.001).

The age at which the crimes were committed ranged from 15 to 60 years (M=30.1; Mdn = 28; SD= 9.7) for the whole sample. The distribution of serious violence in the course of life does not differ much from the data for delinquent activity in general (see bar graph in Figure 2). With the exception of the occasional offenders, who rarely committed severe violent crimes, the same could be found for the individual career types. Figure 3 gives a general idea of the age-related crime rate in each group. The box plots specify the range as well as the 25th, 50th (median) and 75th percentile for each group, and the width of the boxes indicates the respective share in the overall frequency of violent crime.

Figure 3 shows marked differences between the groups not only with regard to the probability of severe violence but also with regard to

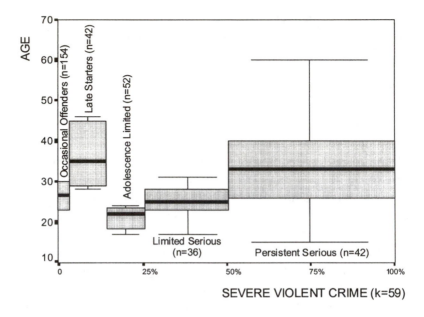

FIGURE 3: ACTS OF SEVERE VIOLENT CRIME IN THE COURSE OF LIFE

different life phases of particular risks. The differences clearly correspond to the specific trajectories of delinquent activity of the respective careers and appear to be highly significant. A Kruskal-Wallis test of the differences resulted in a chi-square of about 25 (χ^2 = 24.6; df=4; p<.001). Moreover, the temporal spread of offences clearly differed between the five groups (Levene's F=4.2; p<.005). The persistent serious offender group clearly showed the widest spread with a standard deviation of 10.4 years (M=33.4 years) and an age range of 15 to 60 years. In fact, the group appeared to be "life-course-persistent" in the literal sense of the word.

Finally, some brief remarks should be made about the sexual offences of the sample. A total of 22 subjects committed this type of crime, and this was too small a number for statistical analysis. However, it was striking that 12 of 13 cases of rape could be allocated to the two serious offender groups, and, in all of these cases, rape was one type of crime among others. The only exception was a late-starter, who began at the age of 28 a career of repeated rape and continued until he was 46 (when he got imprisoned for about 10 years). In contrast to this, isolated cases of child sexual abuse (altogether 9 cases) could be found in every group.

NOTES

1　We believe that the retrospective data are gaining reliability by referring them systematically to the findings from prospective studies. In this respect our study is based on these findings and tries to continue them.

2　A hierarchical cluster analysis estimated the proper number of identifiable clusters. Its results formed the initial cluster centres for subsequent k-means analysis, which optimized the allocations. A discriminant analysis tested the methodological stability of the results with an overall accuracy of 92%.

3　The choice of this particular age limit and range of single steps relates to the age limits defined in the German penal code.

4　Older age groups were slightly overrepresented among the "late starters". There was a disproportionately high number of subjects who spent their childhood during World War II. Some hazards were associated with the age of the subjects and the influences of war (e.g. loss of father). However, these particular types of burden did not affect the later outcome.

5　However, please note that our sample comprises only subjects who got imprisoned at least once at the minimum age of 21 and thus does not include the "typical" adolescence-limited offender.

REFERENCES

Buikhuisen, W. (1990). Der Täter in seinen biosozialen Bezügen. In H.-J. Kerner & G. Kaiser (eds.), *Kriminalität: Persönlichkeit, Lebensgeschichte und Verhalten* (pp. 65–79). Berlin: Springer.

Dahle, K.-P. (1998). Straffälligkeit im Lebenslängsschnitt. In H.-L. Kröber & K.-P. Dahle (eds.), *Sexualstraftaten und Gewaltdelinquenz* (pp. 47–56). Heidelberg: Kriminalistik.

Dumas, J.E. (1992). Conduct disorders. In S.M. Turner, K.S. Calhoun & H.E. Adams (eds.), *Handbook of clinical behavior therapy* (pp. 285–316). New York: Wiley.

Farrington, D.P. (1996). Psychosocial Influences on the Development of Antisocial Personality. In G. Davies, S. Lloyd-Bostock, M. McMurran & C. Wilson (eds.), *Psychology, Law and Criminal Justice: International Developments in Research and Practice* (pp. 424–444). Berlin, New York: DeGruyter.

Hare, R.D., McPherson, L.M. & Forth, A.E. (1988). Male Psychopaths and Their Criminal Careers. *Journal of Consulting and Clinical Psychology*, 56, 710–714.

Loeber, R. (1990). Development in risk factors of juvenile antisocial behavior and delinquency. *Clinical Psychology Review*, 10, 1–41.

Lösel, F. & Bender, D. (1998). Aggressives und delinquentes Verhalten von Kindern und Jugendlichen: Kenntnisstand und Forschungsperspektiven. In H.-L. Kröber & K.-P. Dahle (eds.), *Sexualstraftaten und Gewaltdelinquenz* (pp. 13–37). Heidelberg: Kriminalistik.

Moffitt, T.E. (1993). Adolescence-Limited and Life-Course-Persistent Antisocial Behavior: A Developmental Taxonomy. *Psychological Review*, 100, 674–701.

Chapter 13

CAN POLICE PREVENT DOMESTIC VIOLENCE?

Anna L. Stewart

Twenty-five years ago the prevailing attitude toward domestic violence was that, except in exceptional circumstances, police had little role to play in this 'private' or 'family' problem. As a result, the criminal justice system had a very 'hands off' approach to policing violence in the home. In recent years, in response both to strong pressure by women's groups and an increasing understanding of the extent and severity of violence in the home, there have been substantial changes in legislation relating to domestic violence and the police enforcement of this legislation. These changes have been predicated on the belief that domestic violence offending will be prevented by a strong consistent traditional law enforcement approach. Unfortunately, despite these changes there is little evidence that domestic violence is less of a problem now than 25 years ago (Snider, 1998).

The failure of changes in legislation and policing practices to reduce the incidence and prevalence of domestic violence is seen by some as evidence that police are still failing to respond appropriately to the seriousness of domestic violence. Consequently, there are continuing calls for increased criminalisation and 'get tough on crime' approaches to policing domestic violence (Jones, 1994). These approaches include the use of mandated police responses, compelling witnesses to testify, not allowing prosecutions to be withdrawn, and tougher sentencing policies. These strategies limit the discretion of both police and victims as to the arrest and prosecution of offenders.

In recent years there has been an interest in ways of changing policing strategies to increase the preventative aspects of the law enforcement approach. This has involved the implementation of a range of innovative policing strategies that have the potential to increase police effectiveness in preventing domestic violence. These innovative solutions have involved police in implementing additional crime prevention strategies to the traditional, 'arrest, prosecute and sentence' approach to law enforcement. It is important to note that these strategies are not necessarily alternatives to the traditional policing role but rather an extension of their current role. These new prevention strategies emphasise the use of situational and community prevention strategies.

The aims of this chapter are twofold. The first is to examine our current theoretical and empirical understandings of the necessary conditions for a law enforcement approach to crime prevention. It will be argued that, because of the nature of domestic violence, a traditional law enforcement approach does not and can not meet these conditions. The second aim of the chapter is to explore the less traditional police role in some of the recent innovative crime prevention strategies aimed at preventing crime.

LAW ENFORCEMENT AS A CRIME PREVENTION STRATEGY

Tonry and Farrington (1995) identified law enforcement as one of four major crime prevention strategies. Laws are enacted and enforced to achieve one or more of the following four aims of the criminal justice system; retribution, deterrence, incapacitation and rehabilitation. The first of these four aims, retribution, has no preventative function. Offenders are punished to extract revenge for the wrongdoing and the suffering caused to the victims. It is postulated that the other three aims, deterrence, incapacitation and rehabilitation all have a role in the prevention of crime. Crime is prevented both directly and indirectly by the enforcement of laws. Indirect prevention occurs because of the impact of the law on the overall socialisation of individuals. Individuals do not commit crimes because it is illegal (and therefore wrong) to do so. Direct prevention involves the processes of deterrence, rehabilitation and incapacitation. Deterrence operates in two different ways, general deterrence and specific deterrence. General deterrence occurs when the punishment of criminal offenders serves as an example to the general public and discourages offending behaviour. Specific deterrence occurs when the punishment of an individual offender discourages them from further offending. Incapacitation usually involves a period of incarceration and prevents crime by removing the offenders from the situation. Rehabilitation of offenders refers to the use by the criminal justice system of some form of vocational, educational or therapeutic training or treatment to prevent future offending.

Police play a critical role in the law enforcement approach to the prevention of crime, as they are the gatekeepers to the criminal justice system. They make decisions concerning whether a law has been broken, whether arrest is the appropriate course of action and, if there is sufficient evidence of a crime, to proceed with a prosecution. They are also responsible for investigating and developing the prosecution case. An efficient police service is supposed to catch most of the serious offenders who then proceed through the criminal justice system and are punished. As a result, the offenders are deterred, rehabilitated or incapacitated and a message is sent out to the community that this behaviour is not tolerated and will be punished.

Unlike Tonry and Farrington's (1995) other three crime prevention strategies, developmental, community and situational prevention, law enforcement is predominantly a tertiary crime prevention strategy. That is, in order for it to be implemented a crime must be committed. The other three crime prevention strategies are predominantly primary prevention strategies in that they reduce the likelihood of crime occurring in the first place. Developmental crime prevention reduces the likelihood of an individual committing a crime by focusing on their developmental risk and protective factors. Community crime prevention focuses on interventions that change the social conditions. Situational prevention strategies reduce the opportunities and increase the risks to the potential offender of committing a crime.

The focus of this chapter is on the role of police in the prevention of domestic violence. The empirical literature examining the impact of the traditional law enforcement approach of arrest, prosecution and sentencing to the prevention of domestic violence will be examined. In addition the police role in both situational and community crime prevention strategies will be explored. However, before examining police responses to domestic violence the nature of the calls received by police to respond to will be examined.

THE NATURE OF DOMESTIC DISTURBANCES AND DOMESTIC VIOLENCE

McKean and Hendricks (1997) identified a number of dubious assumptions made in much of the literature examining the police response to domestic violence. These assumptions were that a call to the police for a domestic disturbance usually involved criminal violence, that this violence was usually by a man against a woman, and therefore the best way for the police to respond was by arresting the assailant. However, police get called to a range of domestic disturbances of which only one-third involve some form of criminal violence among family members (Elliot, 1986). The other calls include situations that call for order maintenance or peace keeping but not law enforcement. These include incidents such as loud verbal arguments with no violence, property damage, drunk and disorderly, and trespassing. Stewart (2000b) found similar results in her investigation of 18 months of police calls for service in a predominately residential police division. She examined calls that related to interpersonal violence but not to disturbances. Of the calls received, 9% (n = 616) concerned interpersonal violence and the majority of these were domestic violence. However, after the police had visited these calls only one-third were classified as domestic violence. A substantial proportion (25%) was downgraded to a disturbance, indicating there was no evidence of violence. In addition, arrest was not a viable option in approximately 20% of calls because by the time the police arrived the offender had left the scene. This finding, that an arrest is not made because the offender had left the scene at the time of the police arrival, has also been observed by other researchers (Hirschel & Hutchinson, 1992; Sherman, 1992).

Arrest may not be an option for police even in situations where there appears to be criminal violence. According to the Queensland Police Service Operations Procedure Manual, the discretionary decisions of who gets arrested and eventually prosecuted, are based primarily on the 'sufficiency of evidence' test (Section 3.4.1). Sufficiency of evidence is satisfied if there is a reasonable prospect of the defendant being found guilty when the case is presented in court. One of the key factors in this assessment is an evaluation of the availability of credible and co-operative witnesses. Stewart (2000b) found that when the victim made the call or there was evidence of physical violence the police were more likely to verify the incident as domestic violence.

These findings indicate that when police are called to a domestic disturbance or assault they are confronted with a wide range of possible situations (Hutchison, Hirschel & Peasackis, 1994). Not all of these situations will meet the criteria necessary for the offender to be arrested. In many situations they will not even involve domestic violence. In the next section the deterrence impact of arrest in domestic violence situations will be examinined.

Arrest, deterrence and domestic violence
The majority of work examining the law enforcement approach to preventing domestic violence has focused on deterrence and the arrest of domestic violence offenders. Interest in the deterrence impact of arrest in preventing future domestic violence was initially generated by the Minneapolis Domestic Violence Experiment (Sherman and Berk, 1984). This experiment compared three police responses to domestic violence; arrest, separation of the victim and assailant, and advice and mediation.

Sherman and Berk concluded, using a six-month follow-up period, that arrest was more effective at deterring violence than the other police responses. In addition at this time research was appearing that indicated that police were not responding as seriously to domestic assault as non-domestic assault cases (Black, 1980; Oppenlander, 1982). As a result of these findings, and litigation against police for not responding appropriately to domestic violence (*Thurman v. City of Torringrton*, 1984), mandatory arrest policies were adopted in many United States jurisdictions and arrest became the predominant response to domestic violence (Sherman, Smith, Schmidt, & Rogan, 1992).

Deterrence, both general and specific, was the rationale behind the adoption of arrest as the predominant response to domestic violence. Specific deterrence assumes that the swift arrest and strict application of criminal justice sanctions will prevent future criminal behaviour. Consequently, the arrest of a domestic violence offender indicates to the offender that domestic violence is a crime and therefore deters them from further offending. Also, this arrest sends out the message to the general population that it is a crime. Subsequent research has focused on the impact of arrest on domestic violence recidivism and changes in police behaviour in response to these changes in legislation and policy. This research has found that the impact of arrest in deterring future offending is not as clear-cut as the original findings indicated. In addition, despite the introduction of mandated arrest responses, there is substantial evidence that police are still not arresting domestic violence offenders.

Attempts at replicating the results of Sherman and Berk's original domestic violence experiment have provided conflicting results. In reviewing these replications Sherman et al. (1992) reported that in economically stable areas where unemployment was low and poverty less acute, arrest resulted in a reduction on re-offending. However, among unemployed and unmarried assailants arrest actually increased the rates of domestic assaults. Sherman et al. (1992) concluded that arrest deterred offenders who had a 'stake in conformity' and for whom contact with the criminal justice system was combined with a range of informal social controls (p. 680). Similar conclusions were provided by Fagan (1989) who suggested that criminal justice sanctions are more effective for first time offenders but have little impact on persistent offenders. From these findings it appears that a law enforcement approach to domestic violence may deter some offenders from re-offending but for other offenders it may escalate the violence experienced by the victim. Consequently, Schmidt & Sherman (1993) have argued that removing police discretion and mandating police responses to violence may have the impact of increasing the risk of assault for some women.

Despite substantial changes in the laws and the training of police officers there is still evidence that many reports to police of domestic violence do not result in arrest. Even after the introduction of mandatory arrest Ferraro (1989) observed that arrest occurred in only 18% of incidents. In jurisdictions with a preferred arrest policy the figures vary from 23% (Feder, 1998), 28.8% (Bourg & Stock, 1994) to 43% (Hoyle, 1998) of incidents resulting in arrest. These figures have been interpreted as indicting that domestic violence is treated more leniently by the criminal justice system than other interpersonal violence cases. Recent research comparing the arrest rates of domestic violence cases with other interpersonal violence cases has suggested that this is not true. Feder (1998) found that domestic assault calls were almost twice as likely to result in the arrest of the offender than were non-domestic assault calls although the rates were still fairly low (23% versus 13%). Stewart and Maddren (1997) found that police reported being more likely to arrest when the victim was the spouse of the perpetrator than when the victim was a male relative. Elliot (1989) found little evidence that different factors were involved in the decision to prosecute family violence cases compared to stranger violence crimes. It appears that it may be the nature of interpersonal violence that makes it difficult for police to arrest and prosecute rather than the relationship of the victim to the perpetrator.

The deterrence impact of arrest has been questioned. For some offenders it appears that arrest may impact on their future offending behaviour. However, for other offenders this may not be the case. In addition it appears that the nature of domestic violence makes it difficult for police to proceed through the criminal justice system. In the following sections the deterrence impact of prosecution and sentencing for domestic violence will be examined.

Prosecution and sentencing, deterrence and domestic violence

It has been suggested that the failure of arrest to deter offenders occurs partly because many offenders do not proceed through the criminal justice process from arrest to prosecution and sentencing. Not only do offenders need to be arrested; they also need the strict application of criminal justice sanctions to prevent future criminal behaviour. However, recent research indicates that even if a suspected offender is arrested, charges are laid in only 36% (Hoyle, 1998) of cases, and only 32% of cases where charges are laid (Thistlewaite, Wooldredge & Gibbs, 1998) result in a conviction and the subsequent punishment. Psychological research has identified a number of conditions necessary for punishment to be effective at changing behaviour. The punishment must be delivered immediately after the behaviour, it must be delivered every time the behaviour occurs, it must be sufficiently severe, and there must be no escape from the punishment (e.g. by lying or a superficial apology) (Van Houten, 1983; Sandon, Montgomery, Gault, Gridley & Thomson, 1996). In this section, the research on prosecution and sentencing of domestic violence offenders will be examined within the framework of the necessary conditions for effective punishment. Following this some of the negative side effects of punishment will be examined.

The first condition of a successful punishment response, the punishment must be delivered immediately after the behaviour, is never met by traditional law enforcement processes. The delays between when an offender is arrested, prosecuted and then sentenced are considerable. It may be that arrest can be considered a punishment in situations where the offender has a high stake in conformity. However, as most domestic violence perpetrators have already had extensive contact with the criminal justice system for violent offences both inside and outside the family (Stewart, 2000a) arrest is unlikely to be providing an immediate punishment.

The second condition, that the punishment is delivered every time it occurs, is also unlikely to be met. Dutton, Hart, Kennedy, and Williams (1992) examined offenders' perceptions of the likelihood of criminal sanctions. Among assaulters who had not been arrested, their perception of the likelihood of arrest for assault was low. The experience of arrest and subsequent prosecution heightened the offenders' perceived risk of legal sanctions but not necessarily their perceived risk of social sanctions such as loss of partner or social disapproval.

The third condition, that the punishment be sufficiently severe, has been examined. There has been limited research examining the effectiveness of different sentences for preventing future violence. Davis, Smith and Nickles (1998) showed no effect of type of disposition (non-continuation, dismissals, probation with batterer treatment program, and jail sentences) on the likelihood of recidivism over a six-month period. Ford and Regoli (1993) found that the chance of a man re-assaulting his partner is unaffected by whether he is prosecuted under policies calling for harsh punishment or for rehabilitative treatment. Conversely, Thistlethwaite et al. (1998) found that more severe sentences did correspond with lower recidivism rates. However, in accordance with Sherman et al. (1992), severe sentences appeared most effective for persons with greater stakes in conformity. It appears that the concept of severity differs with different offenders.

Psychological theory also has provided evidence of a range of negative side effects of punishment including observational learning, cycles of retaliation, strong emotional responses, and avoidance behaviour (Van Houten, 1983). Many of these side effects are evident in domestic violence offenders' responses to a criminal justice system intervention. There is substantial evidence of the inter-generational transmission of violence both from being a victim and experiencing violence (Gelles, 1998). Sherman et al. (1992) provided evidence that, for some offenders, police intervention resulted in an escalation of violence. Evidence of avoidance behaviour can be found in the observation that, following police intervention in a violent relationship, some offenders continue the violence in a new relationship (Stewart, 2000a).

Given the nature of domestic violence, that it frequently occurs in the home, between people who have, or have had an intimate relationship, and it occurs repeatedly, it is unlikely that the available criminal justice sanctions will meet the conditions necessary for effective deterrence. One of the critical factors in this is the victim–offender relationship. In the next section this will be discussed.

Victim's role in the criminal justice system
The domestic violence victim plays a critical role in the criminal justice response to domestic violence. Unlike other crimes the victim is often the only witness to the crime. Consequently, it is the victim who must contact the police with the report of violence and who must act as the primary witness in any prosecution. The vast majority of domestic violence incidences are not reported to the police. Victimisation surveys have consistently reported that only a minority of incidences are reported to the police (Australian Bureau of Statistics, 1996; Mirrlees-Black, 1999). Under-reporting to the police severely limits their ability to protect women. Furthermore, it seriously undermines the ability of the criminal justice system to effectively deliver a deterrence message. Despite changes in policing strategies, community attitudes to domestic violence and numerous public education campaigns, it appears that women are as reluctant to report violence to police now as they were 20 years ago (Australian Bureau of Statistics, 1996).

Traditional law enforcement advocates argue that the reason why women do not report to the police is because they perceive the police to be ineffective (Dobash and Dobash, 1992). However, the Women's Safety Survey (Australian Bureau of Statistics, 1996) asked women why they do not report to the police. Almost half (42.2%) said they dealt with it themselves and a quarter (26.5%) said they did not regard it as a serious offence. Only 8% said that they felt that the police could not do anything, while 4% said they did not want the perpetrator arrested and 2.6% said they were fearful of the perpetrator. The British Crime Survey found that of female victims, only 20% defined the violence as a crime. The two reasons suggested to explain this finding were that infrequent low level violence is not perceived as warranting a criminal justice system intervention and that victims who are reluctant to pursue a case are also reluctant to define the behaviour as a crime (Mirrlees-Black, 1999). Victims who regarded the incidences as crimes were more likely to report to the police. Mirrlees-Black (1999) reported that the police usually came to know about incidences when the woman was particularly frightened or injured, and where children overheard or saw the assault. However, an investigation of spousal homicide cases found that police had been contacted in less than half the cases in which there was evidence of previous violence (Easteal, 1993).

The predominant reason given for the attrition of domestic violence cases through the criminal justice system is victim unwillingness to proceed with both arrest and charges. Dunford, Huizinga and Elliott (1990), in the Omaha replication of the Minneapolis domestic violence experiment, reported that 60% of the arrests made in the experimental situation were against the women's expressed wishes. In non-experimental settings police regard the complainants' or victims' preferences as a major consideration in decisions whether or not to make an arrest. In many situations the victim is the only witness and without victim co-operation police are reluctant to proceed with the case (Hoyle, 1998). Furthermore, domestic violence victims make uncertain witnesses with many withdrawing their support for the prosecution, refusing to testify or changing their story. A range of reasons why women do not wish to proceed with a criminal justice response have been identified. Hoyle (1998) found women gave three reasons not to involve the police. First, women did not want to break up the relationship or the family unit. Second, they were afraid of retaliatory violence and, third, they had no faith in the criminal justice system (Hoyle, 1998). In some jurisdictions the victim's decision is not taken into account when deciding to proceed with a prosecution and in a few jurisdictions victims have been compelled by law to act as witnesses.

However, Ford (1991) has also suggested that some victims do use the criminal justice system as a 'rational power strategy' in that they use the range of sanctions available as threats to manage the violence (p. 313). These findings are supported by Dutton, Hart, Kennedy and Williams (1992) who suggested that arrest reduces domestic violence by altering the power dynamic in the relationship and by making a private event public. Ford and Regoli (1993) suggest that women should be empowered by allowing them to make choices in the prosecution process (i.e. whether to drop charges). These choices can result in an increase in their safety. Women are aware that while they live in the home, police are limited in their ability to protect them (Hoyle, 1998). However, women do not want to leave their abusive situations for a wide variety of financial, family, and cultural reasons (Ferrero, 1993). Consequently, the focus of the criminal justice system's response should be on providing victims with information and protection needed for them to make truly free choices.

Based on increasing research evidence, it appears that calls for increasing sentences and mandating police responses are unlikely to be effective in preventing violence. The last two aims of the criminal justice system, incapacitation and rehabilitation will be briefly examined.

Incapacitation and rehabilitation as crime prevention strategies
Incapacitation and rehabilitation are two additional strategies included within the law enforcement approach for the prevention of domestic violence. These strategies will be briefly examined. There has been little research on the effectiveness of incapacitation in preventing domestic violence. First, it appears that few domestic violence offenders are ever sent to jail (Hoyle, 1998). Moreover, despite substantial increases in the prison population there is no evidence that there has been a corresponding reduction in crime. While incapacitation may protect women while the offenders are incarcerated, this strategy is unlikely to provide any long-term change in offending behaviour.

Australia has been slow to develop programs designed to rehabilitate domestic violence perpetrators. There are a number of community-based programs available. However, participation in these programs is generally voluntary rather than mandated as a sentencing option. Gondolf (1997) reviewed the issues arising from perpetrator treatment programs. He identified a wide range of programs that differ in their approaches, formats and objectives. He concluded that the effectiveness and appropriateness of these programs in preventing violence have not yet been determined and that further research is needed. However, given that most programs are short-term interventions, it is unlikely that they will be effective in treating what is often a chronic and severe problem (Holtzworth-Munroe, Beatty, & Anglin, 1995).

It is important to continue to try to improve the traditional law enforcement approach to domestic violence. In a number of communities the criminal justice system is working with other agencies to develop a co-ordinated community response to domestic violence (e.g. Duluth Domestic Violence Intervention Program). In Australia similar programs have been trialed both in Canberra and in Townsville. Hirschel, Hutchison, Dean, and Mills (1992) in their review of these programs in the USA noted that these programs have generally been introduced in small cities with only relatively modest crime and domestic violence rates. As yet, no evidence has been provided that these programs reduce domestic violence. The primary aim of these programs is to improve the traditional law enforcement response.

One of the major criticisms of the traditional criminal justice response to domestic violence is that it has been typically reactive, responding only after the offences have occurred. In recent years there have been calls for police to take a stronger proactive policing role in preventing crime (Moore, 1992). Rather than attempting to achieve greater operational effectiveness through improvements in organisation and management, new approaches such as 'problem-orientated policing' (Goldstein, 1979) have been suggested. These approaches involve devising tailor-made solutions for individual problems through the detailed analyses of the situation. In response to increasing understanding about the repeat nature of crime (Farrell, 1995) a range of problem-orientated policing strategies have been identified and implemented. The phenomenon of repeat victimisation has identified that a small proportion of households repeatedly making calls account for a large proportion of all calls received by police. Furthermore, these repeat calls are more likely to occur soon after the initial call. Many of the problem-orientated policing strategies can be classified as situational crime prevention strategies as they attempt to reduce the opportunities and increase the risks to the perpetrators (Clarke, 1999). In the next section the application of situational strategies to domestic violence will be discussed.

Situational crime prevention strategies
Two projects involving the police utilising situational strategies have been implemented and evaluated by the Home Office. These are the Merseyside domestic violence prevention project (Lloyd, Farrell & Pease, 1994) and

the Killingbeck domestic violence and repeat victimisation project (Hanmer, Griffiths, & Jerwood, 1999).

The Merseyside domestic violence prevention project involved a rapid response system to domestic violence (Lloyd et al., 1994). Based on an understanding of repeat victimisation, women who were considered to be at risk of domestic violence were provided with a prevention package. The centrepiece of this package was a portable quick-response pendant alarm. These alarms were provided to women who had been the victim of domestic violence. They were directly linked to the police control room. Consequently, if the women suffered a repeat victimisation police responded rapidly to the women's call. In addition, a domestic violence incidence database was established ensuring police arrived at the incident well briefed. These alarms were not used in isolation. A community based domestic violence worker assisted the woman to address her long-term needs. An evaluation of the women's opinions of the alarms found that these women reported a reduction in fear, a reduction in violence and an increase in positive attitudes to police (Lloyd et al., 1994).

The Killingbeck domestic violence and repeat victimisation project (Hanmer et al., 1999) was a more sophisticated project than the Merseyside project and focused equally on both the victimised woman and the offending man. Three levels of police operational interventions, increasing in intensity, were developed. These interventions included official warnings, information letters, visits by the community constable and domestic violence officer, cocoon watch and police watch. Cocoon watch involves the police requesting the help and support of neighbours, family and relevant agencies to further protect the victim by contacting the police immediately. A cocoon watch was only implemented with the informed consent of the victim, and the perpetrator is made aware of the actions. Police watch involved providing a visible police presence to both the victim and offender with police patrolling within the vicinity of the incident on a twice weekly basis following a reported incidence. Evaluation of the program indicated a reduction in the number of repeat attendances and increased time intervals between attendances.

These projects appear to result in increased efficiency of the police response to domestic violence. However, they are proactive rather than reactive. They enhance the effectiveness of deterrence, and therefore prevent the offence from occurring, by increasing the perceived costs to the individual offender and reducing the opportunities for him to commit the offence. However, they also appear to increase the victim's satisfaction with the police and women are more willing to contact the police. This can be problematic if a reduction in calls to the police is seen as a measure of the effectiveness of the response.

Community crime prevention strategies, indigenous communities and the policing of domestic violence

The major challenge in Australia to the effective policing of domestic violence is the policing in indigenous communities in which violence is endemic. Strang (1993) found that indigenous people comprised 21% of homicide victims but they only make up 2.4% of the Australian population. Ferrante, Morgan, Indermaur, and Harding (1996) reported that the rates of domestic violence for Aborigines are up to 45 times those of non-Aboriginal Australians.

In Queensland the highest rates of violence occur in remote communities that are predominantly indigenous communities (Criminal Justice Commission, 1997). Figure 1 is a map of Queensland that indicates the rates of crime against the person by police division. Queensland is the second largest state in Australia (1,727,200 square kilometres) and is very sparsely populated. The majority of the population of 3 million people live in the southeast corner or on the eastern coast of the state. Over 80% of the population live in urban regions. From Figure 1 it is clear that the highest levels of interpersonal violence are experienced in the remote indigenous communities such as Doomadgee, Aurukun and Mornington Island.

Not only are these indigenous communities extraordinarily isolated but they are also very diverse both in language and culture. There are over 250 Aboriginal languages. After 200 years of colonisation, which has included the loss of land and the forced removal of children, there is substantial mistrust of the criminal justice system. Policing these remote and rural communities using traditional approaches to law enforcement is extremely difficult. There is currently a substantial debate about the appropriate policing of domestic violence (Robertson, 2000). In some communities there is a call for a more aggressive policing response. In other communities criminal justice interventions are seen as contributing to the substantial over-representation of Aboriginal people in correctional institutions. Furthermore, in these remote communities there are few additional support services such as refuges, women's legal aid, or women's health services.

In remote indigenous communities, community development or community crime prevention offers some hope in addressing the social conditions that cause the endemic violence experienced by these

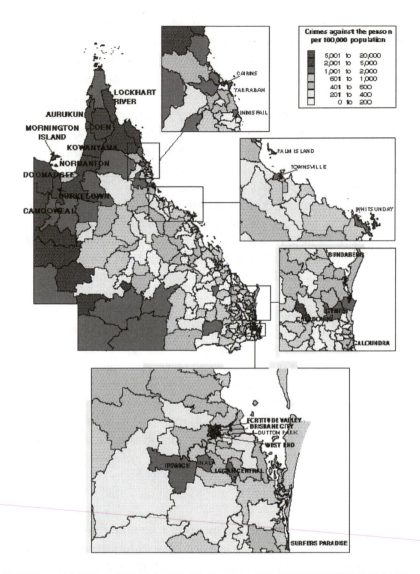

FIGURE 1: ANNUAL AVERAGE RATES OF CRIMES AGAINST THE PERSON BY POLICE DIVISION
Note: From *Snapshot of Crime in Queensland* (Research Paper Series, Vol 5, No 1.) (p. 5), by Criminal Justice Commission. Reprinted with permission.

communities (Homel, Lincoln & Herd, 1999). Community crime prevention does not focus on individual offenders or their victims but rather on changing the social conditions that are believed to sustain crime in residential communities (Hope, 1995). Police have a role in working with rural and remote communities in developing policing responses that are culturally sensitive and meet the needs of the individuals in the communities. In Queensland an example of such a program is provided through the Community Justice Program. This program which is currently running in 30 Aboriginal communities involves local Aboriginal people working in conjunction with the relevant criminal justice agencies to plan successful programs that go well beyond the criminal justice system (Department of Aboriginal and Torres Strait Island Policy and Development, 1998). An example of such an initiative is the night patrols by elders of the community to monitor disturbances, mediate disputes and keep juveniles out of trouble. Police make a radio available for the patrol and provide back-up support. Other initiatives include the strengthening of languages, culture and customary law, addressing health and alcohol related issues, dealing with truancy and the development of meaningful employment programs (d'Abbs, Hunter, Reser & Martin, 1994).

These programs involve an extension of the community policing role (Moore, 1995) which centres on creating partnerships between people and police in an attempt to solve problems. A community crime prevention model requires co-operation between police and members of the community in an attempt to change the criminogenic conditions of the community. The most powerful crime prevention strategies often depend on informal rather than formal social control processes. Consequently, the major aim of preventative policing should be to strengthen informal controls (Homel, 1994). This will often mean the transfer of some of the police power either to the victims (as in the situational strategies) or to members of the community.

SUMMARY

There is no simple answer to the question Can police prevent domestic violence? Without doubt, the traditional law enforcement approach of arrest, prosecution and sentencing is important in the management of domestic violence. This legal response to domestic violence may have a general deterrent impact as it conveys the message of societal intolerance towards domestic violence. Furthermore, in most jurisdictions the police are the only 24-hour service available to provide immediate protection for women. However, as it is a response that occurs only after the offence has been committed, the question is Does it prevent future offending? It would appear that for some men in some situations this response is effective in deterring future violence. Consequently, it is important to continue to improve the traditional law enforcement approach to domestic violence. Police officers need to receive support and training, cases need to be efficiently processed through the criminal justice system, and rehabilitation programmes need to be developed and evaluated. Furthermore, co-ordination between the police and the various agencies need to be developed and sustained to ensure the police response is consistent and efficient.

However, recent research has questioned the effectiveness of the criminal justice objectives of deterrence, incapacitation and rehabilitation for preventing further violence. There is an increasing body of research evidence that suggests that 'more of the same' is unlikely to produce the desired reductions in domestic violence. Furthermore, recent research has indicated that there are a number of serious unintended consequences of criminal justice interventions. Following police intervention it appears that some domestic violence perpetrators may increase the violence or, if the opportunities to victimise are blocked, move to another victim. Consequently, there is a need to explore and examine innovative policing and law enforcement strategies that extend the traditional reactive policing role. In extending the traditional law enforcement model, police need to utilise other crime prevention strategies such as community and situational prevention approaches. These crime prevention strategies need to strengthen informal controls and require police to be involved in 'power sharing'. This would require a substantial change in the current police culture and practices.

Finally, law enforcement alone will never truly prevent domestic violence. At its best it can only provide a 'Band-Aid' approach to the prevention of violence. Violence in the family should be prevented before it starts, which is long before it comes to the attention of the criminal justice system. To do this requires a shift from the focus on criminalisation of and law enforcement approaches for controlling violence to examining how to create less violent people, families, communities and societies.

REFERENCES

Australian Bureau of Statistics (1996). *Australian Women's Safety Survey No. 4128.* Canberra: Author.

Black, D. (1980). *The manner and customs of the police.* New York: Academic Press.

Clarke, R. V. (1999). *Situational crime prevention: Successful case studies.* New York: Harrow and Heston.

Criminal Justice Commission (1997). *A Snapshot of Crime in Queensland.* (Research Paper Series, Vol. 5. No. 1). Brisbane: Author.

d'Abbs, P., Hunter, E. Reser, J. & Martin, D. (1994). *Alcohol-related violence in Aboriginal and Torres Strait Islander communities: A literature review.* Canberra: Australian Government Publisher.

Davis, R. C., Smith, B. E. & Nickles, L. B. (1998). The deterrent effect of prosecuting domestic violence misdemeanours. *Crime and Delinquency, 44,* 434–442.

Department of Aboriginal and Torres Strait Islander Policy and Development (1998). *Local Justice Initiates Program: Interim Assessment of Community Justice Groups, Draft Report.* Brisbane: Author.

Dobash R. E., & Dobash, R. P. (1992). *Women, violence and social change.* London: Routledge.

Dutton, D. G., Hart, S. D. Kennedy, L. W. & Williams, K. R. (1992). Arrest and the reduction of repeat wife assault. In E. S. Buzawa & C. G. Buzawa (Eds.), *Domestic violence: The changing criminal justice response.* (pp. 111–127). Westport, Connecticut: Auburn House.

Dunford, F. W., Huizinga, D., & Elliott, D. S. (1990). The role of arrest in domestic assault: the Omaha police experiment. *Criminology 28,* 183–206.

Easteal, P. W. (1993). *Killing the beloved: Homicide between adult sexual intimates.* Canberra: Australian Institute of Criminology.

Elliott, D. S. (1989). Criminal justice procedures in family violence crimes. In L. Ohlin & M. Tonry (Eds.), *Family violence, Vol 11: Crime and justice, An annual review of research.* Chicago: University of Chicago Press.

Fagan, J. (1989). Cessation of family violence: Deterrence and dissuasion. In L. Ohlin & M. Tonry (Eds.). *Family violence (Volume 11: Crime and justice: An annual review of research).* Chicago: University of Chicago Press.

Fagan, J. & Browne, A. (1994). Violence between spouses and intimates: Physical aggression between women and men in intimate relationships. In A. J. Reiss, & J. A. Roth. (Eds.), *Understanding and preventing violence: Volume 3: Social influences.* Washington: National Academy Press.

Farrell, G. (1995). Preventing repeat victimization. In M. Tonry and D. P. Farrington (Eds.) *Building a safer society: strategic approaches to crime prevention.* Chicago: University of Chicago Press.

Farrington, D. P. (1992). Psychological contributions to the explanation, prevention and treatment of offending. In F. Losel, D. Bender, T Bliesener (Eds.). *Psychology and law: International perspectives.* Berlin: W. de Gruyter.

Feder, L. (1998). Police handling of domestic and nondomestic assault calls: Is there a case for discrimination. *Crime and Delinquency, 44,* 335–349.

Ferrante, A., Morgan, F., Indermaur, D. & Harding, R. (1996). *Measuring the extent of domestic violence.* Sydney: Hawkins Press.

Ferrero, K. J. (1993). Cops, courts and women battering. In P. B. Hart and E. G. Morgan (eds.). *Violence Against Women: The Bloody Footprint.* Newbury Park CA: Sage.

Ford, D. A. (1991). Prosecution as a victim power resource: A note on empowering women in violent conjugal relationships. *Law and Society Review, 25,* 313–334.

Ford, D. A. & Regoli, M. J. (1993). The criminal prosecution of wife assaulters: Process, problems and effects. In Z. N. Hilton (Ed.), *The legal responses to wife assault: Current trends and evaluation.* (pp. 127–164). Newbury Park: Sage.

Gelles, R. J. (1998). Family violence. In M. Tonry (Ed.), *The handbook of crime and punishment.* New York: Oxford University Press.

Goldstein, H. (1979). Improving policing: A problem-orientated approach. *Crime and Delinquency, 25,* 36–58.

Gondolf, E. W. (1997). Batterer programs: What we know and need to know. *Journal of Interpersonal Violence, 12,* 83–99.

Hanmer, J., Griffiths, S. & Jerwood, S. (1999). *Arresting evidences: Domestic violence and repeat victimisation. Police research series paper 104.* London: Home Office.

Hirschel, J. D., Hutchison, I. W., Dean, C. W. Mills, A. (1992) Review essay on the law enforcement response to spouse abuse: Past, present and future. *Justice Quarterly, 9,* 247–283.

Holtzworth-Munroe, A., Beatty, S. B., & Anglin, K. (1995). The assessment and treatment of marital violence. In N. S. Jacobson & A. S. Gurman (Eds.), *Clinical handbook of couple therapy* (2nd ed.; pp. 317–339). New York: Guilford.

Homel, R. (1994). Can police prevent crime? In K. Bryett, & C. Lewis. *Un-peeling tradition: Contemporary policing.* South Melbourne: Macmillan Education.

Homel, R. Lincoln, R. & Herd, B. (1999). Risk and resilience: crime and violence prevention in aboriginal communities. *Australian and New Zealand Journal of Criminology, 32,* 182–197.

Hope, T. (1995). Community crime prevention. In M. Tonry and D. P. Farrington (eds.) *Building a safer society: strategic approaches to crime prevention.* Chicago: University of Chicago Press.

Hoyle, C. (1998). *Negotiating domestic violence.* Oxford: Clarendon Press.

Hutchison, I. W., Hirschel, J. D., & Peasackis, C. E. (1994). Family violence and police utilization. *Violence and Victims, 9,* 299–313.

Jones. A. (1994). *Next time she will be dead: Battering and how to stop it.* Boston, MA: Beacon Press.

Johnson, M. P. (1995). Patriarchal terrorism and common couple violence: Two forms of violence against women. *Journal of Marriage and the Family, 57,* 283–294.

Lloyd, S., Farrell, G. & Pease, K. (1994). *Prevention of domestic violence: a demonstration project on Merseyside. Police Research Group Crime Prevention Unit Series No. 49.* London: Home Office

McKean, J. & Hendricks, J.E. (1997). The role of crisis intervention on the police response to domestic disturbances. *Criminal Justice Policy Review, 8,* 269–294.

Mirrlees-Black, C. (1999). *Domestic violence: Findings from a new British Crime Survey self-completion questionnaire. Home Office Research Study No. 191.* London: Home Office.

Moore, M. H. (1992). Problem-solving and community policing. In M. Tonry & N. Morris (Eds.), *Modern policing. (Crime and justice A review of research Vol 15).* (pp. 99–158). Chicago: University of Chicago Press.

Oppenlander, N. (1982). Coping or copping out: police service delivery in domestic disputes. *Criminology, 20,* 449–465.

Robertson, B. (2000). *The Aboriginal and Torres Strait Islands Women's Task Force on Domestic Violence Report.* Queensland Government Press: Brisbane.

Sandon, A., Montgomery, B., Gault, U., Gridley, H. and Thomson, D. (1996). Punishment and behaviour change: An Australian Psychological Society position paper. *Australian Psychologist, 31,* 157–165.

Schmidt, J. D., & Sherman, L. W. (1993). Does arrest deter domestic violence? *American Behavioral Scientist, 36,* 601–609.

Sherman, L. W., & Berk, R. A. (1984). The specific deterrent effects of arrest for domestic assault. *American Sociological Review, 49,* 261–272.

Sherman, L. W., Smith, D. A. Schmidt, J. D. & Rogan, D. P. (1992). Crime, punishment, and stake in conformity: legal and informal control of domestic violence. *American Sociological Review, 57,* 680–690.

Snider, L. (1998). Towards safer societies: Punishment, masculinities and violence against women. *The British Journal of Criminology, 38,* 1–39.

Stewart, A. L. (2000a). Who are the perpetrators of domestic violence? *Australian and New Zealand Journal of Criminology, 33,* 77–90.

Stewart, A. L. (2000b). *Interpersonal violence: analyses of police calls for service.* Manuscript in preparation.

Stewart, A. L. & Maddren, K. (1997). Police officers' judgement of blame in family violence: the impact of gender and alcohol. *Sex Roles, 37,* 921–935.

Strang, H. (1993). *Homicides in Australia 1990–91.* Canberra: Australian Institute of Criminology.

Straus, M. A. (1996). Identifying offenders in criminal justice research on domestic violence.

In E. S. Buzawa and C. G. Buzawa (Eds.), *Do arrests and restraining orders work?* (pp. 14–29). Thousand Oaks: Sage.

Thistlewaite, A. , Wooldredge, J., Gibbs. D. (1998). Severity of dispositions and domestic violence recidivism. *Crime and Delinquency, 44*, 388–389.

Thurman v. City of Torringrton 595 F. Supp. 1521 (D Conn 1984).

Tonry M. & Farrington, D. P. (1995). Strategic approaches in crime prevention. In M. Tonry and D. P. Farrington (Eds.) *Building a safer society: strategic approaches to crime prevention.* Chicago: University of Chicago Press.

Van Houten, R. (1983). Punishment: From the animal laboratory to the applied setting. In S. Axelrod & J. Apsche (Eds.). *The effects of punishment on human behavior.* (pp. 13–44). New York: Academic Press.

Chapter 14

MUTILATION-MURDER CASES IN JAPAN

Kazumi Watanabe and Masayuki Tamura

Although the overall number of murder cases has decreased in Japan since 1945, the number of such cases involving mutilation has risen sharply in the last decade (Figure 1). The occurrence of mutilation-murder is still rare relative to other offences. Official task forces investigated, on average, almost six cases per year in the last decade. Despite the increase in mutilation-murder cases, there has been little statistical analysis of these offences. There are only a few medical-legal case reports, such as the work of Sugiyama et al. (1995) on four cases in Osaka prefecture between 1984 and 1993. Thus, compiling a database and investigating the characteristics of mutilation murder are important directions for research.

This chapter explores mutilation-murder cases as part of a broader project on criminal-offender profiling. Holmes (1990) suggested that lust and mutilation murder is one of the crime types most appropriate for psychological profiling, because of the possibility that dismemberment has some sexual meaning. Ressler et al.'s (1986, 1988) F.B.I. research on mutilation-murder cases also focused on cases involving sexual aspects.

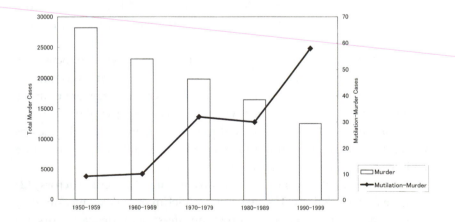

FIGURE 1: TRENDS OF TOTAL MURDER AND MUTILATION–MURDER CASES

Watanabe and Tamura (1998) suggested from their analysis of cases in Japan from 1947 to 1996 that most offenders dismember their victims in order to dispose of or destroy physical evidence. Our data set contained three cases involving sexual motives by three serial offenders. However, in many cases we could not distinguish whether sexual fantasy was involved since the body parts were found long after the victim's death and/or had become severely decomposed. For these reasons our current study analyzes all mutilation-murder cases even if a sexual motive can not be determined.

The purpose of this study is to explore the relationship among victim, offence and offender factors in mutilation-murder cases. Furthermore, we investigate the usefulness of frames for predicting victim–offender relationships and traits of mutilation murderers based on victim and offence characteristics.

METHOD

We define mutilation-murder cases as homicides where the offenders dismember the victims. By this definition, 134 mutilation-murder cases (104 solved cases and 30 unsolved cases) were investigated by official task forces between 1947 and 1998. We collected the records of those cases reported to the National Police Agency. This data does not include all mutilation-murder cases in Japan, since cases not investigated by official task forces are not reported to the National Police Agency. The clearance rate for mutilation-murder cases reported to the National Police Agency is 78.0%, and it is lower than the almost 90.0% clearance rate for all murder cases. The difference lies in the difficulties in victim identification in mutilation murders when compared with other murder cases.

Our study excludes fourteen cases due to missing data, and focuses on the 90 solved cases. In almost 80.0% of the cases, perpetrators committed the homicide without an accomplice. In cases where there were multiple offenders, one significant offender was selected as a subject of the analysis. Most of the cases (95.6%) involved only one victim. In the three cases where more than one victim was involved, one significant victim whose body was mutilated was selected for each case.

This study analyzes the relationships among (1) Victim factors, (2) Offence factors, and (3) Offender factors. Victim factors are measured by four variables: sex, age, occupation, and life-style. Offence factors are measured by nine variables: site where the body was found (in a body of water, buried etc.), the number of sites where the body parts were found, causes of death, the number of body parts removed, from which part of the body removed, removal of muscles and adipose tissues, removal of internal organs, removal of genitals, and whether the body was burned. Offender factors consist of six variables: age, occupation, victim–offender relationship, was the offender living with the victim, the motivation for killing, and the number of offenders. The sex of the offender was excluded from the study due to limited variation (e.g., female offenders committed only six cases).

Based on nonlinear canonical correlation analysis (OVERALS), mutilation-murder cases could be divided into three groups: those with victims less than 20 years old; those where the victims were females aged 20 or older; and those where the victims were males aged 20 or older (Watanabe and Tamura, 2000). The remainder of this article examines the differences among these three groups according to victim–offender relationships and offence factors, and investigates mutilation-murder cases in their respective groups.

SAMPLE DESCRIPTION

Victim Demographics
The range in victims' ages was between 5 and 79 years old, with a mean age of 38.8 years. In terms of gender distribution, 47.8% of victims were male. The majority of the victims were Japanese; only 8.9% of the victims were non-Japanese.

Crime Scene Demographics
In almost half of the cases the number of body parts removed was between two and five (45.6%). In 43.3% of the cases more than five body parts were removed. Although in the majority of the cases the offender cut the victim's body into multiple pieces, in 55.6% of the cases the body parts were found at one place. In 80.0% of the cases, the body parts were abandoned in the same pattern. In one-third of the cases, the victim's body parts were found in a body of water such as river, lake, sea or port. Roughly 16.7% of the body parts were buried while 22.2% were left on the ground or floor unattended. In 10.0% of the cases the victim's body parts were burned.

In fifteen cases, autopsy failed to reveal the cause of death. Where a clear cause could be determined, 52.2% involved body injury, 26.0% involved suffocation, and 16.7% were due to other causes.

Victim–Offender Relationships

The majority of the victims knew the offender (86.7%). Almost 40% of the cases were committed by kin or lovers of the victims. In one-third of the cases, the victim lived with the offender at the time of the incident (31.1%).

Offender Demographics

The age of offenders ranged between 14 and 72 years old, with a mean age of 39.8 years. In terms of gender distribution, 93.3% of offenders were male. The majority of the offenders were Japanese; 12.2% of the offenders were non-Japanese.

RESULTS

Differences among Three Groups of Victims

Comparison of V-O Relationship: These three groups reveal statistically significant differences in Offender factors as predicted by Victim and Offence factors. Victim–offender relationships are examined in Table 1. The data in Table 1 suggest that the distribution of victim–offender relationships is different among the 3 groups (χ^2=50.31, df=6, p<.001). Offenders who did not know their victims comprised the largest proportion of the cases in which the victim was less than 20 years old. This group has no cases in which the offender was a family member of the victim. In those cases where the female victim was 20 or more years old, the largest proportion of offenders consisted of lovers or spouses of the victim. In this group, cases where the offender and victim were strangers were rare. Offenders in those cases where the male victim was 20 or more years old were predominantly acquaintances. Although there is no statistically significant difference in the proportion of the cases where the victim lived with the offender among the three groups, in almost 44% of the cases in which the female victim was 20 or more years old the victim lived with the offender prior to the homicide. This proportion is large compared with that of the other victim types.

Comparison of Offender Traits: We compared the traits of offenders in the 3 types of mutilation-murder along three dimensions: the age of offenders, number of offenders, and occupation of offenders. As shown in Table 2, the distribution of offenders by age differed for the three groups (χ^2=28.62, df=12, p<.01). In cases where the victim was less than 20 years old, almost 60.0% of the offenders were between the ages of 20 and 29. When the victims were older than 19, the largest proportion of cases involving female victims were committed by offenders aged 40 and

Table 1: Victim–Offender Relationship by Victim Type

	Victim Type			
	Victim less than 20 years	Female victim 20 years or more	Male victim 20 years or more	All victims
Victim–Offender Relationship***				
Kinship		8 19.5%	4 10.0%	12 13.3%
Lover	1 11.1%	22 53.7%	4 10.0%	27 30.0%
Acquaintance	2 22.2%	9 22.0%	28 70.0%	39 43.3%
Stranger	6 66.7%	2 4.9%	4 10.0%	12 13.3%
Total	9 100.0%	41 100.0%	40 100.0%	90 100.0%

***p<.001

older. In male-victim cases, the offenders were predominantly between the ages of 30 and 49. The number of offenders was also different among the three victim types (χ^2=10.75, df=4, p<.05). In all of the cases where the victim was less than 20 years old, the offenders acted without an accomplice. The proportion of cases with more than one offender is largest in the case of male victims 20 and older. The occupation of offenders did not differ across the type of victim.

Comparison of Motivation for Killing: The relationships between motivation for killing and victim type are examined in Table 3. These results suggest that the distribution of the motivation for killing also differs by type of victim (χ^2=52.20, df=14, P<.001). In 75.0% of the cases where the victim was less than 20 years old, the offender's motivation for killing involved sex. In the cases of female victims older than 19, 60.0% were killed because of quarrel or brawl between lovers or spouses. Where male victims older than 19 were killed and mutilated, almost one half of the cases involved money or money trouble with acquaintances. In this group, the distribution of the motivation for killing varied more extensively when compared with other two groups.

This section of the chapter revealed statistically significant differences in offender variables as predicted by victim and offence factors. These findings suggest that an analytical frame based on the sex and age of victim also may have validity. Therefore, characteristics of the cases in three groups by victim's sex and age are shown below.

Characteristics of Mutilation-Murder Cases in three Groups
Victims less than 20 years old: This group with victims less than 20 years old consists of nine cases. Table 4 shows characteristics of all cases in this group. In each case, one male offender murdered one victim. The victims' ages ranged from five to 19 years old. The victims had no relationship

Table 2: Offender Traits by Victim Type in Mutilation-Murder Cases

	Victim Type			
	Victim less than 20 years N=9	Female victim 20 years or more N=41	Male victim 20 years or more N=40	All victims N=90
Age of Offender**				
~19 years	1 11.1%	3 7.3%	9 22.5%	1 1.1%
20~29 years	5 55.6%	12 29.3%	13 32.5%	17 18.9%
30~39 years	1 11.1%	12 29.3%	14 35.0%	26 28.9%
40~49 years	2 22.2%	12 29.3%	4 10.0%	28 31.1%
50~59 years		2 4.9%		16 17.8%
60~ years				2 2.2%
Occupation of Offender				
No occupation	1 11.1%	18 43.9%	13 32.5%	32 35.6%
Has occupation	7 77.8%	23 56.1%	26 65.0%	56 62.2%
Student	1 11.1%		1 2.5%	2 2.2%
Number of Offenders*				
1	9 100.0%	35 85.4%	25 62.5%	69 76.7%
2~3		6 14.6%	11 27.5%	17 18.9%
4-6			4 10.0%	4 4.4%

**p<.01, *p<.05

Table 3: Motivation for Killing by Victim Type in Mutilation-Murder Cases

	Victim Type							
	Victim less than 20 years		Female victim 20 years or more		Male victim 20 years or more		All victims	
Motivation for Killing***								
Sex	6	66.7%	2	4.9%	1	2.5%	9	10.0%
Money			7	17.1%	11	27.5%	18	20.0%
Lovers' Quarrel or Brawl	2	22.2%	26	63.4%	11	27.5%	39	43.3%
Money Trouble with Acquaintances			2	4.9%	6	15.0%	8	8.9%
Revenge			1	2.4%	2	5.0%	3	3.3%
Lynching					3	7.5%	3	3.3%
Other Quarrel or Brawl	1	1.11%	2	4.9%	3	7.5%	6	6.7%
Others			1	2.4%	3	7.5%	4	4.4%
Total	9	100.0%	41	100.0%	40	100.0%	90	100.0%

***p<.001

with the offenders prior to the homicide in 66.7% of the cases. This finding suggests that the investigation of mutilation-murder cases involving younger victims is likely to be more difficult when compared with other cases.

The nine cases can be divided into three groups based on the motivation for killing. The first group involves one case, which took place between foreign co-workers living in the same dormitory. In this case the body was found at a murder site, the dormitory. The second group consists of two cases, in which the offenders had friendly ties and some type of sexual relationship with the victims prior to the offence. All of the victims in these cases were 19 years old and the motivation for the homicide stemmed from trouble between the offender and the victim. All offenders in this group abandoned the body near the victim's house.

The third group consists of six that have some sexual dimension. Although five cases revealed that the offenders killed their victims as part of sexual activities (such as rape before death, rape after death or molestation), only one case reveals that that the offender knew, killed and mutilated his victim for experimentation and sexual satisfaction. This latter case of a juvenile lust murderer who killed and dismembered his acquaintance is a new trend in this category.

Most of the offenders in these groups were distinguished by high criminality. Two were serial killers, one was a serial rapist, one was a serial child molester, one had a criminal record of rape murder and body disposal, and only one had no criminal record. Most of the offenders used a car to abandon the body in locations more than 2 kilometers apart from victim's residences.

Although our results suggest that the location of body disposal is related to the offender's motivation for murder and the victim–offender relationship, this finding reflects the analysis of only a small number of cases and requires further data collection and research.

Female victims 20 years old or more: This group with female victims 20 and older consists of 41 cases. Almost 90.0% of the cases involved a single offender. In most of the cases involving an accomplice, the offender killed a spouse or a lover of their family member. With the exception of one case where the offender dismembered the body of his wife after he killed his wife and child, offenders victimized one female in each case in this group. The case where husband and wife killed and dismembered was classified into a group of male victims 20 years or more. Half of the cases involved victims between the ages of 20 and 39, while the other half consisted of victims 40 and older.

Table 4: Characteristics of the Cases in which Victim was Under 20 Years of Age

| Case NO. | Body disposal locations | Victim | | | | Offender | | |
		Age, Sex	Occupation	V-O Relationship	Motive	Age, Sex	Occupation	Other traits
1	Victim's residence	19M	Factory Worker	Peer	Quarrel or Brawl	27M	Factory Worker	Both victim and offender are foreigners
2	Near the victim's residence	19F	Farmer	Stranger (misidentify stranger with ex-lover)	Lovers' Quarrel or Brawl	29M	Craftsman	Misidentify stranger with ex-lover
3	Near the victim's residence	19F	Hairdresser	Lover	Lovers' Quarrel or Brawl	28M	No Occupation	
4	Near the victim's residence	11M	Elementary School Child	Acquaintance	Sex	14M	Junior School Student	Serial killer
5	Far from the victim's residence	17F	High School Student	Stranger	Sex	42M	Factory Worker	Has crime history of rape murder
6	Far from the victim's residence	5F	Pre-school Child	Stranger	Sex	27M	Factory Worker	Serial killer
7	Far from the victim's residence	14F	Junior School Student	Stranger	Sex	29M	Mechanic	Serial rapist
8	Far from the victim's residence	12M	Elementary School Child	Stranger	Sex	31M	No Occupation	Serial child molester, Schizophrenia
9	Far from the victim's residence	17F	No Occupation	Stranger	Sex	41M	Restaurant Manager	No crime history

In all of the cases the offenders met with and spent several hours with the victims just before the murder. In almost one half of the cases, the victims worked in businesses affecting public morals (e.g., as prostitutes or bar hostesses) and their murders stemmed from sex-related disputes. In 72.0% of the cases, the victims were killed by either family members or lovers. Distinguishing this group from those where the victim–offender relationship was not as strong is important for the decision making of investigators. Discriminant analysis was conducted with eight variables of victim and offence factors such as:

1. removal of muscles and adipose tissue
2. body parts were buried
3. cause of death was body injury
4. victim was working as a hostess
5. victim was living alone
6. removal of the head
7. victim was 40–49 years old
8. the number of body parts removed was between 2 and 5

In almost 90.0% of the cases where family members or lovers were the offenders, these cases could be discriminated from the other cases of victim–offender relations (eigenvalue = .735, correlation coefficient = .651).

The victims' ages ranged from between 20 to 70 years old in both groups. Although the distribution of the offenders' ages was correlated with that of the victims' ages in the group in which the offenders were not family members or lovers of the victims, the majority of the offenders in the other group were between 30 and 50 years old. Except for one case committed by two offenders, a father and his son, all of the cases in the group "victims killed and mutilated by their family members or lovers" involved offenders acting without accomplices. By comparison, the proportion of the cases committed by the offenders with an accomplice in the other group is large (45.5%).

The majority of the cases in which female victims aged 20 years and older were killed and mutilated by non-family members/lovers of the victims occurred in the last decade (63.6%), and these cases have become a new trend of this adult female group.

Male victims 20 years old or more: This group with male victims 20 years old or more consists of 40 cases. The percentage of cases committed by offenders acting alone (62.5%) is the lowest of the three groups. In contrast to the other two groups of victims, the offender's motive and relationship with the victim in this group of cases reveals less clear patterns.

The primary motivations for killing in this group were "money" (27.5%) and "lovers' quarrel or brawl" (27.5%). Although discriminant analysis was conducted with the variables of victim and offence factors, all of the cases in which offender's primary motivation for killing was to get money were not discriminated clearly from the other cases. All of the cases in which offender's motivation for killing was a quarrel or brawl between lovers were not discriminated clearly from the other cases as well. These results suggest that further analysis on the typology of this group is needed. The case descriptions were shown below by V-O relationships.

Eighty percent of the cases consisted of offences commited by acquaintances. In contrast to the adult female victim cases, the offenders and victims were rarely lovers (10.0%) but were more likely to be acquainted through their jobs (40.0%). The most frequent motive for the homicide was robbery murder.

Kinship ties were very rare in this group; only four cases were found. One case in 1963 revealed that the offender was the victim's schizophrenic brother. A second case in 1997 revealed that the offender was the victim's wife and had a criminal record of robbery murder. The third case in 1998 involved an offender who was the victim's wife. She had no criminal record and killed her husband in a quarrel over money. In the fourth case in 1998, the offender was a son of the victim, and the offender had beaten his father to death. In the last decade this kinship type of case has increased.

There were only four cases where the victims did not know the offenders. In two of these cases, the offenders were serial killers. The first case in 1958 revealed that the male offender killed a day laborer in order to disguise himself as the victim. The offender was a murder suspect and on the run. In the second case in 1989 the male offender killed a homeless elder male for the purpose of molestation. The two other cases had weaker V-O relationships. In one case in 1976, the male offender met with the male victim at the pub and then spent time drinking in the victim's house prior to a robbery-homicide. He killed the victim because he wanted to make certain that evidence of his theft was destroyed. The last case in 1998 revealed that the male offender and his accomplice knew the victim's wife. The offenders all belonged to criminal organizations and killed the victim to get money.

CONCLUSION

This chapter is based on the first statistical analysis of mutilation-murder cases in Japan. Because the occurrence of such cases is rare, the study collected data as reported to the National Police Agency over almost the past fifty years.

The difficulties and costs for the offenders in dismembering their victims lead to the hypothesis that the offenders had a strong relation with their victims. Investigators commonly hold this hypothesis when dealing with mutilation-murder cases. Our results suggest that this hypothesis is not applicable to all mutilation-murder cases, and instead holds more for cases involving adult female victims.

Revealing statistically significant differences in offender variables as predicted by victim and offence factors, those three groups are useful frames for the profiling of mutilation-murderers. When the victim's age is under 20, all of the cases, except for those where the victims were 19 years old, were carried out by strangers and for sexual reasons. All of the cases in which adult female victims were killed and mutilated by their family members or lovers were discriminated by victim and offence factors from other cases. The adult female victims group, except for the cases where the victim was killed by kinship or lover, is considered to be a new trend in mutilation-murder cases. The adult male victims group is most difficult to analyze because of the diversity of the cases. As the sample size is small in every group, further research is needed to test this analytical frame. Also the cases in which the victim was less than 20 years of age suggest that geographic information analysis of body disposal locations is needed.

REFERENCES

Holmes, R.M. and Holmes, S.T. (1996). *Profiling Violent Crimes: An Investigative Tool,* Sage.

National Police Agency (1956–1999). Criminal Statistics.

Ressler, R.K., Burgess, A.W., Hartman, C.R., Douglas, J.E. and MaCormack, A. (1986). Murderers Who Rape and Mutilate. *Journal of Interpersonal Violence,* Vol.1, No.3, 273–287.

Ressler, R.K., Burgess, A.W. and Douglas, J.E. (1988). *Sexual Homicide: Patterns and Motives,* Lexington Books.

Sugiyama, S., Tatsumi, S., Noda, H., Yamaguchi, M., Furutani, A., Izumi, M., Wakatsuki, R. and Yoshimura, M. (1995). Investigation of Dismembered Corpses Found during the Past 10 Years in Osaka. *Acta Criminologiae et Medicinae Legalis Japonica,* 61, 5, 192–200.

Watanabe, K. and Tamura, M. (1998). Analysis on the Characteristics of Mutilation-Murder Cases in the last 50 Years. *Reports of the National Research Institute of Police Science (Research on Prevention of Crime and Delinquency),* 39, 52–65.

Watanabe, K. and Tamura, M. (1999). Profiling on Mutilation-Murder Cases. *Reports of the National Research Institute of Police Science (Research on Prevention of Crime and Delinquency)*, 40, 1–19.

Chapter 15

CHASING GHOSTS: OFFENDER PROFILING AND TERRORISM

Andrew Silke

Offender profiling is one of the most distinctive areas in contemporary forensic psychology. It is also one of the most controversial. It is unlikely that there is any other topic in the area on which so much has been written on the basis of so little research. Probably less than 2% of qualified forensic psychologists will ever actually construct an offender profile and even fewer will publish research on the subject. Yet despite such fringe credentials, offender profiling has emerged as one of the consistently 'hot' topics in the discipline for nearly two decades.

Recent years in particular have seen forensic psychologists begin to dominate the literature on the subject more. However, it is a somewhat worrying sign that this growing contribution from psychologists is primarily taking the form of books, rather than research articles in peer-reviewed journals. It is one of the deep concerns with the entire area that it often seems that there are as many books published on the topic each year as there are research papers. Journals use peer reviewing as their primary and most important method of quality control. A wealth of research testifies to the fact that if reviewers are concerned about the quality of a research paper then it is very unlikely that the editors will decide to publish. Even a cursory review of forensic psychology conferences shows that a reasonable amount of related research appears to be happening in the area. At the EAPL conference in Dublin for example, there were at least nine papers on the subject. However, there is a depressing failure for most of this research effort to transfer into journal articles. In the three-year period from 1997 to 1999 there were at least eleven separate research papers on offender profiling presented at conferences held in the UK. In contrast, during these same years only one research paper on the subject actually made it into a mainstream UK forensic psychology journal (i.e. Cantor and Fritzon, 1998).

This tendency for research to apparently fall by the wayside raises understandable questions about quality. Traditionally, offender profiling research has been dominated by case study analysis, research which focuses on peripheral aspects of the subject or research which focuses on more central issues but relies on obtuse or obscure methodologies to analyse and report findings. The overall result is that while the wider interest in the area has continued to thrive, in research terms the field has been stifled and constantly left exposed to justified criticism.

Nevertheless, a truly remarkable feature of offender profiling is that despite the lamentable state of its research base, as a technique used in the real world it has not only endured but has actually thrived. Surveys in both the USA and the UK have consistently shown that law enforcement agencies are using offender profiling techniques more regularly than ever before. Indeed, the growth and acceptance of the practice in applied settings has been nothing short of phenomenal. Not only are the techniques used more frequently for the offences for which they were first developed, there has been a growing trend to use the same techniques in relation to an ever widening range of criminal activities. It is the spread of these techniques into terrorist investigations which is the focus of this chapter. As we shall see, there are a number of well-documented cases describing how profiles of terrorists have been produced in an effort to assist police investigations. This chapter reviews the success and failure of these profiles and considers the implications for future offences.

WHAT EXACTLY IS OFFENDER PROFILING?

This is becoming an increasingly difficult question to answer. There are two main reasons for this. One is because of the nebulous nature of the research literature on the subject. There is not a lot of it and what there is tends to be focused on a surprisingly disparate range of topics. Overall, there is a relatively poor level of synthesis with past work. The situation is not helped by conceptual confusion over definitions. Depending on the author in question, profiling is variously referred to as: psychological profiling, criminal personality profiling, criminal personality assessment, criminal behaviour profiling, offender profiling, criminal profiling or investigative profiling. As a result, the conceptual framework which should hold the area together lacks rigour. No solid benchmarks or conceptual definitions have been established, so there is no widely agreed context for new writers or researchers to place their work into. Further, serious personality clashes abound leading to an extremely high level of acrimony and hostility between individual profilers, both as practitioners and as researchers. A culture of backbiting and closed-mindedness has come to dominate in both the USA and the UK and this has seriously undermined efforts to establish a solid research base and to set conceptual definitions and standards.

The second reason why it is difficult to say what it is, lies in the fact that offender profiling is very much a victim of its own success. As already indicated, there has been impressive applied growth in the area and offender profilers as practitioners are being used more and more frequently. However, just as importantly, the roles they play are expanding and changing and the types of crimes they are involved in are also beginning to vary considerably. As a term, 'offender profiling' is struggling badly to keep pace.

This chapter though follows the succinct view of Hazelwood, Ressler, Depue and Douglas (1995) that a "profile (characteristics and traits of an unidentified person) is a series of subjective opinions about the unknown person(s) responsible for a crime or a series of crimes" (p. 123). The traditional account of profiling is that it works on the premise that an offender's behaviour at the crime scene can reveal aspects of his or her personality, work background, family history, social life, criminal history and age. Under ideal circumstances, a profile is normally generated only after extensive examination has been made of crime scene photographs, victim background reports, autopsy reports and other police reports on the crime.

The original aim of profiling was simply to help law enforcement focus investigations – either by narrowing an overwhelming list of suspects to a small subgroup or by providing new avenues of inquiry. The growing reputation of profiling is largely due to the widespread belief that it is used to identify specific offenders, but the reality is that the technique is rarely this effective. As experienced FBI profilers point out, "profiles have led directly to the solution of a case, but this is the exception rather than the rule. The primary purpose of a profile is to help the investigators narrow the focus of their investigation" (Hazelwood et al., 1995, p. 124). As has already been noted, other uses for the technique have now been found, including providing advice on how best to interrogate a suspect, or advice for prosecutors on how to question defendants when they give evidence in court (Homant and Kennedy, 1998).

A wide range of activities and approaches have now fallen under the umbrella term profiling. In general all approaches to profiling have the same starting point: a focus on the available crime scene evidence. However, once this initial data has been collected, what happens next will vary depending on the approach advocated by the specific profiler.

Conceptually, it is probably fair to say that there are currently three broad approaches in use. The first approach could be termed the *FBI Method*. This is the dominant approach in the United States and is used within the FBI and also by the large number of profilers who have been trained by the FBI but work in other agencies. Having collected the raw crime scene data, the profiler then draws upon past experience of similar cases to reach a conclusion regarding the characteristics of the offender. The FBI have carried out some limited research to help improve the reliability of this method (e.g. Ressler, Burgess and Douglas, 1988) but the profiler's past experience is considered the most important factor. There is also a healthy respect for the role and value of intuition in the development of a profile.

The second approach could broadly be described as the *statistical method*. This is also sometimes referred to as the scientific approach and certainly it is the most objective of the available systems. It is probably fair to say that this standpoint has been pioneered mainly within the UK (e.g. Canter, 1994). Profiles using this approach are derived based on probabilities which are known from experimental research. Large databases of specific types of crime are created and analysed to identify relationships and patterns which can be used to make predictions of future crimes. Indeed, no assumptions about the motivation or personality are necessary (Homant and Kennedy, 1998). In theory, this approach should produce more reliable profiles and be less prone to spurious conclusions. However, problems arise as the technique averages across large numbers of cases and can miss salient features of individual cases (Bekerian and Jackson, 1997).

The final main approach can be described as the *Clinical method*. This is something of a half-way house between the other two approaches. It is objective in that it draws upon established principles in clinical psychology and forensic psychiatry and also draws heavily on personality theory but it does not rely on probabilities. Instead, each case is treated as unique. Like the FBI approach, conclusions about the offender are based on the profiler's own experience and knowledge of numerous previous cases and experiences (Bekerian and Jackson, 1997).

HOW EFFECTIVE IS IT?

Available in the US since 1974, the demand for profiling has increased enormously in the past 25 years. The FBI produced some 300 profiles on average each year in the early to mid-1980s. Currently they are now producing over 1,000 profiles every year and at least as many profiles again are being requested in the US by non-FBI profilers (Homant and Kennedy, 1998). The UK has been somewhat more restrained in utilising profilers. In the mid-1980s, the British police were using profilers on around four cases per year. By the mid-1990s, profilers were being called in on over 75 cases each year (Copson, 1995). If nothing else the workload being invested in the practice has increased enormously. Yet is this increased investment warranted?

It is somewhat disturbing to learn that, despite the increasing popularity of profiling, very little research has been carried out to check its effectiveness. More disturbing still is the realisation that what little research which does exist supplies less than impressive results.

Successful case studies are frequently cited in defence of profiling. Certainly, there are a small number of police investigations described in the literature which probably would not have been solved if an offender profile had not been available. The existence of these cases does provide some justification for a wider use of profiling in general. However, one must be cautious when presented with case studies as evidence that profiling works. Just as adherents cite specific cases where profiling succeeded dramatically, it is much easier for critics to find cases to illustrate the failings of the process. Jenkins (1994) for example, notes that even the most respected and experienced profilers have provided hopelessly inaccurate profiles and goes on to note that there still exists dissension within the ranks of the FBI itself as to the value and effectiveness of profiles.

The most cited study on the effectiveness of profiling was one conducted by the FBI's Institutional Research and Development Unit (IRDU) in 1981. The IRDU surveyed user agencies as to the investigative value of profiles prepared in 192 cases. The overall findings of this survey convinced the FBI to continue investing in profiling, but the specific results of the survey have been misquoted and misinterpreted repeatedly in the literature. For example, Grubin (1995, p. 260) reports that the survey found that profiling led directly to the identification of suspects in 46% of 192 cases. However, the actual success rate was just 7.8% (Hazelwood, Ressler, Depue and Douglas, 1995).

A similarly poor performance was found by Copson (1995) who reviewed 184 cases where profiling was used in the UK. Copson's study was a more detailed one than the earlier FBI effort. He found that in only 2.7% of cases did the profile lead to the identification of the offender. Yet despite the relatively poor performance of the profiles on this measure, both studies reported that profiling was viewed very positively by the investigating teams. The FBI recorded that "all users overwhelmingly agreed that the service should be continued" (Hazelwood et al. 1995, p. 125) and Copson's more detailed assessment found that 92.4% of the UK police officers would *definitely* or *probably* use profiling again. Only four of the 184 investigators said they would definitely not use profiling again. While profiling had a generally poor performance in identifying offenders the officers were clearly perceiving other benefits. The American police reported that the profiles "helped focus the investigation" and "insured a complete investigation was conducted." Copson found that the UK police investigators found that profiles increased their understanding of the offence/offender (60.9%) and also reassured officers about their own judgements of the case (51.6%). Much more limited research elsewhere has generally supported this favourable reception for profiles among police investigators (e.g. Jackson, van den Eshof and de Kleuver, 1997).

While the FBI survey just explored the reception of FBI produced profiles, Copson's study also distinguished between different types of profiler. Copson found that the success rate of individual profilers varied enormously. In a follow-up to the original research, Copson revealed that "the aggregate accuracy ratio of the information contained in the profiles was found to be 2.2: 1 (that is 2.2 points correct to each 1 incorrect)" (Gudjonsson and Copson, 1997, p. 73). He found differences depending on the background of the profilers. Significantly clinical profilers had the highest average of 2.9: 1, while statistical profilers were lower at just 1.8: 1. The range among individual profilers was considerable, going from a low of just 1.5: 1 to an impressive high of 6.8: 1.

PROFILING TERRORISTS

Numerous authors have claimed that profiling is not a suitable tool for all criminal investigations. In general, profiles have usually been most efficient in cases where an unknown offender has displayed indications of psychopathology. According to Holmes and Holmes (1996) the types of crimes most appropriate for psychological profiling are sexually motivated crimes and crimes with satanic or ritualistic aspects. Generally, offenders involved in such crimes tend to have distinctive personality characteristics and these distinctive characteristics tend to result in distinctive behaviours. 'Distinctive' in these terms has generally been associated with some form of psychopathology on the part of the offender. It is also generally recommended that there should be a sufficient database of known offenders from previous similar cases (McCann, 1992). Such caveats would appear to limit profiling to serial rape and serial murder cases and indeed this is generally what has happened. In total around 90% of profiles have been generated for murder or rape cases (Howlett, Hanfland and Ressler, 1986).

However, profiling has also been used in cases of arson, bombing, hostage-taking, stalking, bank robbery and even computer crime (Homant and Kennedy, 1998; Casey, 1999). To date, what limited validation research that has been conducted on profiling has been done with regard to cases involving sexual homicide or rape. There has been no systematic research on its effectiveness for other crimes but a number of case studies have been documented which show that it can be of demonstrable benefit for a wider range of crimes than previously believed (e.g. Boon, 1997).

As we have already seen, the evidence attesting to the reliability and effectiveness of profiling as a technique for directing investigations and identifying possible suspects is less than impressive. There have been some successes but in general profiles do not seem to have had a significant impact. Nevertheless, for a variety of ancillary reasons profiles are generally viewed by law enforcement officers who use them as having had a positive input into investigations. The result of this common perception is that profiling inevitably gains wider acceptance and is used more and more regularly for a wider variety of offences.

What then is the potential for the technique with regard to terrorist offences? Terrorist violence – as viewed in this chapter – is essentially a strategy of the weak, adopted by individuals or groups "with little numerical, physical or direct political power in order to effect political or social change" (Friedland, 1992). In practical terms, terrorists are either lone individuals or members of small covert groups engaged in an organised campaign of often extreme violence. The terrorists themselves tend to live isolated and stressful lives and enjoy varying levels of wider support.

Terrorist violence is typically carefully planned and well-organised with a consequence that effective post-event investigation can be surpassingly difficult. For example, consider the experience of the Greek police in trying to deal with *Revolutionary Organization 17 November*, a terrorist group which has been operating in and around Athens since 1975 (Corsun, 1991). In that time, the group has carried out over 100 violent attacks which have killed a total of twenty-three people and left hundreds more injured. The group made headlines recently when they assassinated the military attaché to the British embassy in Athens (Gaunt, 2000 June 9).

Yet despite the numerous attacks against high level targets, no member of the group has ever been captured by police investigators. Considering both the prevalence and lethality of terrorism and the diversity of actors responsible for this violence, there is a constant need to develop more effective investigative methods in response to terrorist incidents.

Can offender profiling really be used to help investigations of terrorist incidents? The potential is certainly there. The FBI, for example, have a long history of using profiling in arson cases, where many of the principles developed could theoretically be readily transferred to considerations of terrorist behaviour. Consider the following from Turvey (1999a):

"Take the behaviors of fire setting and explosives use. They can be analyzed just like any other offender behaviour. They can occur in a variety of contexts, and satisfy or be motivated by multiple offender needs. They are not limited to use in a particular kind of criminal offense or against any particular type of victim. Their use in a particular offence is constrained only by offender motive, offender intent, offender skill level, and the availability of materials" (p. 269).

He goes on to add:

"The use of fire and explosives are an extension of an offender's will to use force. They are agents of an offender's will . . . In order to interpret their motivational origins, like any other behaviour, close attention needs to be paid to their context in terms of victimology and crime-scene characteristics" (pp. 270–271).

As can be inferred from these latter comments, a major aim of many profiles (and certainly those in the FBI and clinical schools) is to uncover the motivations of the offender. Once the motivations have been identified, they can reveal other characteristics of the offender. With regard to sex crimes, profilers have found that motivations can act as the key to describing offenders in terms of a particular typology (Hazelwood and Burgess, 1995).

Typologies order a multitude of objects and/or phenomena and make them manageable for analysis. However, there are enormous difficulties in attempting to categorise terrorists. A review of international media reports for any given week quickly makes it clear that the spectrum terrorism covers is vast and includes a wide range of very different groups and individuals. For example, the cultural, economic and educational background of the average Provisional IRA member is quite different to that of the average Red Army Faction member. Both of these in turn are quite different to the average Hamas member, and so forth, yet all are supposedly engaged in '*terrorism*'. This enormous variety means that any attempt to classify or categorise is difficult.

Certainly some attempts to create meaningful profiles of terrorists have occurred in the past thirty years. For example, Russell and Miller (1977) surveyed the known membership variables of fifteen separate terrorist groups and produced a general terrorist profile. However, as the characteristics were averaged across the different groups, essential information regarding some of the groups was lost. For example, the final overall profile provided a very poor description of the average IRA terrorist. Russell and Miller recognised this weakness and did draw attention to the fact that some groups did not fit the typical profile. A further serious weakness with Russell and Miller's work was that they relied on media reports for most of their information. Later research showed that such sources did not provide a representative sample of many of the terrorist groups and in particular with regard to the Middle East groups. Merari (1991) heavily criticised the profiles, noting that they were extremely inaccurate when they were compared with thousands of proven members of various PLO groups captured in Lebanon and Israel. Russell and Miller had claimed that Palestinian terrorists tended to be highly educated, well-travelled and have urban upbringings. In actuality, most Palestinian terrorists are poorly educated, have never left the region where they have grown up, and rather than having urban backgrounds a very high proportion are from rural areas or refugee camps.

Nevertheless, even the critics recognise that the value of reliable profiles of terrorist group members would be immense and a small – but steady – stream of work has since tried to develop reliable profiles of particular groups (e.g. Handler, 1990; Smith and Morgan, 1994; Dingley, 1997).

The secret to identifying information useful to an investigation is to focus on the targets of terrorists attacks (victimology) and to also take advantage of the more distinct aspects of terrorism such as public statements made by the terrorists. Unlike sexual criminals, terrorists are motivated by a political agenda and thus are interested in a much higher public profile – and a much more explicit one – than individual criminals. As a result they are likely to eventually make public statements and these can be analysed to provide a window into their motivations and general backgrounds.

A particular problem which is being increasingly faced by investigators of terrorist incidents is to determine whether a group or a lone individual is responsible. Both the UK and the USA are learning the hard way that terrorist acts committed by lone individuals are becoming increasingly common. Yet, from the investigators' point of view it can be very difficult to differentiate between a group effort and that of a loner. The series of nail-bombing attacks carried out in London in 1999 illustrate this problem very well. The bombings were widely believed to have been carried out by a right-wing extremist group, with suspicion being strongest that a splinter element of the neo-nazi group, Combat-18, was behind the attacks. However, when the offender, David Copeland, was eventually arrested, it was quickly apparent that he was operating entirely by himself and that he had no formal links to any of the right-wing groups under suspicion.

Considering this rise in lone terrorism, it is disturbing that virtually nothing has been written on profiling individual terrorists (the limited writings of Russell and Miller and the others have all had a group focus). However, a small number of cases exist where profiling has been used for such terrorists. An examination of these cases can be useful in illustrating the practical issues raised by any attempt to profile terrorists and to show the more special problems raised by lone terrorists in particular.

REAL-LIFE CASES

That the potential to profile terrorists exists is something that actual terrorists themselves have recognised. Consider the following statement from an IRA terrorist:

> "There are certain traits and behavioural characteristics surrounding operations which identify the operators"

The IRA man had been ordered to carry out a one-man bombing campaign in England, and this statement underlined his expectation that it would only be a matter of time before the security forces had identified him. He had carried out numerous 'operations' in Northern Ireland and thus the security forces had a recognisable pattern to compare the UK campaign with. However, security force intelligence on Northern Irish terrorism is superb by international standards. Most investigators will not have the benefit of such intelligence to draw upon. This is especially a problem with lone terrorists who can emerge suddenly and unexpectedly and present investigators with little or no advance intelligence to draw upon.

The Mad Bomber

The first documented case of offender profiling being used to help identify the individual behind a terrorist campaign is also the first widely acknowledged case of psychological profiling. In the 1940s and 1950s there were a series of bomb attacks in New York city in what came to be known as the 'Mad Bomber' case (Jackson and Bekerian, 1997). In total at least 37 explosive devices were detonated in train stations and theatres all over the city. In an effort to assist the police investigation, a psychiatrist, James Brussel, reviewed the letters which were believed to have been sent by the bomber and also reviewed crime scene photographs. Brussel predicted that the bomber would be an Eastern European male, 40 to 50 years old, who lived with a maiden aunt or sister. Brussel diagnosed the bomber as a paranoiac who was meticulous in his personal habits, and he predicted that when he was found he would be wearing a buttoned up double-breasted suit. When the perpetrator, George Metesky, was eventually captured (a few years after Brussel had submitted his profile) the predictions turned out to be incredibly accurate, right down to the suit (though Metesky actually lived with two maiden sisters) (Brussel, 1968).

Brussel's performance in the Mad Bomber case is now the stuff of profiling legend, but it was not the only time profiling would be used for such offences. As the incidence of domestic terrorism has steadily increased in the United States, the use of profiling for such purposes has increased also.

The Unabomber

The case of the Unabomber involves an even longer running bombing campaign. By the time a suspect was arrested in April 1996, the Unabomber was responsible for a 17-year-long bombing campaign. In that time, the Unabomber had carried out a total of 16 attacks which left three people dead and a further 23 injured. The investigation of the bombing campaign cost over $50 million, making it the most expensive manhunt in US history.

An offender profile of the bomber was first developed by the FBI as early as 1980. This predicted that the bomber was a reclusive, lone individual in his 30s. As the attacks continued more profiles were continuously produced by a variety of sources. In 1995, shortly before the Unabomber's capture the FBI released a twelve-item profile of the suspected bomber. A summarised copy of this profile can be seen in Table 1. When Theodore Kaczynski was arrested in April 1996 for the bombings, he matched this profile on seven of the twelve counts and as the table shows there were some important points which the profile got very wrong. For example, the FBI's profile predicted that the bomber would be a '*neat dresser with a meticulously organized life*'. In stark contrast Kaczynski was a slovenly dresser who lived in an isolated one-room cabin without running water or electricity. A review of the literature indicates that other more accurate profiles possibly existed but these do not seem to have impacted on the profile which was released publicly.

Did the profile have a role to play in the identification and apprehension of the suspect? Probably not. The most important development in the case was the publication of the manifesto by the Unabomber in national newspapers in September 1995. The bomber's brother recognised similarities in phrases and ideas in the 35,000 word

Table 1: The Unabomber Profile and the Offender

FBI profile	Ted Kaczynski
Race, sex	
White, male	White, male
Age	
Late 30s, early 40s	55
Height	
5′ 10″ to 6′	5′9″
Weight	
165 pounds	143 pounds
Physical features	
Reddish-blonde hair, thin moustache, ruddy complexion	Brown hair, bearded, pale skin
Personality	
Neat dresser with meticulously organized life; reclusive; most likely has had problems dealing with women	Slovenly, according to acquaintances; reclusive; no known relationships with women
Education	
At least high school, familiar with university life	Harvard graduate, 1962; U.C. Berkeley: assistant professor

manifest and the writings of Kaczynski. He consulted a hand-writing expert who felt the concerns were well-founded (Hubert, 1997). The authorities were contacted and shortly afterwards Kaczynski was arrested.

In the wake of Kaczynski's arrest and trial, various profilers were quick to take credit for producing accurate profiles of Kaczynski. The only published profile had a hit ratio of just 1.4: 1. Accounts of other profiles discussed after the arrest are difficult to assess. For example, forensic psychiatrist Park Dietz is credited with constructing a profile of the Unabomber used by the FBI (Toufexis, 1999). However, it remains unclear if this is the one published in 1995 or a more accurate version which remained unpublished. What is clear is that a relatively large number of profiles were produced over the course of the eighteen-year investigation, which ultimately had little if any impact in apprehending the suspect.

The Atlanta Olympics bombing
At 1:20 a.m. on Saturday July 27, 1996 a 40-lb. bomb exploded in Centennial Olympic Park in Atlanta during the Summer Olympics. The explosion killed one person and injured over a hundred. A second person died at the scene shortly afterwards due to a heart attack. The bomb had been placed in a backpack and was a home-made device packed with a large number of masonry nails.

Richard Jewell was a security guard working in the park and was the first to notice the suspicious backpack. He alerted police to the suspicious bag and was helping to evacuate the area when the bomb exploded. Initially Jewell was hailed by the media as a hero, but within days it emerged that the FBI considered the 34-year-old security guard to be the main suspect to the bombing.

Jewell apparently matched closely a psychological profile which described the bomber as a former policeman who longed for heroism. Items taken from Jewell's home during the service of search warrants, such as a collection of newspaper clippings describing Jewell as a hero, added fuel to the media fire. However, the search warrants failed to produce any physical evidence whatsoever to link Jewell to the bombing and the FBI lied to Jewell when they brought him in for questioning. After a prolonged period, Jewell was finally informed that '*barring any newly discovered evidence*' he was no longer considered a suspect.

The FBI agent who had leaked the information to the press regarding the psychological profile was reprimanded and given a five-day suspension. However, an indication of the investigators' persisting belief of Jewell's guilt can be seen from the fact that the agent was applauded by several dozen people when he returned to the Atlanta FBI headquarters after serving his suspension (Turvey, 1999b).

Park Dietz was again used by the FBI to construct a detailed profile of the Atlanta Olympics bomber. It is claimed that Dietz helped to tie the explosion to a number of subsequent explosions, including two others in Atlanta and a third attack on a women's health clinic in Birmingham. These latter attacks were believed to have been carried out by elements of the extremist Army of God group. Dietz's profile of the bomber apparently led to the identification of Eric Rudolph as the chief suspect for the Atlanta bombing (Toufexis, 1999). Rudolph's truck had been seen by witnesses at the scene of the Birmingham bombing, and shortly afterwards a man wearing a wig was seen driving off at speed. The truck was found abandoned and Rudolph disappeared (Mason, 1999). However, other sources indicate that the major reasons for linking these crimes was not because of a psychological profile but because of the close similarities in the construction of the explosive devices in all four attacks (Mason, 1999). As Rudolph was already wanted for questioning with regard to the Birmingham attack, it was no great leap of the imagination to link him with the other three attacks.

POTENTIALS AND PITFALLS

While the vast majority of terrorists do not suffer from psychological disorders (Silke, 1998), the spread of profiling beyond the sex crimes will inevitably continue and the high media impact of terrorism means that it is always likely to be a source of interest for profilers. While the general concepts of profiling can transfer readily to virtually any activity, the usefulness of the spread remains open to question. Without having proven itself for its original task, it is prudent to be cautious during any attempts to profile terrorists.

The problems of attempting to profile terrorist attacks are well demonstrated in the above examples. These problems can be roughly divided into two camps: (1) problems of accuracy and (2) problems of impact.

The problems of accuracy are well illustrated by the profiling fiasco surrounding the Atlanta bombing. The original profile seems to have been generated explicitly with the unfortunate Jewell in mind. Profilers are not supposed to be made aware of possible suspects of an investigation for fear that it may unconsciously bias the profile produced. In hindsight it seems possible that the original profile produced was a 'contaminated' one. Once developed, this profile certainly had a high impact on the investigation, as the investigative effort focused almost entirely on finding evidence to confirm Jewell's guilt. When this corroborative evidence failed to materialise, the FBI were very slow to revise the significance of the original profile and focus the investigation elsewhere. Indeed the reaction and comments of many of those involved in the investigation make it clear that many continued to regard Jewell as the most likely culprit. The misleading initial profile and its strong focus on Jewell diverted the investigation down a fruitless cul-de-sac and valuable months passed before the investigation began to seriously search for the actual perpetrator. It would take three more bombings and another death for the investigators to finally link Atlanta to elements within the Army of God.

Metesky's case is almost the opposite of Atlanta. Here an impressively accurate profile of the offender was produced but it seems to have had very little impact on the investigation. The bomber was uncovered as a result of detective work which was not explicitly guided or influenced by the profile. The Unabomber case lies somewhere between the other two cases. The profile was not as accurate as the one describing Metesky but it was certainly more accurate than the initial Atlanta profile. The profile appears to have been seriously attended to by the investigation team but this does not appear to have helped them much. When the profile was published in 1995, this did not prompt anyone who knew Kaczynski to inform the authorities that he could be a possible suspect. It was only in 1996, after his brother had read the Unabomber's manifesto and noted similarities with letters from Kaczynski, that the ageing recluse finally became a suspect. A few sources claim that the profile was an influencing factor in the brother's decision to contact the authorities, but this is far from certain. What is clear from the brother's own account is that reading the manifesto was by far the most important factor (Hubert, 1997). If he had not seen that, he would not have contacted the authorities.

The experiences outlined here demonstrate that while profiling has been used in terrorist cases, its impact has tended to be either negligible or detrimental to the investigation. This is not to suggest that the potential for a significant and positive impact does not exist. A profile which combined the *accuracy* of the Metesky profile with the *impact* of the initial Atlanta profile could be of powerful benefit to any investigation. The potential is certainly there, but it is a potential that in all probability will not be realised in most cases. This is partly due to the inherent problems and flaws in the profiling process as it currently exists, and partly due to the difficulties presented by terrorists. Lone terrorists in particular present exceptional problems. By avoiding membership of established groups they also avoid the current intelligence and surveillance activities of the security forces. Further, the underlining simplicity of home-made weapons limits the amount of forensic evidence which can be gathered and used.

Despite the many misgivings, ultimately profiling will continue to be used in terrorist cases. While there is much to be cautious about, there are also reasons to express at least a little optimism. Profiling in general is still in its infancy and the profiling of terrorists is hugely underexplored. The initial cases have not been inspiring from an investigative point of view, but they have shown that terrorist profiles can be accurate and that they can have an impact. As the literature develops on this aspect of profiling, better guidelines will inevitably emerge. For now, all that can be reliably said is that a potential exists, but as with the rest of profiling, it is far from clear if this can ever be fully realised.

REFERENCES

Beckerian, D. and Jackson, J. (1997). Critical issues in offender profiling. In J. Jackson and D. Bekerian (eds.), *Offender Profiling: Theory, Research and Practice* (pp. 209–220). Chichester: Wiley.

Boon, J. (1997). The contribution of personality theories to psychological profiling. In J. Jackson and D. Bekerian (Eds.), *Offender Profiling: Theory, Research and Practice* (pp. 43–60). Chichester: Wiley.

Canter, D. (1994). *Criminal Shadows: Inside the Mind of the Serial Killer*. London: Harper Collins.

Canter, D. and Fritzon, K. (1998). Differentiating arsonists: A model of firesetting actions and characteristics. *Legal and Criminological Psychology*, 3, 73–96.

Casey, E. (1999). Cyberpatterns: Criminal behavior on the Internet. In B. Turvey (Ed.), *Criminal Profiling: An Introduction to Behavioural Evidence Analysis* (pp. 299–327). London: Academic Press.

Copson, G. (1995). *Coals to Newcastle? Part 1: A study of offender profiling* (Paper 7). London: Police Research Group Special Interest Series, Home Office.

Corsun, A. (1991). Group profile: The Revolutionary Organization 17 November in Greece. *Studies in Conflict and Terrorism*, 14, 77–104.

Dingley, J. (1997). The terrorist – developing a profile. *International Journal of Risk, Security and Crime Prevention*, 2, 25–37.

Friedland, N. (1992). Becoming a terrorist: Social and individual antecedents. In L. Howard (Ed.), *Terrorism; Roots, Impact, Responses* (pp. 81–93). London: Praeger.

Gaunt, J. (2000 June 9). 'November 17 Says It Killed British Diplomat'. http://dailynews.yahoo.com/h/nm/20000609/wl/greece_britain_dc_13.html

Grubin, D. (1995). Offender profiling. *Journal of Forensic Psychiatry*, 6, 259–263.

Gudjonsson, G. and Copson, G. (1997). The role of the expert in criminal investigation. In

J. Jackson and D. Bekerian (Eds.), *Offender Profiling: Theory, Research and Practice* (pp. 61–76). Chichester: Wiley.

Handler, J. (1990). Socioeconomic profile of an American terrorist: 1960s and 1970s. *Terrorism*, 13, 195–213.

Hazelwood, R. (1995). Analyzing the rape and profiling the offender. In R. Hazelwood and A. Burgess (Eds.), *Practical Aspects of Rape Investigation* (2nd edition) (pp. 155–182). London: CRC Press.

Hazelwood, R. and Burgess, A. (1995). The behavioral-oriented interview of rape victims: The key to profiling. In R. Hazelwood and A. Burgess (Eds.), *Practical Aspects of Rape Investigation* (2nd edition) (pp. 139–154). London: CRC Press.

Hazelwood, R., Ressler, R., Depue, R. and Douglas, J. (1995). Criminal investigative analysis: An overview. In R. Hazelwood and A. Burgess (Eds.), *Practical Aspects of Rape Investigation* (2nd edition) (pp. 115–126). London: CRC Press.

Holmes, R. And Holmes, S. (1996). *Profiling Violent Crimes: An Investigative Tool* (2nd Ed.). London: Sage.

Homant, R. And Kennedy, D. (1998). Psychological aspects of crime scene profiling. *Criminal Justice and Behavior*, 25, 319–343.

Howlett, J., Hanfland, K. And Ressler, R. (1986). The violent criminal apprehension program. *FBI Law Enforcement Bulletin*, 55, 14–18.

Hubert, C. (1997, 19 January). Role in capture haunts Kaczynski's brother. *Sacramento Bee*.

Jackson, J., van den Eshof, P. and de Kleuver, E. (1997). A research approach to offender profiling. In J. Jackson and D. Bekerian (Eds.), *Offender Profiling: Theory, Research and Practice* (pp. 107–132). Chichester: Wiley.

Jenkins, P. (1994). *Using Murder: The Social Construction of Serial Homicide*. New York: Aldine de Gruyter.

Mason, S. (1999). *The Secret World of Cults*. Godalming, UK: Bramley.

McCann, J. (1992). Criminal personality profiling in the investigation of violent crime: Recent advances and future directions. *Behavioral Sciences and the Law*, 10, 475–481.

Merari, A. (1991). Academic research and government policy on terrorism. *Terrorism and Political Violence*, 3, 88–102.

Ressler, R., Burgess, A. and Douglas, J. (1988). *Sexual Homicide: Patterns and Motives*. New York: Lexington Books.

Russell, C. and Miller, B. (1977). Profile of a terrorist. *Terrorism*, 1, 17–34.

Shafritz, J., Gibbons, E. Jr. and Scott, G. (1991). *Almanac of Modern Terrorism*. Oxford: Facts on File.

Silke, A. (1998). Cheshire-cat logic: The recurring theme of terrorist abnormality in psychological research. *Psychology, Crime and Law*, 4, 51–69.

Smith, B. and Morgan, K. (1994). Terrorists right and left: Empirical issues in profiling American terrorists. *Studies in Conflict and Terrorism*, 17, 39–57.

Toufexis, A. (1999). Dancing with devils. *Psychology Today*, 32, 54–58,78–79,85.

Turvey, B. (1999a). Use of fire and explosives. In B. Turvey (Ed.), *Criminal Profiling: An Introduction to behavioural Evidence Analysis* (pp.269–284). London: Academic Press.

Turvey, B. (1999b). Ethics and the criminal profiler. In B. Turvey (Ed.), *Criminal Profiling: An Introduction to behavioural Evidence Analysis* (pp. 235–246). London: Academic Press.

Chapter 16

IMPRISONMENT FOR HOMICIDE: EUROPEAN PERSPECTIVES CONCERNING HUMAN RIGHTS

Nicholas McGeorge and Hartmut-Michael Weber

All the countries of Europe which are members of the Council of Europe have undertaken not to use the death penalty. As a consequence the use of life imprisonment has expanded. The variations in its use and its meaning in different European countries, however, raise issues about the purposes of such sentences, and whether such sentences are violating human rights.

This study examines: the crimes for which such a sentence is given; whether the sentence is mandatory or discretionary; the minimum age at which life imprisonment can be imposed; procedures for assessment for release of life sentence prisoners; whether such sentences mean the prisoner will die in prison; and the involvement of Government ministers or Heads of State in the process.

A recent development has been the expansion of indeterminate and life sentences, for example, in France, Germany and the United Kingdom. In the United Kingdom, the law has been changed to introduce a mandatory life sentence for offenders being found guilty a second time of certain offences.

Such mandatory life sentences for crimes that on their own would not merit life imprisonment would appear to contradict views expressed by the European Court of Human Rights. The Court determined that one of the crucial differences between mandatory and discretionary life sentences is that a mandatory sentence is imposed due to the nature of the crime, but a discretionary sentence is imposed because of the offender's perceived dangerousness or mental instability.

There are countries in Europe, however, such as Spain, where life imprisonment has been abolished and only fixed length sentences can be given.

The argument that the risk assessment procedures for release of prisoners convicted of homicide from indeterminate life imprisonment reduce the risk of serious re-offending, compared with the release of prisoners with the same offence from fixed terms of imprisonment, is shown to be false.

The case is presented that the abolition of indeterminate life imprisonment and its replacement with a fixed maximum term:

A) would not increase the risk of serious re-offending,
B) would remove political influence concerning the release of prisoners with indeterminate sentences,
C) would serve as a major step in removing much of the infringement of human rights suffered under the laws and procedures of many European countries.

LIFE IMPRISONMENT AND THE EUROPEAN DIMENSION – A QUESTION OF HUMAN RIGHTS

Life imprisonment means by its definition that a person shall be kept in prison until the end of his or her life. Compared with countries providing capital punishment, however, life imprisonment is usually seen as the 'milder' punishment, although the Dutch Humanist Coornhert invented it in 1587 because it would deter more effectively than capital punishment (de Jonge 1993).

In Western European countries life imprisonment does not generally mean imprisonment until death. On the other hand it has retained its indeterminate character. Life imprisonment can vary in length from 8 or 9 years and up to 45 to 50 years. In Germany for example, the average is 21 years for a life sentence. However, about one fifth of lifers die in prison (Weber 1999). In England and Wales, the Home Secretary has decided that over 20 life sentence prisoners will die in prison. They really do serve 'natural life'.

Studies on life imprisonment also need to take into account its equivalent: the maximum determinate sentences in countries which do not have life imprisonment. In addition there are orders for indeterminate secure preventative detention in a prison-like establishment or for indeterminate detention in a psychiatric hospital. These indeterminate sentences also represent the peak of the states' power over the individual.

The European Convention of Human Rights, now with seven protocol amendments, came into being in 1953. In 1983 capital punishment was abolished by the 6th protocol amendment of this Convention. Its replacement by such a powerful and unusual sentence as life imprisonment needs to be examined as to whether it is compatible with human rights.

This examination becomes increasingly important as several European countries have abolished the sentence of life imprisonment and replaced it with sentences of determinate length.

LIFE IMPRISONMENT – EUROPEAN VARIATIONS[1]

A comparison between various European countries in the application and use of the severest sentence shows remarkably wide divergences.

The lowest age at which the severest sentence can be given is seven years old in Ireland to 21 years old in Sweden.

The number of offences for which a country's maximum sentence can be given is from three in Spain to nearly 70 in England and Wales.

Even when there is a mandatory sentence of life imprisonment for murder, the definition of murder can alter the frequency with which the sentence is given. In England and Wales the essential element is premeditation, whilst in Germany there has to be in addition one of seven specific motives.

The maximum sentence for murder varies from 20 years to imprisonment until death.

The release of prisoners with indeterminate sentences can be achieved through clemency from the Head of State, determined by a Government minister with total discretion, through the quasi-judicial parole board, or through judicial review.

Countries without life imprisonment

There are four countries in Europe which do not have life imprisonment. They are Portugal, Spain, Norway, and Cyprus. Portugal's maximum sentence is imprisonment for 25 years, Spain has a maximum sentence of 30 years and Norway's maximum sentence is 21 years. Cyprus, however, is a special case of an abolitionist country. Offenders can be sentenced to life imprisonment, but the prerogative of the President has made the upper limit 20 years. Therefore it is appropriate to subsume Cyprus in the abolitionist countries. In addition there is a fifth country, Italy, which has *de facto* a maximum sentence of 27 years for their life sentence prisoners. All other European countries have indeterminate life imprisonment.

Age of liability for imposing maximum prison sentences

The minimum age at which a person can be sent to prison varies dramatically from country to country in Europe.

Table 1 shows however that the age of criminal liability is much lower among countries retaining life imprisonment than in abolitionist countries;

Table 1: Retentionist and Abolitionist Countries by Age of Criminal Responsibility for Maximum Prison Terms

Countries providing life imprisonment (retentionist countries)		Countries providing maximum determinate imprisonment (abolitionist countries)	
England & Wales	10 years	Cyprus	14 years
Scotland	10 years	Spain	18 years
Northern Ireland	10 years	Norway	18 years
France	16 years	Portugal	16 years
The Netherlands	16 years		
Austria	20 years		
Germany	18 years		
Italy	18 years		
Sweden	21 years		
Czech Republic	18 years		
Ireland	7 years		

Ireland has an exceptionally low age of 7 years, followed by England & Wales, Scotland and Northern Ireland at 10 years (Table 1).

Type of offences carrying maximum prison sentences
Some of the retentionist countries have very lengthy lists of offences (e.g. England & Wales with nearly 70 offences), others a briefer list of offences (e.g. Austria with ten offences) which qualify for life sentences. This is also true for countries with a determinate maximum sentence, but their range is much smaller. Here, Norway offers a long list (27 offences) and Spain, after the penal reform of November 1995, a short list of only three offences attracting the maximum penalty of thirty years (incitement to cause a serious rebellion, murder by terrorist attack; and genocide). The maximum penalty for any other offences, including murder, is twenty years.

Retentionist countries do not differ markedly from abolitionist countries in the range of offences for which the severest punishment can be given. However, it is not only intentional homicide that attracts the maximum penalty.

However, there is no agreement about what makes a particular offence qualify for the maximum penalty or about how dangerous it is. While the life sentence in England & Wales can be imposed for such offences as removing a corpse from a grave, aggravated and attempted burglary, or failing in the duty to assist constables, in other countries such offences are punished with a relatively mild prison sentence or are not punishable at all.

Mandatory and discretionary maximum prison sentences: special relevance to murder

Some countries emphasise the penalty factor for one or more specific offences by making the maximum penalty mandatory for such offences. Thus in England & Wales, Scotland, Northern Ireland, and Cyprus, mandatory life sentences exist for murder. In Germany a life sentence is mandatory for murder, aggravated manslaughter and genocide. In Austria a life sentence is mandatory for genocide.

As the circumstances of the individual case have to be ignored with mandatory sentences, such sentences are by definition unjust.

In contrast, other countries leave it to the discretion of the courts to use the maximum penalty.

Use of maximum prison sentences for intentional homicide

Practice shows that particular importance is attached to intentional homicides, especially murder, when using the maximum sentence.

Table 2 shows figures obtained for six retentionist countries (England & Wales, Scotland, France, The Netherlands, Austria, Federal Republic of Germany) and three abolitionist (Spain, Norway, Cyprus). Data relate to the period 1988 to 1993. See Table 2.

Firstly, there are wide variations in the rates of use of maximum sentences (per 100,000 inhabitants) for all sentenced offenders, as well as the rates of those sentenced for intentional homicide.

The retentionist countries, however, show a range of variations which is much higher (from zero to 0.6 for all sentenced; zero to 0.59 for those sentenced for intentional homicide) than that of the abolitionist countries (0.03 up to 0.16 for all sentenced; 0.02 up to 0.05 for those sentenced for intentional homicide).

Secondly, the imposition of life sentences is mostly linked to committing intentional homicide (France is an exception in this respect) and this pattern is much more characteristic for retentionist than for abolitionist countries. Cyprus, which abolished life imprisonment but still provides life sentences, fits more into the retentionist pattern, because its courts imposed these sentences only for intentional homicide.

These findings raise questions about what is the definition of intentional homicide.

Definitions of homicide (murder) and their impact on sentencing for life imprisonment

There is no European standard definition of murder. Definitions are not primarily based on 'objective' elements of the offence, but instead on

Table 2: Mean Rates of Persons Sentenced to Life Imprisonment (Retentionist countries) or to the Respective Maximum Determinate Sentence (Abolitionist countries). Rates per 100.000 of inhabitants, broken down by overall figures and figures for intentional homicide (murder/manslaughter).

Country	Retentionist countries						Abolitionist countries			
	E & W	SCOT	F	NL	A	D	CY	SP	NO
All sentenced	0.44	0.60	0.15	0.00	0.12	0.10	0.03	0.16	0.11
Sentenced for homicide	0.36	0.59	0.07*	0.00	0.12	0.10	0.03	0.05	0.02
Sent. for homicide in percent of all sentenced	82 %	98 %	47 %	n.a	100 %	100 %	100 %	31 %	18 %

* Including also *attempted* murder, figures excluding attempted murder are not available

subjective motives of the offender. Table 3 gives an overview of these indicators, which are used by both retentionist and abolitionist countries. The consequences, however, of using such indicators have clearly different outcomes in abolitionist countries compared with retentionist countries. In the latter they legitimise sentences of unknown length.

There is no agreement about what psychological motives cause a finding of murder to be made. Examples of motives which can turn manslaughter into murder are "committed for lust to kill", "committed for inferior (contemptible) motives" and "committed maliciously" (Germany), "displaying wicked recklessness" (Scotland) or "performed in an especially contemptible manner" (Czech Republic). There is also the very strange motive of the "intention to do serious bodily harm" (England & Wales), which is clearly less serious than an intention to kill.

An example for such ascriptions in the "old" (former) Federal Republic of Germany is in Table 4 (Weber 1996). This table illustrates the least used and the most used 'motives' by the courts in each federal state for defining a homicide as murder. These wide disparities are difficult to explain, other than by the influence of local developed norms, based on arbitrary interpretations, that can be altered on the way from the prosecutor to the judge (Sessar 1980).

It appears, however, that the need to ascribe specific types of motive in Germany significantly reduces the proportion of homicides designated as murder compared with England and Wales, despite not dissimilar homicide rates.

Criteria for earlier release from maximum imprisonment

i) *Retentionist countries*: In *England & Wales* there is no provision by law for early release from life imprisonment. In its place the Home Secretary uses procedures for decisions about early release by clemency (mercy). This can be seen as entirely political decision making. This is illustrated by the rate of refusal by the Home Secretary to accept the recommendations of the Parole Board for the release, under licence, of life sentence prisoners. In the early 1980s, the probability of a life sentence prisoner being released after review was 1 in 3. By 1992 the ratio had dropped to 1 in 5 (McGeorge, 1995). By 1995 the ratio had dropped further to 1 in 6. The Home Secretaries during that period were members of a Government that supported more punitive approaches to offenders.

"Mandatory lifers" are those sentenced for murder, and "discretionary lifers" are those condemned for manslaughter or other offences where the

Table 3: Objective and Subjective Elements of Murder

Legal system	'Objective' (external) elements	'Subjective' (mental, normative) elements
Austria France	nil	• intention
aggravated murder (assassinat)	nil • victim aged under 15	• premeditation • in order to prepare or to facilitate another offence
murder	• victim a relative or adopted • victim a particular vulnerable person • victim a public agent • preceding, accompanying or following another offence	• in order to interfere with the course of justice
Germany	• using means dangerous to the public	• committed for lust to kill • for satisfaction of sexual needs • for greed (property benefits) • for inferior (contemptible) motives • committed cruelty • maliciously • intention to conceal or facilitate another crime
Netherlands	nil	• intention • premeditation
England & Wales	• victim dead within 1 year and 1 day	• intention to kill • to do serious bodily harm
Scotland	nil	• intention to kill • displaying wicked recklessness
Czech Republic	• more than one victim • committed repeatedly • victim aged 15 or under • victim a public agent or committed because of the agent or committed because of the exercise of a public agent	• intention to gain property benefits • intention to conceal or facilitate another crime • performed extremely brutally or tormentingly • performed in an especially contemptible manner
Norway	• committed repeatedly • especially aggravating circumstances (not defined)	• premeditation or • in order to facilitate or to conceal another felony or to evade the penalty of such felony • especially aggravating circumstances (not defined)

Spain	• offence caused by flooding, arson, poisoning or explosives	• aware of premeditation • performed maliciously • committed for property values • performed with hate • performed augmenting deliberately and inhumane pain to the victim
Cyprus	nil	• premeditation

Table 4: Ascribed Individual Elements of Murder in Percent of the Total Ascribed Indicators for Murder by Federal States of Germany (including Berlin-West)

Element of murder	Most rare ascription in percent	Most frequent ascription in percent
Lust to kill	0.0 Schleswig-Holstein Rhenish Palatinate	5.8 Bavaria 5.8
Satisfaction of sexual needs	0.0 Schleswig-Holstein Bremen Saarland	9.4 Bavaria
Greed (for property benefits)	7.4 Bremen	4.17 Bavaria
Inferior motives	15.7 Berlin	40.7 Bremen
Committed maliciously	2.8 Bavaria	32.6 Hesse
Committed cruelly	0.8 Bavaria	26.0 Hamburg
Using means dangerous to the public	less than 1.0	less than 1.0
In order to facilitate another offence	2.5 Bremen	17.9 Berlin
In order to conceal another offence	4.9 Bremen	17.5 Saarland

Calculated according to Table "Häufigkeitsverteilung der qualifizierenden Merkmale des § 211 StGB in den einzelnen Bundesländern einschliesslich Berlin-West zwischen 1945–1975 (zusammengestellt nach der Umfrage des Bundesverfassungsgerichts)" (Rasch/Hinz 1980, 378).

life sentence is optional. In both instances there is a punitive phase (tariff), namely the minimum time to serve (or "time for crime") set by the judge, in which are anchored the notions of retribution and deterrence. This can be followed by an extended sentence if the offender is still considered to be a danger to the public.

For "discretionary lifers" the decision for release is taken by the Parole Board, once the 'tariff' set by the trial judge has been completed. This Board decides whether such a prisoner needs to stay longer in prison.

For "mandatory lifers" the Home Secretary can increase the 'tariff' (without any judicial appeal) set by the judge and has the discretion to include other factors besides retribution and deterrence which accompany the minimum time to be served, such as the apparent public demand for longer sentences. The Home Secretary has also specified a group of over 20 life sentence prisoners who are to die in prison.

The Home Secretary's precise criteria for further preventative detention of "mandatory lifers" are not known.

In *France* lifers may be conditionally released by the court after a minimum of 15 years. If at the point of their trial such prisoners received an additional "mesure de sûreté" (extra time as security measure) between 18 and 22 years, the judge has to present the prisoner for assessment by a commission in the Ministry of Justice. The Minister of Justice decides about such cases (political procedure). An early release is determined by a favourable prediction about dangerousness (psychiatric report), a positive prognosis of reintegration and by the conduct of the prisoner during his detention. The "mesure de sûreté" may only be used for premeditated murder and other cases of homicide.

Since 1994, however, life sentences can be combined with an exceptional security measure of 30 years which cannot be reversed by any court. This penalty was introduced for severe recidivism (murder, rape) for people who had similar previous offences and were deemed to be dangerous and difficult to reintegrate. Only the President, and no one else, may convert such a security measure into a determinate sentence.

In *The Netherlands*, the conversion of the life sentence into a determinate sentence is only possible as release by clemency (mercy) of the Queen. In practice it is the judge's report which determines a pardon. In addition, the public mood has to be tested, which might demonstrate strong objections to release. Whether such a public expression of abhorrence might outweigh all the factors in favour of release is difficult to assess.

In *Austria*, there are three significant criteria in the court's review of suspension of the sentence: (1) a minimum time served of 15 years, (2) that "continuing detention is no longer necessary to deter others from committing punishable offences" and (3) a favourable risk prediction (generally made by a psychiatrist). Pardons by clemency are possible but are hardly ever implemented.

In *Germany*, both parole under clemency and parole regulated by court review are available and are used. The penal code sets the following criteria for conditional release. (1) A minimum time served of 15 years. (2) The "particular gravity of guilt [as shown by the seriousness of the offence] does no longer necessitate life imprisonment". (3) A favourable prognosis must be given, particularly about the risk of committing further homicides. The courts are not allowed to suspend a sentence without having ordered an expert's report (usually by a psychiatrist).

ii) *Abolitionist countries*: In *Cyprus*, due to the prerogative of the president, the latest time for release is when 20 years' imprisonment has been served. The prison administration's report of the prisoner's conduct, physical and mental health and other information are presented to the public prosecutor who then makes recommendations to the president. Good conduct and a good work record are known to have a positive effect for early release.

In *Spain*, according to the penal reform of November 1995, conditions for early release are the prisoner being in an open prison, having displayed good conduct and having received a favourable prognosis for reintegration. There are two different types of procedures, i.e. a standard procedure after having served at least three quarters of the sentence, and a special procedure after having served at least two thirds of the sentence. For a successful special procedure there must be evidence of continuous participation in rehabilitation. There are no special release criteria for those who have received a maximum sentence for homicide.

In *Portugal*, both release on grounds of clemency and release by court review are available. Release procedures of maximum determinate prisoners are the same as those for other prisoners. The court has total discretion about ordering an expert's risk assessment report. Such a report, however, is the exception, not the rule. Prisoners who have committed murder have a relatively good chance to be conditionally released after one half of their term, particularly in cases of domestic murder.

In *Norway*, a minimum of twelve years has to be served when sentenced to more than eighteen years. In special cases, early release may be granted after half of the sentence has been completed. Release will not be granted, when the circumstances or the behaviour of the prisoner does not deem this to be advisable. However, this does not affect the right to pardon by the King.

From this summary, risk assessment review is shown as a major feature in retentionist countries in deciding whether to release a prisoner with an indeterminate sentence. Abolitionist countries have no special provisions for releasing prisoners who serve a maximum determinate term for homicide.

Retentionist countries would argue in defence of indeterminate sentences that their citizens are better protected than those in abolitionist countries. The following section examines penal justifications for life imprisonment.

MAJOR PENAL JUSTIFICATIONS OF LIFE IMPRISONMENT

Incapacitation and deterrence are in the forefront of the justifications for life imprisonment, with additional justifications being linked to them. Rehabilitation, for instance, is linked to incapacitation when a person is held under rehabilitative detention until this person is no longer seen as dangerous.

Retribution and defence of the legal order are related to deterrence, because both arguments are aimed at the public and normally used to justify harsher sentences.

INCAPACITATION

Firstly, the numbers of re-convictions with homicide are decisive in judging the risk to the public from releasing homicide offenders.

In *England & Wales*, according to NACRO (1990), 1.1% of those released from 'life sentences' (of which about 83% were sentenced for homicide) were reconvicted with homicide. Furthermore, Thomas found that of 6,000 persons sentenced for homicide, only six persons were reconvicted for murder during a period of ten years (House of Lords 1989). This represents a reconviction rate of 0.1%. The reason for this being so low could be that only reconvictions for murder and not for other homicides were considered.

The likelihood of a murderer already having served an earlier prison sentence for other offences is higher than for the general population.

According to research by Tournier/Barre (1983), in *France*, of 471 released 'lifers' who had been convicted not only for homicide but also for other offences to life imprisonment, a total of only two were reconvicted (0.42%). Furthermore, Kensey/Tournier examined a cohort of 121 released prisoners, who had a sentence for murder, four years after their release. They did not come across one single reconviction for homicide (1994, pages 58ff).

In *Germany* ("old" Federal Republic) the reconviction rate for homicide for released 'lifers' (of those 99% sentenced for homicide) is 0.68%. For those released from a determinate sentence with an average of 6.6 years' duration the comparable rate is 1.44% (Weber 1999).

These low reconviction rates are supported by respective findings in countries inside and outside Europe (Kerner 1974; Wulf 1979; Laubenthal 1987).

Secondly, the question of predictions of dangerousness can be seen as central to the question of incapacitation. However, such predictions are only useful if individuals who would commit further homicides can be identified accurately.

The methodological dilemma of risk assessment is the *false positive* prediction which keeps a lifer in prison. The prediction cannot be tested under conditions outside of prison. Naturally, on the other hand, a strong effort is being made to avoid 'false negative' forecasts (projected behaviour not dangerous, but offender commits a grave offence) and the consequent sensational reporting by the media.

Beside other factors (Sweetland 1974; Monahan 1975; Gohde/Wolff 1992) the major pitfalls for false predictions from the overestimation of 'dangerous' behaviour are *low base rates* (rates of frequencies) of criterion variables. For example, if a criterion variable is the occurrence of a homicide following a lifer's release, the rate of false predictions is extremely high, because of the extreme rarity of such homicides. Accurate predictions in such cases would demand clairvoyant abilities of high order from those making the predictions.

The overestimation of 'dangerousness' cannot be demonstrated more forcefully than in the famous Baxstrom case, the classic 'natural' experiment (Steadman/Cocozza 1974). On behalf of a judgement of the Supreme Court in 1966 a total of 967 'most dangerous patients' in New York State had to be released from two high security institutions for psychiatric offenders. Of those, a sample of 929 men was studied during their stay in the hospital and after their release (follow-up study being made 4.5 years later). Under the assumption that these men were dangerous and would commit grave offences if released, and using the rate of those subsequently returned to closed establishments as a criterion for dangerousness, a 'false positive' rate of 97.4% would have been the result (i.e. 24 people out of 929 were returned). If they had been predicted as homicidally dangerous, the rate would have even been higher at 99.7% (i.e. 3 out of 929). Furthermore, the Baxstrom study demonstrated that the over-estimation of dangerousness *rose* when increasingly tighter criteria for dangerousness were used.

A similar 'natural experiment', the so-called *'Dixon Patients'* in the 1970s, confirms the findings of the Baxstrom study for Pennsylvania (Thornberry/Jacoby 1979).

Deterrence

Deterrence addresses the public. There is an untested assumption by the supporters of life imprisonment for murder that the public (as potential offenders) will be more generally deterred from committing homicides by the threat of life imprisonment than by fixed length sentences. The offender is thus merely the instrument for deterrence. The underlying assumption is that the public is in need of such coercive education, otherwise homicide rates would rise.

The difficulties in testing a possible deterrent effect of life imprisonment start with controlling all major intervening variables which could have an impact on stopping people committing homicide. Without such controls, the specific deterrent effects of life imprisonment cannot be demonstrated. There are long lists of such variables such as risk of detection, probability of punishment, social class, copying the behaviour of others, religious allegiances etc. (Schumann at al. 1987).

In addition, further requirements to conduct valid research on deterrence lead to empirical dilemmas. These include a sample size of many thousands of people from the general population so that enough homicide offenders can eventually be included to compare the incidence of such offenders among those who had believed a life sentence was necessary compared with those who had believed a long fixed sentence was sufficient, after excluding all other variables.

In addition, such research must be a longitudinal study which lasts as long as life imprisonment lasts. Such a design should include self-reports from people committing unrecorded homicides – a challenging task to any researcher (Weber 1999).

There are, on the other hand, two arguments which indicate support for the case that penal severity of life imprisonment is not likely to serve as a deterrent: findings of research whether the death penalty is a deterrent and general findings of deterrence research.

The effectiveness of the death penalty as a deterrent has been researched by, among others, Liepmann (1912), Sellin (1959), and Archer/Gardner (1984), who did the most ambitious deterrent research and looked at 14 US states where the death penalty had been abolished. They compared the homicide rates (1) one year before and one year after abolition, (2) five years before and five years after abolition (3) of the longest possible interval before and after abolition and (4) undertook a contrast analysis of death penalty sanctions upon the homicide rates and the rates for other grave, non-capital offences (manslaughter, rape, bodily harm, robbery, theft) for all those periods mentioned above. They concluded that under none of the given conditions could the deterrence hypothesis be proven.

Findings of deterrence research on offending in general raise grave doubts about the effectiveness of the severity of the penalty. Risk of discovery, likelihood of punishment and informal sanctions, even though they are considered to be statistically somewhat insignificant as deterrence factors, do not show the same irrelevance as the severity of the sentence.

For instance, in Germany, the risk of discovery for homicides is very high, and clear-up rates of 95% are continually achieved. Equally high is the likelihood of punishment; for example in 1986, 88% for manslaughter and 90% for murder (including manslaughter attempts or murder respectively). Of all variables which could confound deterrent effects, the very pronounced normative value of the prohibition to kill is most likely the one to be emphasised with a normative value of 99.96% (Popitz 1968).

Furthermore, homicides belong to those offences, "which through socialisation and other moral systems (eg religion) are already rendered taboo" (Schumann et al. 1987), They also reported that the public at large made little distinction about the severity of prison sentences once the sentence exceeds three years.

LIFE IMPRISONMENT – AN EFFECTIVE MEANS TO PROTECT THE PUBLIC?

Empirical research (Weber 1996) on intentional homicides in retentionist and abolitionist countries revealed some interesting results.

Data from nine countries were available for analysis. Of these six were retentionist (England & Wales; Scotland; France; The Netherlands; Austria; Germany ("old" Federal Republic)) and three were abolitionist (Spain; Norway; Cyprus). Data related to the period 1988 to 1993.

This comparison between retentionist and abolitionist countries showed that:

- abolitionist countries have a lower rate of intentional homicide than retentionist countries;
- the more severe the punishments, the higher the rate of intentional homicide;
- abolitionist countries use tariffs in the upper ranges of punishments considerably less often than retentionist countries.

Retentionist countries have at their disposal, therefore, great discretion in reducing punishment, and using this discretion would not increase any risk to public safety.

In respect of preventative (secure) detention and detention in psychiatric institutions for indeterminate periods, the analysis showed that:

- equivalents to life imprisonment in abolitionist countries are not applied with the intent to compensate for the absence of life sentences; and furthermore
- even when these equivalents are considered together with respective maximum sentences, the total rate of those detained under the maximum determinate sentence and those with indeterminate detention in abolitionist countries is lower than the total rate of those sentenced to life imprisonment and those indeterminately detained in retentionist countries.

LIFE IMPRISONMENT AND HUMAN RIGHTS: SOME CONCLUSIONS

In examining the work of the International Law Commission at its meeting in 1991 on the use of life imprisonment as a sentence by international criminal courts, van Zyl Smit (1997) remarked "When the spectrum of jurisprudence about life imprisonment in different countries and regions is examined together with the debate about life imprisonment in the International Law Commission it soon becomes clear that the arguments against life imprisonment are strongly founded in general human rights norms that are recognised as principles of international human rights law."

Taking into account the indeterminacy and incalculability of life imprisonment, it is understandable that such extreme interventions in individual lives by the state can be considered as structurally opposed to human rights.

Human rights are designed as a tool of defence against the state's power. Applying long-term detention, especially indeterminate detention in total institutions, can lead to infringements in the following fields of human rights:

- human rights for the protection of dignity and personal expression (safeguarding human dignity, right to personal development, protection from inhumane and degrading punishment and treatment);
- human rights for the protection of privacy (safeguarding the institution of marriage and family, correspondence and telecommunication, the inviolability of one's home);
- human rights for the protection of communication (safeguarding freedom of opinion, information, press, other media);
- legal human rights (enumerated by Seidel 1996).

Legal human rights
In member countries of the Council of Europe prison sentences and other forms of detention on grounds of criminal offences are only allowed to be imposed and to be administered on the basis of law and of legal procedures. It is decisive therefore, whether by ordering and implementing life imprisonment and its equivalents such legal human rights could be violated.

Firstly, the requirement of legality is essential to legal human rights. There shall be no punishment without law and without court (*nullum crimen, nulla poena sine lege*). Beside the fact that there are countries which do not provide laws for the release of lifers (e.g. England & Wales, Scotland, France, The Netherlands, Cyprus) the criteria for imposing life imprisonment for murder are subjective or psychological, and therefore open to the discretion and arbitrariness of the court. The mere existence of a law does not therefore automatically fulfil the requirement of legality. However, even if there were clear provisions for offences carrying life imprisonment, this punishment itself stands for the utmost indeterminacy which cannot be in accord with the principle of legality.

Countries which do not have life imprisonment are much less likely to infringe such a principle.

Secondly, the fundamental requirement of certainty of the punishment and its implementation, which comes from the requirement of legality, is neither fulfilled by the provisions of offences carrying life imprisonment nor by the procedures for conditional release of lifers. It needs to be emphasised that in particular the procedures of risk assessment and their effects – whether regulated by law or administrative rules – yet again reflect the uncertainty of murder provisions and of indeterminate imprisonment. To keep people in prison (after they have served 'their term') on the assumption that they could commit a further homicide (which has not yet happened!) can be seen as a fundamental infringement of sentencing certainty. Only events which have already occurred should be of judicial concern.

Thirdly, such assumptive predictions infringe therefore also the prohibition of multiple punishments for the same offence (*ne bis in idem*).

But Spain offers a blueprint. Its penal reform of 8/11/1995 has abolished all indeterminacy and all additional punishments or measures. Furthermore, for offenders found not to be responsible for their actions, detention in a psychiatric hospital cannot last longer than the prison sentence the person should have received if he or she was responsible.

Protection of dignity and personal expression

Human dignity is in its core mostly understood as the right of self-determination. Self-determination means that a human being cannot be treated as a mere object. Using people as examples for deterring others causes two infringements of human dignity: firstly, that the offenders are just seen as instruments (i.e. objects) for the purpose of educating the public; secondly, that human dignity of the people who constitute the public is infringed by the assumption that the public is only able to respect the lives of the other citizens by a coercive system run by the state.

The subjective and psychological elements of murder provisions which lead to life imprisonment and the system of life imprisonment itself (in particular, conditional release based on assumptions of dangerousness) are strong violations of the individual rights of the convicted individual.

Right to personal development

It is obvious that life imprisonment violates personal freedom. Possibilities for personal development are clearly limited. In addition, the Covenant on Civil and Political Rights (New York 1966) defines rehabilitation and re-integration as the main purpose of imprisonment of sentenced prisoners (Article 10 para 3). It is not possible to have rehabilitation without a defined end of imprisonment.

Protection from inhumane and degrading punishment and treatment

According to the European Court of Human Rights sentences which are ordered by a court are not automatically inhumane and degrading. In the so-called "Greek case", however, the ECHR ruled that "inhumane" punishment or treatment consists of intentionally applied psychological or physical harm which cannot be justified by the relevant situation (YB 12 [1969]; Seidel 1996).

As this study shows, these criteria are valid for life imprisonment, because countries which provide life imprisonment do not have lower homicide rates than abolitionist countries.

"Degrading" punishment or treatment means that such a practice evokes feelings of trepidation, of oppressiveness or inferiority and if such punishment is appropriate to humiliate people, to make them contemptible or to break their psychological or physical resistance (Abdulaziz et al. GB, ECHR verdict of 28 May 1985; Seidel 1996). This definition meets the view of life imprisonment expressed in this study as a degrading punishment and its performance as a degrading treatment.

Protection of privacy

This human right consists of safeguarding the institution of marriage and the family, correspondence and telecommunication and the inviolability of one's home. It covers also a general right for the protection of communication, i.e. freedom of opinion, information, press, other media (Seidel 1996).

Clearly there are numerous violations of the protection of privacy resulting from life imprisonment. Freedom of opinion is not allowed when private letters are censored. The numerous broken marriages and families of life sentence prisoners, the impediments to correspondence and telecommunications, and the staff's accessibility to a prisoner's artificial home (his/her cell) indicate these violations.

And finally

Human rights are universal. They apply to prisoners and in particular to life sentence prisoners. They must not be casually or conveniently suspended. Life imprisonment by its very nature leads to human right violations. Determinate maximum sentences reduce such violations and at the same time, as this study illustrates, improve the public's protection from harm.

NOTE

1 Information in this chapter is based on our own research (mostly published in Weber 1996 and McGeorge 1990) unless otherwise stated.

REFERENCES

Gohde, Hellmut / Wolff, Stephan (1992). " 'Gefährlichkeit' vor Gericht." *Kriminologisches Journal* 24: 162–180.

House of Lords (1989): *Report of the Select Committee on Murder and Life imprisonment. Session 1988–89. Vol. I. Report and Appendices.* London: HMSO, 1989, 34.

Jonge, Gerard de (1993). "Lebenslänglich. Ein europäisches Problem braucht eine europäische Lösung." Lebenslange Freiheitsstrafe: Ihr geltendes Konzept, ihre Praxis, ihre Begründung. Erste öffentliche Anhörung 14. bis 16.Mai 1993. Dokumentation. Ed. Komitee für Grundrechte und Demokratie e.V. Köln: *Komitee für Grundrechte*, 71–83.

Kerner, Hans-Jürgen (1974). "Kriminologische Gesichtspunkte bei der Reform der lebenslangen Freiheitsstrafe." *Straf- und Maßregelvollzug. Kriminologische Gegenwartsfragen. Band 11.* Eds. Ehrhardt, H. / Göppinger, H., Stuttgart, 85–93.

Liepmann, Moritz (1912). Die Todesstrafe: Ein Gutachten. *Sonderabdruck aus den Verhandlungen des XXXI. Deutschen Juristentages.* Berlin: Guttentag. Nachdruck 1978.

McGeorge, Nicholas (1990). *A Fair Deal for Lifers: a study on sentencing and review procedures for people sentenced to life imprisonment in Western Europe.* Quaker Council for European Affairs, Brussels.

McGeorge, Nicholas (1995). Lifer Imprisonment. *Criminal Justice* Vol 13, No 2.

Monahan, John (1975). "The Prediction of Violence." In *Violence and Criminal Justice.* Eds. Chappell, Duncan / Monahan, John. Lexington (Mass.): Lexington Books, 15–31.

NACRO (1990). Briefing, September. National Association for the Care and Resettlement of Offenders: London.

Popitz, Heinrich (1968). *Über die Präventivwirkung des Nichtwissens. Dunkelziffer, Norm und Strafe.* Tübingen: Mohr.

Schumann, Karl F. / Berlitz, Claus / Guth, Hans-Werner / Kaulitzki, Reiner (1987). *Jugendkriminalität und die Grenzen der Generalprävention.* Neuwied/Darmstadt: Luchterhand.

Seidel, Gerd (1996). *Handbuch der Grund- und Menschenrechte auf staatlicher, europäischer und universeller Ebene.* Baden-Baden: Nomos, 1996.

Sellin, Thorsten (1959). *The Death Penalty. A Report for the Model Penal Code Project of The American Law Institute.* Philadelphia: The American Law Institute.

Sessar, Klaus (1980). "Die Umgehung der lebenslangen Freiheitsstrafe." *Monatsschrift für Kriminologie und Strafrechtsreform* 63: 193–206.

Steadman, Henry J. / Cocozza, J. (1974). *Careers of the Criminally Insane. Excessive Social Control of Deviance.* Lexington (Mass.): Lexington Books.

Sweetland, John P. (1972). *'Illusory Correlation' and the Estimation of 'Dangerous' Behavior.* Indiana University, Department of Psychology.

Thornberry, Terence P. / Jacoby, Joseph E. (1979). *The Criminally Insane. A Community Follow-up of Mentally Ill Offenders.* Chicago/London: University of Chicago Press.

Tournier, Pierre / Barre, Marie-Danièle (1983). "L' erosion des cohortes des condamnés à mort graciés et des condamnés à une peine perpétuelle libérés entre le 1er janvier 1961 et le 31 décembre 1980." *Revue de science criminelle et de droit pénal vomparé.* No. 3: 505–512.

Trotha, Trutz von (1980). "Generalprävention, zentrale bürokratische Herrschaft und Recht. Überlegungen zu einigen neueren Studien zur Abschreckung und ihren strafrechtspolitischen Implikationen." *Recht und Politik*: 134–143.

Van Zyl Smit, Dirk (1997). "Life imprisonment as the Ultimate Penalty in International Law: a Human Rights Perspective." Unpublished paper. Faculty of Law, University of Cape Town.

Weber, Hartmut-Michael (1996). *Läßt sich die lebenslange Freiheitsstrafe ohne Sicherheitseinbußen abschaffen? Rechtsvergleichendes Gutachten für den Justizminister des Landes Schleswig-Holstein.* Fulda.

Weber, Hartmut-Michael (1999). *Die Abschaffung der lebenslangen Freiheitsstrafe: Für eine Durchsetzung des Verfassungsanspruchs*. Baden-Baden: Nomos.

Wulf, Bernd Rüdiger (1979). *Kriminelle Karrieren von "Lebenslänglichen". Eine empirische Analyse ihrer Verlaufsformen und Strukturen anhand von 141 Straf- und Vollzugsakten*. München.

Index

Aasland, O. G. 72
Abel, G. G. 25–7, 34
Abel Screen for Sexual Interests 24–7
Aborigines 222–4
accommodation syndrome 144
acquired brain damage 71, 75
actuarial prediction 8–11, 13–14; child abuse assessment 61; MacArthur Risk Assessment Study 38–53; sex offenders 27–8, 32–3; SVP laws 114–16; versus clinical 86
Adams, H. E. 30
adolescence-limited offenders 203–4, 207–8
age:victims of mutilation murders 230–1, 232–9; victims of sexual offending 183–4, 185–6, 190
age of criminal liability 261–2
alcohol:risk assessment 72–3, 77–9; victims of sexual offending 186
American Psychiatric Association (APA) 25–6, 85, 109
amnesia, Recovered Memories 123–4
anchoring 88
Andrews, B. 123–4
Andrews, D. A. 12, 15–16
anger, rape 154–5, 166–7, 170–1
anger rape 154–5, 166–7, 170–1
anger-excitation rape 154–5
anger-retaliation rape 154–5
antisocial behaviour, risk assessment 16–18
antisocial personality disorder, SVP laws 109
antisociality, rapist typologies 153–4
anxiety 73

APA see American Psychiatric Association
ARF see Assessment of Risk Form
Arizona Juvenile Risk Assessment Form 8–9
Arling, G. 12
Armelius, B. 92
Army of God 255
arrest, domestic violence 212–15
Ashford, J. B. 8–9
Assessment of Risk Form (ARF) 71, 75–6
Atlanta Olympics bombing 254–7
AUDIT 72, 77–8
Australia 181–91, 219–20, 222–4
Austria 262, 268–9
Avins, A. L. 71

Babor, T. F. 72
Baird, S. C. 12
Ballard, K. B. 8
Barbaree, H. E. 170, 178
Barre, M.-D. 267
Bartlett, A. E. A. 79
base rates, SVP laws 114
Baumeister, R. F. 167–8
Baxstrom case 268
Bebbington, P. 71
Beck, J. L. 9
Becker, Judith V. 109–10
Beckett, G. E. 14
behavioural decision theory 87
Belfrage, H. 83, 87
Bera, W. H. 179–80
Berk, R. A. 213–14
Berlin Crime Study 199–208
Bevans, H. 91–2
biases, clinical judgement 87–8, 97
Binder, R. L. 40
Birnbaum, H. J. 154, 165–8